NATIVE
AMERICAN HISTORY

THE NATIVE AMERICAN SOURCEBOOK

NATIVE AMERICAN HISTORY

EDITED BY J.E. LUEBERING, SENIOR MANAGER

Britannica®
Educational Publishing

IN ASSOCIATION WITH

ROSEN
EDUCATIONAL SERVICES

Published in 2011 by Britannica Educational Publishing
(a trademark of Encyclopædia Britannica, Inc.)
in association with Rosen Educational Services, LLC
29 East 21st Street, New York, NY 10010.

Distributed exclusively by Rosen Educational Services.
For a listing of additional Britannica Educational Publishing titles, call toll free (800) 237-9932.

First Edition

Britannica Educational Publishing
Michael I. Levy: Executive Editor
J.E. Luebering: Senior Manager
Marilyn L. Barton: Senior Coordinator, Production Control
Steven Bosco: Director, Editorial Technologies
Lisa S. Braucher: Senior Producer and Data Editor
Yvette Charboneau: Senior Copy Editor
Kathy Nakamura: Manager, Media Acquisition

Rosen Educational Services
Jeanne Nagle: Senior Editor
Nelson Sá: Art Director
Cindy Reiman: Photography Manager
Matthew Cauli: Designer, Cover Design
Introduction by Sean McCollum

Library of Congress Cataloging-in-Publication Data

Native American history / edited by J.E. Luebering. — 1st ed.
    p. cm. — (The Native American sourcebook)
"In association with Britannica Educational Publishing, Rosen Educational Services."
Includes bibliographical references and index.
ISBN 978-1-61530-130-0 (library binding)
1. Indians of North America—History. I. Luebering, J. E.
E77.N3513 2011
970.004'97—dc22

                                                                    2010011741

Manufactured in the United States of America

CONTENTS

36

40

54

79

91

99

112

124

128

CHAPTER 10: FROM 1492 THROUGH THE 18TH CENTURY 161

153

154

174

212

225

230

ZUSAMMENKUNFT DER REISENDEN MIT MONNITARRI INDIANERN   RENCONTRE DES VOYAGEURS AVEC DES INDIENS MEUNI

If a family story has been forgotten, did the events really occur? If no one knows the function of a stone tool, what has been lost? When it comes to the history of the indigenous peoples of North America, these are more than just academic or philosophical questions. They embody the challenge and hope of piecing together the unique worlds, past and present, of Native Americans.

This book explores the long history of the native peoples of North America, which reaches back more than 10,000 years, and the myriad cultures and languages that emerged over time. It examines closely the consequences of contact between Native Americans and European settlers, who began their conquest of the Americas in the 15th century, with the arrival of Christopher Columbus in the so-called New World. This book also traces the endurance of Native American traditions and culture to the present day and details contemporary expressions by native peoples of their identities and sovereignty.

When the first nomadic hunter-gatherers came to the Americas remains an matter of debate. Archaeological evidence indicates that at least 13,000 years ago humans migrated from northeastern Asia to northwestern North America by way of a land bridge known as Beringia. Nomadic family-based bands of peoples called Paleo-Indians were hunters and gatherers.

Their pursuit of food most likely led them eastward, travelling by foot or boat down the North American coast. Some groups continued their migration along the Pacific coastline, while others worked their way eastward across present-day Alaska and the western Canadian provinces before turning southward.

Archaeologists have established points in time and space for these peoples mostly by examining stone tools. The Monte Verde archaeological site in Chile, dating back to 10,500 BC, and the site near Clovis, N.M., with stone spear points and other artifacts that date to about 9000 BC, have been especially fruitful in this regard. The diversity of languages and cultures that subsequently developed in North America is astonishing. Consider that at the time of European contact, American Indian languages in North America included more than 50 language families made up of about 300 to 500 languages.

Paleo-Indian groups throughout the Western Hemisphere also demonstrated formidable adaptability. Those that drifted northward developed hunting and gathering skills suited to the environmental extremes of the Arctic and sub-Arctic regions. The people of the Old Cordilleran culture of the Pacific Northwest oriented their culture toward the abundance of coastal resources, from salmon to wild berries.

Travellers Meeting with Minatarre Indians near Fort Clark, aquatint by Karl Bodmer, 1842. Library of Congress, Washington, D.C.

Archaeological evidence suggests Native Americans were experimenting with agriculture during the Archaic Period, perhaps as early as 6000 BC. Early Southwest Indians started planting corn (maize) in that semiarid region by about 1200 BC. Over the next millennium, farming practices had taken root in the cultures of many American Indian groups, allowing more sedentary and stratified societies to emerge. Farming cultures included the Adena culture (c. 500 BC–AD 100), in the Ohio River valley, and the nearby Hopewell culture (c. 200 BC–AD 500). Excavations of burial sites in Ohio and Illinois established that these peoples also created widespread trade networks that reached south to the Gulf of Mexico and west to the Rocky Mountains.

After AD 700, a new power rose in the Mississippi valley, and its influence spread rapidly into the southeast and northeast. Known as the Mississippian culture, its most striking remnants are massive temple mounds. These earthen construction often encompassed a large plaza, with important council buildings and temples erected on their level tops. In its heyday, the Mississippian capital city (now known as Cahokia, near present-day St. Louis, Mo.) featured 120 such mounds and a population that some anthropologists estimate might have been as high as 40,000, making it the most expansive urban center north of Middle America (the area from northern Mexico to Nicaragua).

When the ships of Christopher Columbus made landfall on Hispaniola in 1492, events were set in motion that sent shockwaves through virtually every indigenous culture in the Western Hemisphere and shattered many. Columbus's assumption that he had arrived in India also left American Indians with the name that they have borne ever since.

Over the next 200 years, several European powers established footholds in the Americas, vying to expand their empires. Spain, whose monarchs sponsored Columbus's explorations, led the way with waves of military expeditions seeking whatever wealth they could find, especially gold, to prop up the country's struggling economy. Francisco Vázquez de Coronado infiltrated the southwest while Hernando de Soto and his troops wrested control of what is now Florida, making slaves of the native inhabitants and destroying many villages along the way.

Also seeking riches, in order to support its frequent wars around the globe, was France. In 1534, French explorer Jacques Cartier entered the Gulf of St. Lawrence and claimed the region known as New France. Instead of gold, the French found wealth in furs and other trade, and they established settlements along waterways to expedite their enterprises.

England's main objectives focused less on immediate wealth than on territorial gains. King James I approved commercial ventures to pursue English aims, including the Virginia Company and the Massachusetts Bay Company, and offered land grants to religious groups such as the Quakers.

To accomplish their goals, these three European powers approached colonization of North America in different ways. As the Spanish extended their control across present-day Mexico and the American southwest through the 16th–18th centuries, they established a form of feudal system built around plantations and Roman Catholic missions, with Native Americans as serfs. French trappers built strong partnerships with the Huron, Algonquin, and other northern native peoples. These partnerships, which included intermarriage, were designed to further the lucrative fur trade. The English approach, though, had the most success. The right to earn title to property inspired average land-hungry English subjects to leave their homeland to stake claims and build new lives across the Atlantic.

While the indigenous peoples of North America viewed land largely as a resource to be managed and used communally, Europeans believed in outright ownership. While Indian leaders might interpret colonial gifts and tributes as a form of rent, for example, colonists might view them as payment for possession. Often, reconciling these worldviews proved beyond the power of peaceful negotiations. Reducing interactions of the Europeans and American Indians to a two-sided conflict, however, oversimplifies the evolving complexity of the situation. Tribes formed political and military alliances with European factions in efforts to gain advantage over their traditional Native American enemies. In the early 1600s, for example, the Huron and others in coalition with them allied themselves with the French, then used the alliance, as well as European weapons and tactics, to battle the Iroquois Confederacy. The Iroquois, in turn, joined forces with the English.

Two crucial factors contributed to the precipitous decline of the Huron and demonstrate the type of chain reactions that European colonization triggered in North America. Spurred by economic relations with the French, the Huron alliance shifted away from a subsistence economy to one based on trade. When the beaver population declined, however, the Huron were left destitute and starving. Additionally, a smallpox outbreak is thought to have killed as many as two-thirds of the Huron coalition.

It is difficult to overstate the impact disease had on American Indian tribes. In many instances, epidemics of smallpox, measles, typhus, cholera and new strains of flu often played a decisive role in reducing tribes' ability to resist encroachment. Ethnohistorian Henry Dobyns estimated mortality rates as high as 95 percent for some American Indian groups.

Europeans brought more than disease to their contact with Native Americans. In the 1700s Plains Indian tribes such as the Comanche, Cheyenne, and Sioux benefited from the introduction of horses, which were brought to the continent by Spanish conquistadors. Horses made these tribes more mobile and, combined with newly arrived firearms, greatly increased their hunting effectiveness and their ability to wage war, amongst themselves and against European settlers.

In the 19th century, a pattern of Indian removal began in earnest in the United States and Canada. In 1830, the U.S. Congress passed the Indian Removal Act in response to the discovery of gold on Cherokee land in Georgia. Under pressure from Pres. Andrew Jackson, legislation was passed that allowed the president to divest American Indian tribes of land in exchange for land, almost always inferior, in the West. In 1831, the U.S. Supreme Court ruled in *Cherokee Nation v. Georgia* that indigenous peoples on American soil were dependent rather than independent nations. The ruling took away many of the legal avenues tribes might have used to fight these expropriations.

In 1838, tens of thousands of Southeast and Northeast Indians began the march west along the infamous Trail of Tears during relocation west of the Mississippi River. A similar process of relocation was repeated with other tribes throughout much of the 19th century. When they balked, U.S. troops were quickly called out to crush resistance.

With the ending of the American Civil War in 1865, only the tribes of the central and western Plains and American Southwest remained outside of U.S. government control. With the war over, U.S. troops soon moved westward to force these groups onto reservations or kill them. The Plains Indians tried to protect their homes and families but were at a distinct disadvantage. The 1876 annihilation of George Armstrong Custer's 7th Cavalry by an alliance of Dakota and Northern Cheyenne at the Battle of the Little Bighorn proved the most famous Indian victory in this last stand against U.S. power and control. In December of 1890 the rebuilt U.S. 7th Cavalry massacred more than 200 Sioux men, women, and children near Wounded Knee, S.D. It served as the bloody conclusion to the conquest of the North American Indian.

The fate of most Native Americans now entered a new phase featuring the struggle between assimilation into the dominant white American culture and the pursuit of sovereignty, or self-determination. The policy of the U.S. government was one of assimilation. Many officials in the U.S. and Canada believed the best course was, in the words of U.S. Army Capt. Richard Pratt, to "kill the Indian in him, and save the man." Pratt was one of the architects of a system of Indian boarding schools, the most famous of which is the Carlisle Indian Industrial School in Pennsylvania. Indian children were taken from their families, as compelled by law, and shipped to these distant institutions. There they were remade in Euro-American clothes and haircuts, punished for speaking their tribal languages, forced to renounce their religions and convert to Christianity, and managed with military-like discipline. Emotional, physical, and sexual abuse were common; the deaths of students were not uncommon.

Tribes were sequestered on reservations, many of which had been carved out of lands that were infertile and essentially valueless. Another devastating policy, termination, decreed that indigenous individuals in Canada and tribes in the United States could be stripped of their aboriginal status, which freed governments from promised support.

Native Americans, however, refused to vanish, as some observers had predicted they would. Gradually, the pursuit of sovereignty gained momentum. A major shift came in 1934 with the passage of the Indian Reorganization Act by the U.S. Congress. This law included prohibitions against the allotment of tribal lands, the right of tribes to compose written constitutions and charters to manage their affairs, and federal programs to help improve tribal economies, health care, and education.

Many tribes seized upon these opportunities, forming tribal governments that combined traditional leadership practices with parliamentary procedure. They pursued newly opened legal avenues to force the U.S. government to uphold treaty rights. A congressional Indian Claims Commission set up in 1946 considered petitions regarding Indian land claims. These claims often resulted in substantial compensation for the tribes. The civil rights movement of the 1950s and 1960s helped bring additional attention and support to their cause. New laws restored religious freedoms and resource rights as a pan-Indian movement grew.

In the 21st century poverty, underdevelopment, substance abuse, and other economic and social ills still plague many of North America's native peoples. If tribes on reservation lands were considered their own country, they would qualify for "developing nation" status by the World Bank, based on per-capita income. However, the pursuit of self-determination continues to return power and resources to indigenous peoples. The right of sovereignty has progressively restored or established such prerogatives as local control of school curriculum, resource development on tribal lands, and gaming rights. These advances offer the means for tribes and their members to cultivate and pass on cultural traditions, including tribal languages, while helping them participate in and influence the broader society in which they live.

CHAPTER 1

TRACING NATIVE AMERICAN HISTORY

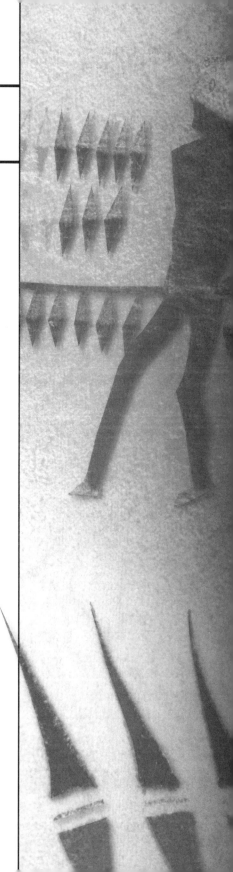

The thoughts and perspectives of indigenous individuals, especially those who lived during the 15th through 19th centuries, have survived in written form less often than is optimal for the historian. Because such documents are extremely rare, those interested in the Native American past also draw information from traditional arts, folk literature, folklore, archaeology, and other sources.

Native American history is made additionally complex by the diverse geographic and cultural backgrounds of the peoples involved. As one would expect, indigenous American farmers living in stratified societies, such as the Natchez, engaged with Europeans differently than did those who relied on hunting and gathering, such as the Apache. Likewise, Spanish conquistadors were engaged in a fundamentally different kind of colonial enterprise than were their counterparts from France or England.

ANCESTRAL ROOTS

The ancestors of contemporary American Indians were members of nomadic hunting and gathering cultures. These peoples traveled in small family-based bands that moved from Asia to North America during the last ice age; from approximately 30,000–12,000 years ago sea levels were so low that a "land bridge" connecting the two continents was exposed. Some bands followed the Pacific coast southward and others followed a glacier-free corridor through the centre of what is now Canada. Although it is clear that both avenues were used, it is not certain which was more important in the peopling of the Americas. Most traces of this episode in human prehistory have been erased by millennia of geological processes: the Pacific has inundated or washed away most of the coastal migration route, and glacial meltwash has destroyed or deeply buried traces of the inland journey.

INDIGENOUS PEOPLES OF NORTH AMERICA

The earliest ancestors of Native Americans are known as Paleo-Indians. They shared certain cultural traits with their Asian contemporaries, such as the use of fire and domesticated dogs; they do not seem to have used other Old World technologies such as grazing animals, domesticated plants, and the wheel.

Early Cultural Development

Archaeological evidence indicates that Paleo-Indians traveling in the interior of Northern America hunted Pleistocene fauna such as woolly mammoths (*Mammuthus* species), giant ground sloths (*Megatherium* species), and a very large species of bison (*Bison antiquus*); those traveling down the coast subsisted on fish, shellfish, and other maritime products. Plant foods undoubtedly

contributed to the Paleo-Indian diet, although the periglacial environment would have narrowed their quantities and varieties to some extent. Plant remains deteriorate quickly in the archaeological record, which can make direct evidence of their use somewhat scarce. However, food remains at Paleo-Indian sites including Gault (Texas) and Jake Bluff (Oklahoma) indicate that these people used a wide variety of plants and animals.

Although the artifacts recovered from many Paleo-Indian sites are predominantly, or even solely, stone tools, it is likely that these groups also made a wide variety of goods from perishable materials that have since disintegrated. Certainly, stone tools alone would have proved inadequate to the challenges these peoples encountered. One of the most distinctive Paleo-Indian artifact types is the Clovis point, the first of which was discovered on a kill site near what is now Clovis, N.M. Clovis points are lance-shaped, partially fluted, and used for killing mammoths and other very large game.

Beginning some 11,500 years ago, the climate in the Northern Hemisphere slowly became warmer and drier. Temperatures rose significantly over the next several thousand years, eventually averaging a few degrees higher than those experienced in the same areas during the early 21st century. Cold-adapted plant species such as birch and spruce retreated to the mountains and the far north, replaced in lower altitudes and

American mastodon   woolly mammoth   African savanna elephant

Mastodons and woolly mammoths were hunted by some Paleo-Indians. These animals were similar in size to modern African elephants but, unlike the modern variety, they were adapted to ice age temperatures. Encyclopædia Britannica, Inc.

latitudes by heat- and drought-resistant species including grasses, forbs, and hardwood trees. Very large animals such as mammoths and giant ground sloths were unable to cope with the change and became extinct. Other species, such as bison, survived by becoming smaller.

ARCHAIC PEOPLES

As the environment changed, so did indigenous economic strategies. The most visible change was a further diversification in subsistence. As megafauna became scarce and cold-weather flora retreated north, groups began to prey upon smaller animals such as deer and elk, to catch fish and collect shellfish from inland rivers and lakes, and to use a wider array of plant foods, including seeds, berries, nuts, and tubers. People became somewhat more settled, tending to live in larger groups for at least part of the year. They often built seasonal residences along waterways. They also developed systems of trade between different geographical areas. These changes in diet and settlement and the development of trade are some of the defining characteristics of the Archaic cultures.

Archaic technology included grinding tools (mortars and pestles), woodworking tools (grooved stone axes and gouges), and items such as plummets whose use is not clear. Archaic hunting tools are distinguished by the introduction of the spear-thrower, which enables a hunter to throw a dart accurately and with great force at a distant target. So-called bird stones may have augmented the hunter's throwing power. Large fluted points became less popular, replaced by smaller side-notched points more appropriate for dart-based hunting.

In adopting a broad array of social, economic, and technological innovations, Archaic peoples enjoyed a long period of relative stability. Although the duration of the Archaic Period varied greatly depending upon location, it persisted from as early as 8000 BC until at least 2000 BC in most of Northern America. In areas that were either unusually prosperous or, conversely, unsuitable for agriculture—the rich microclimates of California and the salmon-rich Plateau and Pacific Northwest in the former case and the cool interior of northern Canada in the latter—foraging societies persisted well into the 19th century AD.

PREHISTORIC AGRICULTURAL PEOPLES

In much of Northern America the transition from the hunting, gathering, and incipient plant use of the Archaic eventually developed into a fully agricultural way of life. In the lush valleys east of the Mississippi River, societies grew increasingly dependent upon plants such as amaranth, sumpweed, sunflower, and squash; their plentiful seeds and flesh provided a rich and ready source of food. Many of these plants were eventually domesticated, sumpweed by approximately 3500 BC and squash and sunflowers by about 3000 BC. By perhaps 500 BC the production of these local cultigens had become the economic foundation upon which the sophisticated Adena and later Hopewell cultures of the Illinois and Ohio river valleys were developed. These village-based peoples created fine sculptures, pottery, basketry, and copperwork; the surplus food they produced also supported a privileged elite and elaborate burial rituals.

By perhaps 100 BC corn (maize) had become a part of the regional economy, and by approximately AD 1000 the peoples of the river valley of the Mississippi and its tributaries had adopted a thoroughly corn-based economy. Known as the Mississippian culture, they built a ceremonial centre at Cahokia, near present-day Saint Louis, Mo., that housed an estimated 10,000–40,000 individuals during its peak period of use. Mississippian peoples had an intricate ritual life involving complex religious ornamentation, specialized ceremonial centres, and an organized priesthood. Many of these features persisted among their descendants, the Northeast Indians and Southeast Indians, and were recorded by Spanish, French, and English explorers in the 16th through 18th centuries.

Early Southwest Indians began to grow corn and squash by approximately 1200 BC, but they could not produce reliable harvests until they had resolved problems arising from the region's relative aridity. Mogollon innovations in the use of small dams to pool rainfall and divert streams for watering crops made agriculture possible, and these innovations were adopted and further developed by the Ancestral Pueblo (Anasazi) peoples. The neighbouring Hohokam also depended on irrigation. In addition to corn and squash, the peoples of this region cultivated several varieties of beans, peppers, and long-staple cotton.

Southwestern cultures came to be characterized by complex pueblo architecture, which consisted of great cliff houses with 20 to 1,000 rooms and up to four stories. A period of increasing aridity beginning in approximately AD 1100 put great stress on these societies, and they abandoned many of their largest settlements by the end of the 14th century.

COLONIZATION AND CONQUEST

Spain, France, England, and Russia colonized Northern America for reasons that differed from one another's and that were reflected in their formal policies concerning indigenous peoples. The Spanish colonized the Southeast, the Southwest, and California. Their goal was to create a local peasant class; indigenous peoples were missionized, relocated, and forced to work for the Spanish crown and church, all under threat of force. The French occupied an area that reached from the present state of Louisiana to Canada and from the Atlantic coast to the Mississippi River, and they claimed territory as far west as the Rocky Mountains. They were primarily interested in extracting saleable goods, and French traders and trappers frequently smoothed the exchange process (and increased their personal safety and comfort) by marrying indigenous women and becoming adoptive tribal members.

The English, by contrast, sought territorial expansion; focusing their initial occupation on the mid- and north-Atlantic coasts and Hudson Bay, they prohibited marriage between British subjects and indigenous peoples. The

Russians sought to supply Chinese markets with rich marine mammal furs from the Northwest Coast and the Arctic; unfamiliar with oceangoing prey, they forced indigenous men to hunt sea otters. These European powers fought territorial wars in Northern America from the 16th through the 18th century and frequently drew indigenous peoples into the conflicts.

During the 19th century, and often only after heated resistance, the governments of the United States and Canada disenfranchised most Northern American tribes of their land and sovereignty. Most indigenous individuals were legally prohibited from leaving their home reservation without specific permission. Having thus confined native peoples, the two countries set about assimilating them into the dominant culture. Perhaps the most insidious instrument of assimilation was the boarding or residential school. The programming at these institutions was generally designed to eliminate any use of traditional language, behaviour, or religion. Upon arrival, for instance, the children's clothes were generally confiscated and replaced with uniforms; the boys were usually subjected to haircuts at this time as well. Students often experienced cruel forms of corporal punishment, verbal abuse, and in some cases sexual abuse; the extent of the mistreatment may best be demonstrated by Canada's 2006 offer of some $2 billion (Canadian) in reparations to former residential school pupils.

Children outside the Indian boarding school at Cantonment, Okla., c. 1909. Library of Congress, Washington, D.C. (Neg. no. LC-USZ62-126134)

Assimilationist strategies were also implemented on reservations. It was not unusual for governmental authorities to prohibit indigenous religious practices such as the potlatch and Sun Dance in the hope that cultural continuity would be broken and Christianity adopted. Many of the hunting, fishing, and gathering rights guaranteed in treaties—which had remained essential to the indigenous economy—were abrogated by a combination of hunting regulations, mobility or "pass" laws, and the depletion of wild resources. In combination these factors demoralized and impoverished many native peoples and created a de facto system of apartheid in Northern America.

Many of these policies were not fully discontinued until the civil rights movements of the 1960s and '70s, the culmination of over a century's efforts by indigenous leaders. By the early 21st century many Native groups in Northern America were engaged in projects promoting cultural revitalization, political empowerment, and economic development.

TRIBE AND BAND

Although many indigenous peoples, particularly those of Canada, have adopted the word *nation* in order to emphasize their sovereign political status, others continue to use the words *tribe* and *band*. Are all these terms interchangeable, or do they have specific meanings? To some extent, the answer to both these questions is yes: the terms

once had specific meanings (and still do in some contexts), but they are now used more or less interchangeably in common speech.

Both *tribe* and *band* are old words. The ancient Romans called a cohesive ethnopolitical unit a *tribus*. Languages as different as Old Norse and Middle French used variants of *band* to describe groups of people that were bound or bonded together. Several other meanings of the word, such as "a decorative stripe" and "a close-fitting piece of attire," denote some of the ways in which such groups expressed their membership, as by collectively wearing garments displaying a colourful stripe or by wearing an armband.

In the Americas, Africa, Australia, and elsewhere, colonial administrators applied these terms to specific groups almost immediately upon contact. In the 19th century, early anthropologists began to use these and other terms, such as *chiefdom* and *state*, to convey a given culture's population and sociopolitical organization. By definition, a band was a small, egalitarian, kin-based group of perhaps 10–50 people, while a tribe comprised a number of bands that were politically integrated (often through a council of elders or other leaders) and shared a language, religious beliefs, and other aspects of culture.

Early scholars discerned a relationship between economics and sociopolitical organization. Hunting-and-gathering cultures and forager-farmers generally organized themselves into

TRIBAL NOMENCLATURE

The past 500 years have seen myriad terms used as referents to indigenous Americans, including American Indian, Native American, First Nation, Eskimo, Inuit, *and* Native Alaskan. *Some of these terms are used almost interchangeably, while others indicate relatively specific entities.*

The term American Indian *is often used to refer to the indigenous cultures of the Western Hemisphere in general; its constituent parts were in use from at least the early 16th century. The word* Indian *came to be used because Christopher Columbus repeatedly expressed the mistaken belief that he had reached the shores of South Asia. Convinced he was correct, Columbus fostered the use of the term* Indios *(originally, "person from the Indus valley") to refer to the peoples of the so-called New World. The term* America *came into use as a referent to the continents of the Western Hemisphere as early as 1507, when the German cartographer Martin Waldseemüller published a map naming them after the Italian explorer Amerigo Vespucci. The word* American *was soon thereafter appended to* Indian *to differentiate the indigenous peoples of these regions from those of South Asia.*

In the 1960s many activists in the United States and Canada rejected the phrase American Indian *because it was seen as a misnomer and sometimes carried racist connotations. In these countries* Native American *soon became the preferred term of reference, although many (and perhaps most) indigenous individuals living north of the Rio Grande continued to refer to themselves as Indians.*

Europeans initially called the peoples of the American Arctic Eskimo, *a term meaning "eaters of raw flesh" in the languages of the neighbouring Abenaki and Ojibwa nations. Finding that referent inappropriate, American Arctic peoples initiated the use of their self-names during the 1960s. Those of southern and western Alaska became known as the Yupik, while those of northern and eastern Alaska and all of Canada became known as the Inuit. The 1960s also witnessed Alaska's aboriginal peoples initiate a variety of land claims. As an expression of unity, these diverse societies, which included not only the Yupik and Inuit but also nations such as the Aleut, and Tanaina, adopted the term* Native Alaskan.

In the 1970s Native Americans in Canada began to use the term First Nation *as their preferred self-referent. The Canadian government adopted this use but did not furnish a legal definition for it. The Métis and Inuit preferred not to be called First Nations, and thus the terms* aboriginal peoples *or* aboriginal nations *are typically used when referring to the Inuit, Métis, and First Nations peoples of Canada in aggregate.*

By the end of the 20th century, native peoples from around the world had begun to encourage others to use tribal self-names when possible (i.e., to refer to an individual as a Hopi, Xavante, or Sami) and the word indigenous *when a descriptor for their shared political identity was more suitable. This preference was recognized by the United Nations when it established the Permanent Forum on Indigenous Issues (2000) and passed the Declaration of the Rights of Indigenous Peoples (2007). In the United States, however, many individuals of indigenous heritage continued to refer to aboriginal Americans, in aggregate, as Indians.*

bands and tribes, while full-time agriculturists tended to organize themselves into chiefdoms or states. When used in this relatively narrow sense, *band* and *tribe* are neutral descriptors, as are those for other forms of organization such as *monarchy* or *county*. However, many terms originating in the social sciences took on derogatory and racist undertones when co-opted by late 19th-century proponents of unilinear cultural evolution, eugenics, and other concepts that have since been discredited.

Historically, the designation of a group as either a tribe or a band was often rather haphazard, as the process usually depended upon colonial administrators who had a poor understanding of indigenous political practices and the fluid nature of traditional social structures. In this context, the Sioux peoples provide a useful example. Their name derives from the derogatory Ojibwa word *Nadouessioux* ("Adder" or "Snake"). Colonial administrators soon shortened *Nadouessioux* to *Sioux* and also made the incorrect assumption that this term referred to a unified people.

Instead, the (notional) Sioux tribe encompassed a diverse group of linguistic and political entities. (Ironically, none of these ever used the ethnonym, or self-name, Sioux.) By the 19th century the speakers of Dakota, Lakota, and Nakota (dialects of a single language within the inappropriately named Siouan language family) were referred to as "bands" because (from the perspective of colonial administrators) they were clearly subdivisions of the larger "Sioux tribe." From a scholarly perspective, however, Dakota, Lakota, and Nakota are the names of linguistic groups that are related to, but quite distinct from, sociopolitical units. Together, these three dialects were spoken by some 40 independent political groups, each of which an anthropologist would consider a tribe. However, those tribes, such as the Sisseton (Dakota), Sicangu (Lakota), and Yankton (Nakota), came to be called bands.

The Sisseton, Sicangu, Yankton, and other independent "bands" in turn comprised numbers of smaller entities that were also (correctly) called bands, each consisting of several households that lived and worked together. Band membership was at this smallest level very fluid and typically coalesced around the bonds of kinship and friendship. Flexibility of residence provided an excellent way to access social support and to cope with the vagaries of a foraging economy. For instance, a given household within the Dakota-speaking Sisseton might move from one (smallest-level) Sisseton band to another, depending on the imminent birth of a child, the availability of food, or other reasons of social support and resource availability; that household might also join another Dakota-speaking tribe, such as the Santee, or friends or kin in a Nakota- or Dakota-speaking group for similar reasons.

The ethnogenesis of the Seminole provides an example of the creation of a new sociopolitical entity. Taking its name from the Creek word *simanóle* (meaning "separatist"), Seminole culture was created in the late 18th century by a diverse assortment of refugees: Native American individuals, some having escaped slavery and others fleeing the destruction caused by the American Revolution and other imperial conflicts; Africans and African Americans, some free and others who had escaped enslavement; Europeans and Euro-Americans who had fled indentured servitude, military service, or the chaos of the war-torn countryside; and a number of individuals whose ethnic heritage included more than one of these groups. Despite many hardships, these people succeeded not only in establishing a common language and new communities in unfamiliar territory but also in holding that territory against Spain and the United States longer than any other Southeast Indian group.

Band and *tribe* continue to be integral parts of the legal vocabulary in the United States and Canada, where many Native American entities include one or the other term in their legal name.

CHAPTER 2

TRIBES OF THE ARCTIC AND THE SUBARCTIC

The Arctic lies near and above the Arctic Circle and includes the northernmost parts of present-day Alaska and Canada. The topography is relatively flat, and the climate is characterized by very cold temperatures for most of the year. The region's extreme northerly location alters the diurnal cycle; on winter days the sun may peek above the horizon for only an hour or two, while the proportion of night to day is reversed during the summer months.

The indigenous peoples of the North American Arctic include the Eskimo (Inuit and Yupik/Yupiit) and Aleut; their traditional languages are in the Eskimo-Aleut family. Many Alaskan groups prefer to be called Native Alaskans rather than Native Americans; Canada's Arctic peoples generally prefer the referent Inuit.

The Arctic peoples of North America relied upon hunting and gathering. Winters were harsh, but the long hours of summer sunlight supported an explosion of vegetation that in turn drew large herds of caribou and other animals to the inland North. On the coasts, sea mammals and fish formed the bulk of the diet. Small mobile bands were the predominant form of social organization; band membership was generally based on kinship and marriage. Dome-shaped houses were common; they were sometimes made of snow and other types of timber covered with earth. Fur clothing, dog sleds, and vivid folklore, mythology, and storytelling traditions were also important aspects of Arctic cultures.

The subarctic lies south of the Arctic and encompasses most of present-day Alaska and most of Canada, excluding the Maritime Provinces (New Brunswick, Nova Scotia, and Prince Edward Island), which are part of the Northeast culture area. Like the Arctic, the topography is relatively flat, but the subarctic climate is cool, and the ecosystem is characterized by a swampy and coniferous boreal forest (taiga) ecosystem.

Prominent tribes include the Innu (Montagnais and Naskapi), Cree, Ojibwa, Chipewyan, Beaver, Slave, Carrier, Gwich'in, Tanaina, and Deg Xinag (Ingalik). Their traditional languages are in the Athabaskan and Algonquian families.

Small kin-based bands were the predominant form of social organization, although seasonal gatherings of larger groups occurred at favoured fishing locales. Moose, caribou, beavers, waterfowl, and fish were taken, and plant foods such as berries, roots, and sap were gathered. In winter people generally resided in snug semisubterranean houses built to withstand extreme weather; summer allowed for more mobility and the use of tents or lean-tos. Snowshoes, toboggans, and fur clothing were other common forms of material culture in the subarctic.

THE ARCTIC

In northernmost North America, only mainland Alaska and a small northwestern corner of Canada remained largely unglaciated during the latest ice age of the Pleistocene (about 2,600,000 to 11,700 years ago); these areas were joined to northeastern Asia—also largely without ice—across land exposed by low sea levels at what is now the Bering Strait. To the east and south, the way into the North American continent was blocked with ice and unnegotiable terrain from about 25,000 to 11,000 BC.

The earliest residents of the American Arctic are known from this area of ice-free Alaska and northwest Canada; they arrived as early as perhaps 12,000 BC and can be referred to as members of the Paleo-Arctic cultural tradition. They made cutting implements in a style common to northeast Asia that was characterized by slender flakes struck from specially prepared stone cores—flakes referred to by archaeologists as "blades," many of them small (less than 2 inches [5 centimetres] in length) and classed as "microblades." Some of these blades were apparently set into the edges of bone or antler batons, thus forming knives or projectile heads. With the latter, the Paleo-Arctic people hunted terrestrial animals. Caribou appear to have been their preferred food, although they also hunted elk, forms of bison now extinct (e.g., *Bison antiquus*), and perhaps mammoths. Blade and microblade tools had appeared earlier on the Asian side of the North Pacific, notably in Siberia and in portions of the Japanese islands; evidence from those regions also suggests a reliance on terrestrial, rather than coastal, resources.

In approximately 11,000 BC, as the thawing of the ice caps began to open access to the rest of North America and to flood the land bridge to Asia, a change occurred in sites in north Alaska. The production of microblades decreased, while small projectile points or knife blades of stone, more fully shaped by chipping than were the microblades, appeared. Some archaeologists have attempted without appreciable success to find the beginning of this change in northeast Siberia. Others have suggested that it represents a development within the early Paleo-Arctic tradition itself or that it is in fact a reflection of people already in the American heartland to the southeast, although the time and manner of their arrival there remains unknown at this time. In any event, by 10,000 BC there was a resurgence of the microblade-producing sites of the Paleo-Arctic tradition. In northern Alaska at the same time there also appeared stone spear points that bear a striking resemblance to the artifacts known from the same period in other parts of North America.

Like its southern counterparts, this material culture and its makers are referred to as Paleo-Indian. Most archaeologists presume the Arctic Paleo-Indians were a new influx of people who moved north from regions to the southeast, probably following (and hunting) herds of bison and other animals as they expanded into the areas where the ice had retreated. That they were in some way descended from people present in Alaska in that earlier interval when microblades were uncommon seems possible but is yet to be demonstrated. The sites used by the Paleo-Arctic (microblade) and Paleo-Indian (spear-point) cultures are in somewhat different areas, and so these groups are thought to have been distinct peoples.

By at least 8000 BC the presence of Paleo-Arctic people can be recognized on the Alaska Peninsula in southern mainland Alaska. At almost exactly the same moment, their characteristic microblade tools appear in a few sites on the coast in southeastern Alaska and British Columbia, suggesting a movement of Paleo-Arctic descendants south. When microblades appear on the central coast of British Columbia, they are found at sites that include distinctively different artifacts. This seems to indicate that the Paleo-Arctic people met with others who were already living in the area. Although food remains from this period are seldom preserved, evidence indicates that the transition from a terrestrial subsistence economy to one based on oceanside resources was complete within a millennium.

Beginning about 7000 BC, sites with blades and microblades appear in the eastern Aleutian Islands. Although food remains are lacking in these sites, it is clear that the occupants lived on ocean resources, as there are no other resources present in any significant quantity. Notably, all of these Paleo-Arctic-related appearances on the coast (of both islands and mainland) occur south of the regions in which coastlines freeze fast during the winter.

The end of the Paleo-Arctic tradition occurred about 5500 BC. Certainly by 5000 BC the signs of remnant Paleo-Arctic-related people had been eclipsed both in the interior and on the southern coast. In the interior, new styles of artifacts constitute the Northern Archaic tradition. In general, Northern Archaic sites are located within what were the expanding northern forests. Although some Northern Archaic people left traces outside the forest limits, they generally avoided the coasts. Their artifacts include fairly large chipped-stone points with stems or notches near the points' base (stemming and notching both facilitate hafting a point to its shaft). Northern Archaic food resources were terrestrial. If the sequence of major tool types in the American Arctic is analogous to that represented to the south, this tradition may have developed from the earlier Paleo-Indian culture of the north, although direct evidence for this has thus far not been presented.

By 5000 BC, changes are also seen at sites along parts of the northernmost Pacific coast, including the eastern Aleutians, where the sea remains open in winter. These sites are characterized by new kinds of artifacts, notably large stone projectile points, stone basins for burning sea-mammal oil, and harpoon heads of bone. When combined with evidence from food remains, these materials clearly indicate that local residents relied heavily upon marine mammals, including those that required the use of boats well offshore. Scholars have not reached consensus on a name for the people represented by this new material culture, but some have referred to them as members of the Ocean Bay tradition.

Up to about 4000 BC this tradition was common to the residents of the Kodiak region and the Aleutian Islands. Shortly thereafter, however, these two groups began to develop in different directions. People in the Aleutians carried aspects of Ocean Bay technology with them as they moved farther and farther west through the chain of islands, arriving at the most distant islands, Agattu and Attu, not later than about 600 BC. On the Pacific coast around Kodiak, on the other hand, the people began to fashion stone artifacts by grinding, a technology that persisted throughout later millennia and was markedly different from that used in the Aleutians.

The first residents of the winter-freezing coasts of the north appeared only after 3000 BC, when people of the Arctic Small Tool tradition began to replace any Northern Archaic people who were exploiting the largely treeless lands immediately inland from the coasts. Predominantly terrestrial in subsistence orientation—hunting especially caribou and musk ox and taking river and lake fish—the people of the Arctic Small Tool tradition also exploited coastal resources on a seasonal basis. These people are thought to have been new immigrants from Neolithic northeast Asia, as their material culture is characterized by diminutive stone artifacts similar to those found in that region, albeit without the pottery that is usually found on Asian sites.

Although leaving evidence of neither sleds nor boats, by 2500 BC the descendants of the Small Tool people had exploded across the Arctic Archipelago of Canada to northernmost Greenland, in some areas turning more and more to coastal resources. At about the same time, they also expanded within Alaska south to the Alaska Peninsula, where their southern limit coincided with that of heavy winter coastal drift ice and intruded in some limited areas to the North Pacific itself near Cook Inlet. Within a few centuries they moved also into the tundra-covered Barren Grounds west of Hudson Bay, displacing earlier peoples who had exploited Barren Grounds caribou. Along the northeastern coast of the continent, they penetrated southward as far as the Gulf of St. Lawrence, again to the southern edge of heavy winter sea ice.

In northern Canada and Greenland the Small Tool folk gradually developed into those of the Dorset culture, who by 800 BC had created techniques for hunting seals through their breathing holes in winter sea ice and developed substantial dwellings of sod and rocks that they heated with lamps of sea-mammal oil. In some areas the Dorset culture is thought to have persisted until about AD 1300.

In Alaska the material culture of the Small Tool people was replaced by that of the Norton culture in approximately 500 BC. These people made pottery similar to that found in contemporary Siberia, and

their substantial villages of semisubterranean houses appeared along the coast from the Bering Sea to the Beaufort Sea, near the present northern border of Alaska with Canada. Norton people hunted sea mammals in open water—some of their harpoons were large enough for whaling—as well as interior animals, including caribou; they also took lake and river fish. On much of the Alaska mainland, people of the Norton tradition endured until the end of the 1st millennium AD, a period when other major developments were taking place in the islands and on the Asian coast near the Bering Strait.

In the area around the strait, an increasing ability to hunt in the open sea led to the development of the Northern Maritime, or Thule, cultural tradition. In this area the tradition, recognizable by AD 200 and in some cases perhaps a century or two earlier, is characterized by ground slate tools, ivory harpoon heads (often decoratively engraved), lamps made of clay or mud, and a heavy reliance on sea mammals. By c. AD 700 the ancestral Thule people (or their culture) had expanded into Alaska north of the Bering Strait, where by AD 900–1000 the mature Thule culture, or Thule proper, appeared.

Thule culture proved to be the most adaptable of the Arctic, expanding rapidly to the coasts of Alaska, the eastern Chukchi Peninsula of Asia, and up the rivers of the Alaska mainland; this culture's use of the large open skin boat, or umiak, for walrus and whale hunting, the kayak for sealing, and the dogsled for winter land transportation enabled the people to increase their subsistence options and geographic range. After AD 1000, perhaps moving in pursuit of whales (whose locations were shifting due to changing ice conditions), they moved rapidly across northernmost Canada to Greenland. In these areas, they established new settlements of stone and sod houses at key locations while also displacing or absorbing the thinly scattered Dorset descendants of the Small Tool people. The Canadian Thule culture carried the Inuit language to Greenland, while Thule-related groups in Alaska spread forms of the closely related Yupik language around the Bering Sea coast and to the North Pacific.

For the next few centuries a warming climate reduced the formation of winter pack ice. Most Arctic communities relied on excursions inland for caribou, river and lake fish, and other resources during the short summer months. Some people also pursued whales during those animals' migrations, and all of them made use of resources such as nonmigratory seals in both summer and winter. After about AD 1400, a period of increasing cold caused the peoples of northern Canada to give up permanent winter settlements, shifting instead to a nomadic seasonal round. This typically included warm-weather caribou hunting and river fishing, activities during which people lived in tents, and cold-weather seal hunting through the sea ice (at the animals' breathing holes), undertaken while people resided in snow houses—essentially the way of life that many people now think of as characteristic of all traditional Eskimo peoples. Because the climate shift was less extreme in areas closer to the coasts of the Pacific (including the Bering Sea) and Atlantic oceans, communities in those areas perpetuated the stable oceanside life established in the Thule period, building permanent dwellings of sod, logs, and stones; they rarely used snow houses except during winter travel, and they hunted through the sea ice chiefly in times of winter famine when stores of other foods had been exhausted.

ESKIMO

Eskimo peoples are a group who, with the closely related Aleuts, constitute the chief element in the indigenous population of the Arctic and subarctic regions of Greenland, Canada, the United States, and far eastern Russia (Siberia).

The self-designations of Eskimo peoples vary with their languages and dialects. They include such names as Inuit, Inupiat, Yupik, and Alutiit, each of which is a regional variant meaning "the people" or "the real people." The name Eskimo, which has been applied to Arctic peoples by Europeans and others since the 16th century, originated with the Innu (Montagnais), a group of Algonquian speakers. Once erroneously thought to mean "eaters of raw flesh," the name is now believed to make reference to snowshoes.

One of the oldest known Eskimo archaeological sites was found on Saglek

Bay, Labrador, and dates to approximately 3,800 years ago. Another was found on Umnak Island in the Aleutians, for which an age of approximately 3,000 years was recorded.

Eskimo people are culturally and biologically distinguishable from neighbouring indigenous groups including American Indians and the Sami of northern Europe. Studies comparing Eskimo-Aleut languages to other indigenous North American languages indicate that the former arose separately from the latter. Physiologically, an appreciable percentage of Eskimo people have the B blood type (ABO system), which seems to be absent from other indigenous American groups. Because blood type is a very stable hereditary trait, it is believed that at least a part of the Eskimo population is of a different origin from other indigenous American peoples.

Culturally, traditional Eskimo life was totally adapted to an extremely cold, snow- and icebound environment in which vegetable foods were almost nonexistent, trees were scarce, and caribou, seal, walrus, and whale meat, whale blubber, and fish were the major food sources. Eskimo people used harpoons to kill seals, which they hunted either on the ice or from kayaks, skin-covered, one-person canoes. Whales were hunted using larger boats called umiaks.

In the summer most Eskimo families hunted caribou and other land animals with bows and arrows. Dogsleds were the basic means of transport on land. Eskimo clothing was fashioned of caribou furs, which provided protection against the extreme cold. Most Eskimo wintered in either snow-block houses called igloos or semisubterranean houses built of stone or sod over wooden or whalebone frameworks. In summer many Eskimo lived in animal-skin tents. Their basic social and economic unit was the nuclear family, and their religion was animistic.

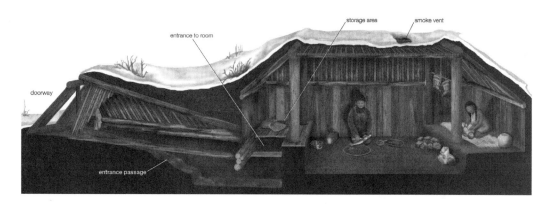

Cross section of a traditional semisubterranean dwelling of the North American Arctic and subarctic peoples. © Encyclopædia Britannica, Inc.; adapted using information from The Field Museum, Chicago

Eskimo life has changed greatly due to increased contact with societies to the south. Snowmobiles have generally replaced dogs for land transport, and rifles have replaced harpoons for hunting purposes. Outboard motors, store-bought clothing, and numerous other manufactured items have entered the culture, and money, unknown in the traditional Eskimo economy, has become a necessity. Many Eskimo have abandoned nomadic hunting and now live in northern towns and cities, often working in mines and oil fields. Others, particularly in Canada, have formed cooperatives to market their handicrafts, fish catches, and tourism ventures. The creation of Nunavut, a new Canadian territory, in 1999 helped to support a revitalization of traditional indigenous culture in North America.

Early 21st-century population estimates indicated more than 135,000 individuals of Eskimo descent, with some 85,000 living in North America, 50,000 in Greenland, and the remainder in Siberia.

ALEUT

Aleuts are natives of the Aleutian Islands and the western portion of the Alaska Peninsula of northwestern North America. The name Aleut derives from the Russian; the people refer to themselves as the Unangas and the Sugpiaq. These two groups speak mutually intelligible dialects and are closely related to the Eskimo in language and culture.

The earliest people in this region, the Paleo-Aleuts, arrived in the Aleutian Islands from the Alaskan mainland about 2000 BC. Ancient Aleut villages were situated on the seashore near fresh water, with a good landing for boats and in a position safe from surprise attack. Village placement in such locations persisted over the long term, as did many other cultural characteristics.

Traditional Aleut villages were usually composed of related families that lived in extended family households in well-insulated, semisubterranean homes. Kinship was reckoned through the mother's line. A chief, generally a seasoned and talented hunter, might govern several villages or an entire island. His rule, however, was based on his wisdom, experience, and ability to build consensus rather than on raw power.

Traditionally, Aleut men hunted seals, sea otters, whales, sea lions, sometimes walrus, and, in some areas, caribou and bears. One-man and two-man skin boats known as *baidarkas*, or kayaks, and large, open, skin boats (Eskimo *umiaks*) were used. Aleut women gathered fish, birds, mollusks, and wild plant foods such as berries and wove fine grass basketry. Stone, bone, and ivory were fashioned into containers, needles and awls, oil lamps, and other objects.

Aleut people first encountered Russian colonizers in 1741, when the expedition led by Vitus Bering reached the Aleutian Islands. Russian rule was quickly established, not least because of

NATIVE AMERICAN SELF-NAMES

Many ethnic groups have more than one name, and this is as much the case for Native Americans as it is for others. Names can originate in a number of ways, and their creation and use are often intertwined with historical events.

The best-known names for many Native American groups were bestowed by their rivals and, when translated into English, can be seen to be quite insulting. When the Ojibwa (Anishinaabe) and Fox (Meskwaki) were asked who lived to their west, French traders were told stories of the Winĭpig, or Winĭpyägohagi—a name that translates roughly to "Filthy (or Stinking) Waters." In 1993, after more than 300 years of this negative appellation, the members of the Wisconsin Winnebago Tribe revised their constitution in order to replace this legal name with the ethnonym Ho-Chunk, meaning the "People of the Big Voice" in Hocąk, their language. Notably, the members of the Winnebago Tribe of Nebraska did not enact a parallel renaming, a valid choice given that these are two entirely independent political entities.

Sometimes a name substitution is undesirable or difficult to effect. Such is the case for the dozens of legally recognized bands or tribes of the Sioux nation. Many members of these tribes and bands prefer the ethnonyms Lakota, Dakota, and Nakota (for the three dialects of their language), because Sioux is a derivation of Nadouessioux—meaning "Adder" or "Snake"—another name bestowed courtesy of traditional rivals. Nonetheless, Sioux remains in common use for several reasons: it provides a convenient referent for the three dialect groups as a whole; it promotes ethnic solidarity; it is used in a variety of other contexts such as history and linguistics (e.g., the so-called Siouan languages); and changing the legal name of a band or tribe is difficult enough that it inevitably diverts energy from other political and social priorities. Rather than abandoning the name Sioux altogether, then, many groups simply refer to themselves in multiple ways. The Rosebud Sioux Tribe, for example, is also known as the Sicangu Lakota Band. Both names are legitimate reflections of the community so named; Rosebud is the name of the group's reservation, while Sicangu and Lakota are the ethnonyms for the people and their dialect.

Periods of cultural rupture or coalescence have also spurred the creation of multiple names. For example, three of the village-dwelling nations of the Plains—the Mandan, the Hidatsa, and the Arikara—were struck by recurring waves of smallpox, whooping cough, and other illnesses from 1780 to 1840. The Mandan suffered horrendously; according to reliable eyewitness accounts, their population plummeted from approximately 10,000–15,000 in the 1730s to perhaps 150 in 1837, a crushing loss. To maintain their viability as a people, Mandan survivors merged with the Hidatsa, their close neighbours and allies; these two tribes were later joined by the Arikara, who had once been their economic and military rivals.

By the late 19th century the three nations had legally merged and had taken a new name, the Three Affiliated Tribes. Yet, even as they worked in concert politically, the original groups created separate ethnic enclaves; well into the early 21st century, most members of this tribe referred to themselves as Mandan, Hidatsa, or Arikara or used a hyphenated ethnicity (e.g., Mandan-Hidatsa). Clearly, the distinct ethnic identities of the three original tribes have survived despite devastating losses, coalescence, and the adoption of a new legal name.

Nineteenth-century Aleut and Eskimo baskets. Library of Congress, Washington, D.C. (neg. no. LC-USZ62-101278)

the depredations of a large party of Russian and Siberian hunters who over-wintered in the Aleutian Islands in 1745; members of the party were later convicted of atrocities in the Russian courts. In subsequent decades, Russian trading companies treated Aleuts as they did their own rural population—as serfs, albeit serfs whose labour was tied to fur production rather than agriculture.

By the 1830s the Aleuts' traditional ways of life had been heavily disrupted. Further disruptions occurred in the later 19th century, when discoveries of gold in Alaska drew prospectors to the region. The Aleut population declined drastically under foreign domination. At the time of first contact there were approximately 25,000 Aleuts, but by the end of the 19th century they numbered only about 2,000. By the late 20th century, however, Aleut people were revitalizing many forms of traditional culture, including language, crafts, and subsistence-oriented hunting and gathering practices. Aleuts and other northern tribes also became more politically active vis-à-vis the federal governments of the United States and Canada during this period.

Early 21st-century population estimates indicated more than 15,000 individuals of Aleut descent.

THE SUBARCTIC

The subarctic can be divided into the western subarctic and the eastern subarctic, primarily on the basis of linguistic difference. Those peoples who speak Athabaskan languages inhabit the former, while those peoples who speak Algonquian languages live in the latter.

INNU

The Innu are peoples who spoke almost identical Algonquian dialects and whose cultures differed chiefly in their adaptation to their respective environments. The southern Innu, or Montagnais, traditionally occupied a large forested area paralleling the northern shores of the Gulf of St. Lawrence, lived in birch-bark wickiups or wigwams, and subsisted on moose, salmon, eel, and seal. The northern Innu, or Naskapi, lived on the vast Labrador plateau of grasslands and tundra, hunted caribou for both food and skins to cover their wickiups, and supplemented their diet with fish and small game. The name Montagnais is French, meaning "mountaineers"; Naskapi is an indigenous name thought to mean "rude, uncivilized people," an apparent reference to their remote frontier life. The Naskapi called themselves Nenenot, meaning "true, real people." In the late 20th century the two closely related groups jointly adopted the name Innu ("people").

Innu people living to the south dressed in robes, loincloths or dresses, leggings, and moccasins, much like their southern neighbours—and ancient enemies—the Iroquois and Micmac. More northerly Innu people wore tailored clothing similar to that of the coastal Eskimo, their only traditional foes. For both groups canoes furnished transportation in summer; snowshoes and dogsleds were used in winter. Religious belief involved animism and centred on manitou, or supernatural power, with much importance also attached to various nature and animal spirits, both evil and benevolent.

Innu people avoided the creation of formal political structures; tribal organization comprised small bands of related families that often shifted in composition as individual leaders rose and fell. After the European colonization of the Americas began, the southern bands formalized their trapping and hunting territories somewhat in order to better engage in the fur trade. The northern territories were larger and more loosely defined.

Population estimates indicated some 9,500 Innu descendants in the early 21st century.

CREE

The domain of the Cree, one of the major Algonquian-speaking tribes, included an immense area from east of the Hudson and James bays to as far west as Alberta and the Great Slave Lake in what is now Canada. Originally inhabiting a smaller nucleus of this area, they expanded rapidly in the 17th and 18th centuries after engaging in the fur trade and acquiring firearms; the name Cree is a truncated form of Kristineaux, a French adaptation of the self-name of the James Bay band. Wars with the Dakota Sioux and Blackfoot and severe smallpox epidemics, notably in 1784 and 1838, reduced their numbers.

At the time of Canada's colonization by the French and English, there were two major divisions of Cree; both were typical American subarctic peoples. Traditionally, the Woodland Cree, also called Swampy Cree or Maskegon, relied for subsistence on hunting, fowling, fishing, and collecting wild plant foods. They preferred hunting larger game such as caribou, moose, bear, and beaver but relied chiefly on hare for subsistence because of the scarcity of the other animals. The periodic scarcity of hare, however, sometimes caused famine. Woodland Cree social organization was based on bands of related families, with large groups coalescing for warfare. Fears of witchcraft and a respect for a variety of taboos and customs relating to the spirits of game animals pervaded historical Cree culture. Shamans wielded great power.

The Plains Cree lived on the northern Great Plains. As with other Plains Indians, their traditional economy focused on bison hunting and gathering wild plant foods. After acquiring horses and firearms, they were more militant than the Woodland Cree, raiding and warring against many other Plains tribes. Reportedly divided into 12 independent bands, each with its own chief, the Plains Cree also had a military system that integrated and organized warriors from all the bands. Religion and ceremony were highly valued as means of fostering success in war and the bison hunt. The Assiniboin were the traditional allies of both the Plains and the Woodland Cree.

Early 21st-century population estimates indicated some 90,000 individuals of Cree descent.

OJIBWA

The Ojibwa, an Algonquian-speaking tribe, lived in what are now Ontario and Manitoba, Can., and Minnesota and North Dakota, U.S., from Lake Huron westward onto the Plains. Their self-name, Anishinaabe, means "original people." They are also called the Chippewa. In Canada those Ojibwa who lived west of Lake Winnipeg are called the Saulteaux. When first reported in the *Relations* of 1640, an annual report by the Jesuit missionaries in New France, the Ojibwa occupied a comparatively restricted region near the St. Mary's River and in the Upper Peninsula of the present state of Michigan. They had moved west as the fur trade expanded, in response to pressure from tribes to their east and new opportunities to their west.

Traditionally, each Ojibwa tribe was divided into migratory bands. In the autumn, bands separated into family units, which dispersed to individual hunting areas. In summer, families gathered

GRAND MEDICINE SOCIETY

According to Ojibwa religion, Grand Medicine Society, or Midewiwin, healing rituals were first performed by various supernatural beings to comfort Minabozho—a culture hero and intercessor between the Great Spirit and mortals—on the death of his brother. Minabozho, having pity on the suffering inherent in the human condition, transmitted the ritual to the spirit-being Otter and, through Otter, to the Ojibwa.

Traditionally, the Grand Medicine Society was an esoteric group consisting at times of more than 1,000 members, including shamans, prophets, and seers, as well as others who successfully undertook the initiation process. The society was thus both a centre of spiritual knowledge and a source of social prestige.

With a complex series of four degrees of initiation that were held within a specially constructed medicine lodge, the society's central acts involved the ritual death and rebirth of the initiate. The powers of an initiate included not only those of healing and causing death but also those of obtaining food for the tribe and victory in battle.

together, usually at fishing sites. The Ojibwa relied on the collection of wild rice for a major part of their diet, and a few bands also cultivated corn. Birch bark was used extensively for canoes, dome-shaped wigwams, and utensils. Clan intermarriage served to connect a people that otherwise avoided overall tribal or national chiefs. Chieftainship of a band was not a powerful office until dealings with fur traders strengthened the position, which then became hereditary through the paternal line. The annual celebration hosted by the Midewiwin (Grand Medicine Society), a secret religious organization open to men and women, was the major Ojibwa ceremonial. Membership was believed to provide supernatural assistance and conferred prestige on its members.

The Ojibwa constituted one of the largest indigenous North American groups in the early 21st century, when population estimates indicated some 175,000 individuals of Ojibwa descent.

CHIPEWYAN

The Chipewyan were an Athabaskan-speaking people of northern Canada. They originally inhabited a large triangular area with a base along the 1,000-mile-long (1,600 km) Churchill River and an apex some 700 miles (1,100 km) to the north; the land comprises boreal forests divided by stretches of barren ground.

Traditionally organized into many independent bands, the Chipewyan were nomads following the seasonal

Chipewyan berry-picking party, photograph by Edward S. Curtis. Library of Congress, Washington, D.C.

movement of the caribou. These animals were their chief source of food and of skins for clothing, tents, nets, and lines, although the Chipewyan also relied upon bison, musk oxen, moose, waterfowl, fish, and wild plants for subsistence.

When the Hudson's Bay Company established a fur-trading post at the mouth of the Churchill River in 1717, the Chipewyan intensified their hunting of fur animals. Members of the tribe also took advantage of their geographic location between the British traders and tribes farther inland, acting as middlemen in the fur exchange by brokering deals with the Yellowknife and Dogrib tribes farther west. Until new trading posts were established in western North America, Chipewyan individuals were able to exact huge profits from this trade. A smallpox epidemic in 1781 decimated the Chipewyan, and subsequent periods of disease and malnutrition further reduced their numbers.

Historically, Chipewyan culture was depicted as rather ruthless. By the mid-20th century such characterizations were generally thought to be inaccurate. Early 21st-century anthropologists characterized traditional Chipewyan culture as one in which individuals typically preferred subtlety to overt action. These anthropologists also described social and individual flexibility (rather than ruthlessness) as important strategies used by the Chipewyan for coping with their difficult northern environment.

Population estimates in the early 21st century indicated more than 1,500 Chipewyan descendants.

BEAVER

The Beaver, a small, Athabaskan-speaking tribe, lived in the mountainous riverine areas of northern Alberta. In the early 18th century they were driven westward into this area by the expanding Cree, who, armed with guns, were exploiting the European fur trade. The name Beaver derives from the Indian name for their main site, Tsades, or "River of Beavers," now called the Peace River.

Traditionally, the Beaver were scattered in many independent nomadic bands, each with its own hunting territory. They hunted moose, caribou, beavers, and bison; lived in skin-covered tepees in winter and brush-covered tepees or lean-tos in summer; and traveled mainly by canoe. Beaver descendants numbered more than 750 in the early 21st century.

SLAVE

The Slave—also called Slavey, Awokanak, or Etchareottine—were a group of Athabaskan-speaking Indians of Canada who originally inhabited the western shores of the Great Slave Lake, the basins of the Mackenzie and Liard rivers, and other neighbouring riverine and forest areas. Their name, Awokanak, or Slave, was given to them by the Cree, who plundered and often enslaved numbers of them, and this name became the familiar one used by the French and English, for the Slave had a general reputation for timidity or pacifism, whether deserved or not.

Like most other Athabaskan tribes, the Slave were separated into a number of independent bands, each of which was rather loosely organized, with only nominal leaders, and was associated with certain hunting territories. An informal council of hunters settled disputes. Women and the aged were treated with a respect and kindness that was not typical of all Athabaskans.

The Slave were inhabitants of the forests and riverbanks. They hunted moose, woodland caribou, and other game but also relied heavily on fish for food. Animal skins were made into robes, shirts, leggings, moccasins, and other clothing. Fringes and ornaments made of antlers, porcupine quills, and other natural materials were popular. Their dwellings consisted of brush-covered tepees in summer and rectangular huts formed of poles and spruce branches in winter.

The Slave believed in guardian spirits, in the power of medicine men, and in an undefined life after death. A common practice was the deathbed confession of sins, thought to contribute to the delay of death.

CARRIER

The Carrier, also called the Takulli or the Dakelh, were an Athabaskan-speaking tribe centred in the upper branches of the Fraser River between the Coast Mountains and the Rocky Mountains in what is now central British Columbia. The name by which they are most commonly known, Carrier (French: Porteur),

derives from the custom whereby widows carried the ashes of their deceased husbands in knapsacks for three years. The name Takulli ("People Who Go upon the Water") is of obscure origin. Although their original territory was significantly inland from the Pacific, traditional Carrier culture shared many of the customs of the Northwest Coast Indians.

The Carrier were semisedentary, moving seasonally between villages and hunting and fishing camps. Southern Carrier people lived in semisubterranean houses. Northern Carrier people made gabled houses of poles and planks, much like those of their coastal neighbours. Both types of dwellings were communal.

Carrier social organization was also much like that of the coastal tribes, though without the slavery commonly practiced among those neighbours. It included elaborate class structures composed of nobles and commoners, usually with complex obligations to marry outside one's lineage, clan, and house. Each subgroup had exclusive rights to its territory, and encroachments by other subgroups constituted grounds for reprisal or compensation. The Carrier practiced the potlatch, the custom of large gift-giving feasts or ceremonies for the recognition of such significant events as marriage.

Carrier economics relied chiefly on the plentiful river salmon, which the people supplemented by hunting various kinds of local game and collecting wild plant foods. They exploited resources from the abundant woodlands and had a woodworking tradition that created highly decorated utilitarian items such as canoes, weapons, and cooking vessels. Carrier craftsmen carved pillars, commonly referred to as totem poles, depicting the crests of noble-status individuals and lineages, as well as spirit-beings from religion, myth, and legend. Carrier religious beliefs centred on a great sky god and many spirits in nature which were contacted through dreams, visions, ritual, and magic. They also believed in both reincarnation and an afterlife.

Early 21st-century population estimates indicated more than 1,000 Carrier descendants.

GWICH'IN

The Gwich'in, a group of Athabaskan-speaking tribes, inhabited the basins of the Yukon and Peel rivers in eastern Alaska and Yukon—a land of coniferous forests interspersed with open, barren ground. The name Gwich'in, meaning "people," is given collectively to an indefinite number of distinct American subarctic peoples, there being no precise agreement among authorities on whom to include under this cover name, which is as much linguistic as cultural.

In traditional Gwich'in social organization, men became chiefs by demonstrating leadership or prowess in hunting or war. Men's major pursuits included battle, fishing, and hunting caribou, moose, and other game. Women's pursuits included making nearly all

household goods, gathering wild plant foods, and transporting their families and material possessions during frequent moves from one camp to another.

The Gwich'in people's most influential neighbours were the Eskimo, or Inuit, with whom they traded and fought and from whom they borrowed such cultural traits as tailored caribou-skin clothing (most conspicuously, the Eskimo hood and mittens), various hunting weapons, and the sled. They also shared many customs with tribes to the south and east—painting their faces and hair, wearing feathers as hair ornaments, and decorating their clothing with fringes and beads. Gwich'in houses were domed structures of poles and fir boughs, banked with snow in winter and ventilated by a smoke hole at the top. Little is known of Gwich'in religion or beliefs, but they were well known for their feasts, games (especially wrestling), singing, and dancing.

Early 21st-century population estimates indicated more than 4,500 individuals of Gwich'in descent.

TANAINA

The Tanaina were the only northern Athabaskan-speaking group occupying extensive portions of the seacoast. They lived chiefly in the drainage areas of Cook Inlet and Clark Lake in what is now southern Alaska. Tanaina, meaning "the people," was their own name for themselves; they have also been called Knaiakhotana ("people of the Kenai Peninsula").

Like other Northwest Coast Indians, the Tanaina traditionally subsisted mainly on salmon and other fish (as well as shellfish). They also hunted bears, mountain sheep and goats, moose, caribou, and other game for both skins and food. Their dwellings consisted of semi-subterranean log-and-sod houses for winter use and a variety of casually built shelters for summer use during the salmon runs; the latter also served as smokehouses for drying the fish catch. For transportation they used the skin-covered kayak and umiak, as well as snowshoes and sleds.

Tanaina society was organized on the basis of kinship and class. Each individual belonged to a clan; membership in a clan was traced through the female line. The clans were grouped into two large phratries, one comprising five clans and the other six clans. Marriages always drew one partner from each phratry. There were also two social classes—nobles and commoners—and each village usually had a chief of sorts. More-organized leadership, with clear leaders and councils, usually developed only for warfare and raiding (their chief foes being the Eskimo or Inuit).

Tanaina individuals and families used the potlatch to increase their prestige through the ostentatious giving of gifts. Animism was at the core of Tanaina religion; they believed that all things in nature were suffused with supernatural powers and that guardian spirits shadowed everyone. Taboos, tokens, and amulets were numerous. Shamanism was also very influential; some shamans were chiefs.

Early 21st-century population estimates indicated some 100 individuals of Tanaina descent.

DEG XINAG

The Deg Xinag, an Athabaskan-speaking tribe of interior Alaska, inhabited the basins of the upper Kuskokwim and lower Yukon rivers. Their region is mountainous, with both woodlands and tundra, and is fairly rich in fish, caribou, bear, moose, and other game on which the Deg Xinag traditionally subsisted—fish, fresh or dried, being central to their diet.

Before colonization, Deg Xinag and Eskimo technology were somewhat similar. The Deg Xinag wore parkas and trousers, built semisubterranean sod houses, and used harpoons, spear throwers, and other weapons like those of the Eskimo. However, in most ways the traditional Deg Xinag were more similar to other American subarctic peoples than to their Eskimo neighbours. The Deg Xinag (or Deg Hit'an) were formerly called the Ingalik, a pejorative term.

Traditionally, the Deg Xinag lived in villages. Permanent winter settlements for a fairly large group were complemented by seasonal fishing and hunting camps that sheltered a few families each. The centre of village life was a large semisubterranean lodge called a *kashim*. The *kashim* served many functions, mostly for men, providing a venue for sweat baths, council meetings, entertainment, funerals, and shamanic rituals. Women's activities tended to take place in family dwellings and in the open air. Deg Xinag people were much given to games and sports, ceremonies, and potlatches. The latter are gift-giving festivities through which the sponsors acquire prestige; potlatches frequently mark life passages such as marriage and death.

Although traditional Deg Xinag religion included a creator, a devil, and other worlds beyond the living, it was more concerned with a kind of supernatural spirit that pervaded all things animate and inanimate in the world. There were several ceremonies, taboos, and superstitions relating to animals and the hunt and to the care of tools and other economic items; as with other societies that practiced animism, the Deg Xinag believed that survival and success required good relations with the things of nature.

Early 21st-century population estimates indicated some 150 individuals of Deg Xinag descent.

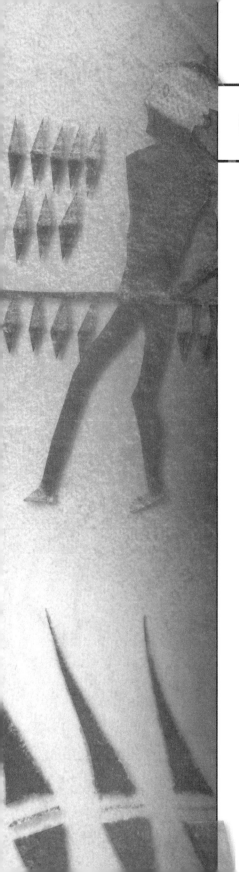

CHAPTER 3

NORTHEAST NATIVE AMERICANS

The Northeast culture area reaches from the present-day Canadian provinces of Quebec, Ontario, and the Maritimes (New Brunswick, Nova Scotia, and Prince Edward Island) south to the Ohio River valley (inland) and to North Carolina (on the Atlantic Coast). The topography is generally rolling, although the Appalachian Mountains include some relatively steep slopes. The climate is temperate, precipitation is moderate, and the predominant ecosystem is the deciduous forest. There is also extensive coastline and an abundance of rivers and lakes.

Prominent tribes include the Algonquin, Iroquois, Huron, Wampanoag, Mohican, Mohegan, Ojibwa, Ho-chunk (Winnebago), Sauk, Fox, and Illinois. The traditional languages of the Northeast are largely of the Iroquoian and Algonquian language families.

Most Northeastern peoples engaged in agriculture, and for them the village of a few dozen to a few hundred persons was the most important social and economic unit in daily life. Groups that had access to reliably plentiful wild foods such as wild rice, salmon, or shellfish generally preferred to live in dispersed hamlets of extended families. Several villages or hamlets formed a tribe, and groups of tribes sometimes organized into powerful confederacies. These alliances were often very complex political organizations and generally took their name from the most powerful member tribe, as with the Iroquois Confederacy.

Cultivated corn, beans, squash, and weedy seed-bearing plants such as *Chenopodium* formed the economic base for farming groups. All northeastern peoples took animals including deer, elk, moose, waterfowl, turkeys, and fish. Houses were wickiups (wigwams) or longhouses. Both house types were constructed of a sapling framework that was covered with rush matting or sheets of bark. Other common aspects of culture included dugouts made of the trunks of whole trees, birchbark canoes, clothing made of pelts and deerskins, and a variety of medicine societies.

ALGONQUIN

The Algonquin, a tribe of closely related Algonquian-speaking bands, originally lived in the dense forest regions of the valley of the Ottawa River and its tributaries in present-day Quebec and Ontario, Can. The tribe should be differentiated from the Algonquian language family, as the latter term refers to a much larger entity composed of at least 24 tribes of Northeast Indians and Plains Indians.

Traditionally, Algonquin people shared many cultural traits with the tribes flanking them on the east, the Innu, and with the Ojibwa to the west. Before colonization by the French, Dutch, and English, the Algonquin were probably organized in bands of patrilineal extended families. Each band resided in a semipermanent longhouse village during the summer, tending gardens of corn, fishing, and collecting wild plant foods. During the winter, bands dispersed across the landscape to hunt terrestrial mammals. In the spring, some Algonquin bands tapped maple trees to make syrup. Military activities, particularly skirmishes with warriors from the Iroquois Confederacy, occurred throughout the year.

During colonization, the Algonquin became heavily involved in the fur trade. As the first tribe upriver from Montreal, they had a strategic market advantage as fur trade intermediaries; in addition to trading pelts they obtained directly from the hunt, the Algonquin traded corn and furs from tribes in the North American interior for French manufactured goods.

Algonquin descendants numbered more than 5,000 in the early 21st century.

IROQUOIS

The name Iroquois embraces those tribes whose members spoke a language of the Iroquoian family—notably the Cayuga, Cherokee, Huron, Mohawk, Oneida, Onondaga, Seneca, and Tuscarora, in addition to the Iroquois proper. The word *Iroquois* is a French derivation of *Irinakhoiw*, meaning "rattlesnakes," their Algonquian enemy's epithet. They call themselves Hodenosaunee, meaning "people of the longhouse." The Iroquoian linguistic groups occupied a continuous territory around Lakes Ontario, Huron, and Erie, in present-day New York state and Pennsylvania (U.S.) and southern Ontario and Quebec (Canada). They should not be confused with the Iroquois

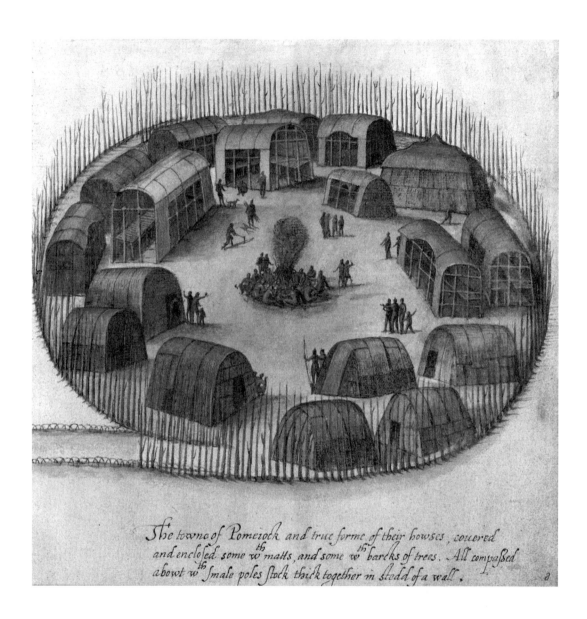

The towne of Pomeiock and true forme of their howses, couered and enclosed some wth matts, and some wth barcks of trees. All compassed abowt wth smale poles stock thick together in stedd of a wall.

Sketch of the Algonquin village of Pomeiock, near present-day Gibbs Creek, N.C., showing huts and longhouses inside a protective palisade, c. 1585; in the British Museum, London. Photos.com/Jupiterimages

Confederacy, as the latter comprised a subset of five, and later six, tribes from within the broader language family.

As was typical of Eastern Woodlands Indians before colonization, the Iroquois were semisedentary agriculturists who palisaded their villages in time of need. Each village typically comprised several hundred persons. Iroquois people dwelt in large longhouses made of saplings and sheathed with elm bark, each housing many families. The longhouse family was the basic unit of traditional Iroquois society, which used a nested form of social organization. Households (each representing a lineage) were divisions of clans, several clans constituted each moiety, and the two moieties combined to create a tribe.

Groups of men built houses and palisades, fished, hunted, and engaged in military activities. Groups of women produced crops of corn, beans, and squash, gathered wild foods, and prepared all clothing and most other residential goods. After the autumn harvest, family deer-hunting parties ranged far into the forests, returning to their villages at midwinter. Spring runs of fish drew families to nearby streams and lake inlets.

Kinship and locality were the bases for traditional Iroquois political life. Iroquois speakers were fond of meetings, spending considerable time in council. Council attendance was determined by locality, sex, age, and the specific question at hand; each council had its own protocol and devices for gaining consensus, which was the primary mode of decision making.

The elaborate religious cosmology of the Iroquois was based on an origin tradition in which a woman fell from the sky. Other parts of the religious tradition featured deluge and earth-diver motifs, supernatural aggression and cruelty, sorcery, torture, cannibalism, star myths, and journeys to the otherworld. The formal ceremonial cycle consisted of six agricultural festivals featuring long prayers of thanks. There were also rites for sanctioning political activity, such as treaty making.

Warfare was important in Iroquois society, and, for men, self-respect depended upon achieving personal glory in war endeavours. War captives were often enslaved or adopted to replace dead family members; losses to battle and disease increased the need for captives, who had become a significant population within Iroquois settlements by the late 17th century.

Early 21st-century population estimates indicated some 80,000 individuals of Iroquois-proper descent; when including the many Iroquois-speaking tribes, these estimates indicated more than 900,000 individuals.

HURON

The Huron, an Iroquoian-speaking people, were living along the St. Lawrence River when contacted by French explorer Jacques Cartier in 1534. They are also called the Wyandot or Wyandotte.

Many aspects of Huron culture were similar to those of other Northeast Indians. Traditionally, the Huron lived in villages of large bark-covered longhouses, each of which housed a matrilineal extended family. Some villages were protected by an encircling palisade. Agriculture was the mainstay of the Huron economy. Men cleared fields and women planted, tended, and harvested crops including corn, beans, squash, and sunflowers. Hunting and fishing supplemented the diet.

The Huron were divided into matrilineal exogamous clans, each headed by a clan chief; all the clan chiefs of a village formed a council, which, with the village chief, decided civil affairs. Villages were grouped into bands (each of which had a band chief and a band council, consisting of village chiefs, to deal with civil matters affecting the entire band), and all the bands together constituted the Huron nation. A large council of band chiefs and their local councils dealt with matters concerning the whole tribe. Women were influential in Huron affairs, as each clan's senior women were responsible for selecting its political leaders.

The Huron were bitter enemies of tribes of the Iroquois Confederacy, with whom they competed in the fur trade. Before the 17th century the Iroquois drove some Huron from the St. Lawrence River westward into what is now Ontario, where related groups seem to have already been resident. Four of these bands (the Rock, Cord, Bear, and Deer peoples) formed a confederacy called the Wendat that was destroyed by Iroquois invasions in 1648–50. The survivors were either captured and forced to settle among their conquerors or driven west and north. The latter remnants drifted back and forth between Michigan, Wisconsin, Ontario, Ohio, and Quebec. During the French and Indian War in the mid-18th century, the Huron allied with the French against the British and the Iroquois Confederacy.

The Huron gradually reestablished some influence in Ohio and Michigan, but the U.S. government eventually forced tribal members to sell their lands. They subsequently migrated to Kansas and then to Indian Territory (present-day Oklahoma).

Early 21st-century population estimates indicated some 4,000 individuals of Huron descent.

WAMPANOAG

The Wampanoag, an Algonquian-speaking people, formerly occupied parts of what are now the states of Rhode Island and Massachusetts, including Martha's Vineyard and adjacent islands. They were traditionally semisedentary, moving seasonally between fixed sites. Corn was the staple of their diet, supplemented by fish and game. The tribe comprised several villages, each with its own local chief, or sachem.

In 1620 the Wampanoag high chief, Massasoit, made a peace treaty with the Pilgrims, who had landed in the tribe's territory; the treaty was observed until

Massasoit's death. Bad treatment by settlers who encroached on tribal lands, however, led his son, Metacom, or Metacomet, known to the English as King Philip, to organize a confederacy of tribes to drive out the colonists. The colonists eventually defeated and killed King Philip and other leading chiefs, and the Wampanoag and Narragansett were almost exterminated. Some survivors fled to the interior, while others moved to the islands of Nantucket and Martha's Vineyard to join kin who had remained neutral during the conflict. Disease and epidemics destroyed most of the indigenous people who lived on Nantucket, but Wampanoag people survive to the present, particularly on Martha's Vineyard.

Early 21st-century population estimates indicated some 4,500 Wampanoag descendants.

MOHICAN

The Mohican, an Algonquian-speaking tribe of what is now the upper Hudson River valley above the Catskill Mountains in New York state, U.S., were known during the colonial period to the Dutch and the English as the River Indians and to the French as the Loups ("Wolves"). Their self-name, Muh-he-con-neok, means "the people of the waters that are never still." The Mohican are not to be confused with the Mohegan, who originally resided in what is now Connecticut and are related to the Pequot.

Before colonization, the Mohican consisted of at least five bands and were further organized by three matrilineal clans; the latter were governed by hereditary sachems, or chiefs, who were assisted by elected counselors. Tribal members lived in strongholds of 20 to 30 houses, situated on hills and enclosed by stockades, as well as in enclosed villages situated between cornfields and woodland.

When first contacted by the Dutch, the Mohican were at war with the Mohawk, and in 1664 they were forced to move from Schodack, near Albany, to what is now Stockbridge, Mass. They gradually sold their territory there, and in 1736 some of them were gathered into a mission at Stockbridge and became known as the Stockbridge band; other groups scattered and merged with other tribes. The Stockbridge band later moved to Wisconsin and were joined by the Munsee band; the two groups were allotted a joint reservation in Wisconsin in the 19th century. The American novelist James Fenimore Cooper drew a romanticized portrait of the Mohican in his book *The Last of the Mohicans* (1826).

Population estimates indicated approximately 3,500 Mohican descendants in the early 21st century.

MOHEGAN

The Mohegan, an Algonquian-speaking people, originally occupied most of the upper Thames valley in what is now Connecticut, U.S. They later seized land from other tribes in Massachusetts and Rhode Island.

KING PHILIP'S WAR

King Philip's War (1675–76) was a war between Native Americans and English settlers, the bloodiest conflict in 17th-century New England, temporarily devastating the frontier communities but eventually eradicating native military resistance to the European colonization of that region.

For years, mutual helpfulness and trade were fostered by both the early Massachusetts colonists and the Indian leader Massasoit, grand sachem of the Wampanoags. The peace was first shattered by the Pequot War in 1637. By the 1660s settlers had outgrown their dependence on the Indians for wilderness survival techniques and had substituted fishing and commerce for the earlier lucrative fur trade. From 1640 to 1675 new waves of land-hungry settlers pushed into Indian territory, particularly in Massachusetts, Connecticut, and Rhode Island. Tribes had to fight to protect their homelands; otherwise they would become "white men's vassals," subject to alien law, humiliating limitations on personal freedom, usurpation of favourite hunting grounds, and regulation by a strict Christian morality.

Upon Massasoit's death (1661) his successor and second son, Metacom (King Philip), vowed to resist further English expansion and attempted to organize a federation of tribes. Eventually Metacom won support from the powerful Narragansett and almost all of the other New England tribes. When three Wampanoags were executed (June 1675) for the murder of an informer, John Sassamon, Metacom could no longer hold his young warriors in check, and bloodshed erupted before either side could coordinate campaign plans.

The war actually resolved itself into a series of ruthless Indian raids on frontier settlements from the Connecticut River to Massachusetts and Narragansett Bay, followed by brutal retaliatory assaults on Indian villages by the colonial militia. By the end of 1675 many frontier towns had been devastated, and the Narragansett had been wiped out in what was called the Great Swamp Fight. The Indians maintained a distinct advantage in the fighting until the spring of 1676, when their efforts were undermined by the threat of starvation after the destruction of their crops and when the English finally agreed to use "Praying Indians" (those who had converted to Christianity) as scouts. Following Metacom's death in August, Indian resistance collapsed, although Articles of Peace were not signed for two years.

King Philip's War was one of the costliest confrontations in colonial history. Edward Randolph, an agent of the crown, estimated that some 600 Europeans and 3,000 Indians lost their lives. It is believed that more than half of the 90 settlements in the region had been attacked and a dozen destroyed. Whole Indian villages were massacred and entire tribes decimated; indigenous refugees fled westward and northward. Thereafter settlers felt free to expand without fear into former Indian territory across southern New England.

The traditional Mohegan economy was based on the cultivation of corn and on hunting and fishing. At the time of the first European settlement of New England early in the 17th century, the Mohegan and the Pequot tribes were ruled jointly by the Pequot chief, Sassacus. Later, a rebellion by the subchief Uncas led to Mohegan independence. After the destruction of the Pequot in 1637, most of the Pequot survivors and the former Pequot territories came under Mohegan control. Uncas strengthened his position by making an alliance with the English. By the end of King Philip's War against the colonists, the Mohegan were the strongest tribe remaining in southern New England. Colonial settlements gradually displaced the Mohegan, and their numbers dwindled from imported diseases and other hardships. Many of them joined other native settlements.

Population estimates indicated some 2,500 Mohegan descendants in the early 21st century.

HO-CHUNK

The Ho-Chunk lived in what is now eastern Wisconsin when encountered in 1634 by French explorer Jean Nicolet. A Siouan-speaking people, they are also called Ho-Chungra or Winnebago. Settled in permanent villages of dome-shaped wickiups (wigwams), the Ho-Chunk cultivated corn, squash, beans, and tobacco. They also participated in communal bison hunts on the prairies to the southwest.

Traditionally, the Ho-Chunk were divided into clans that traced membership through the male line. The clans were organized into two phratries, or groups of unequal size: the Upper (Air) division contained four clans, the Lower (Earth) division eight. A marriage partner was always drawn from the opposite phratry, never from one's own. Some clans had special functions, such as the adjudication of disputes, and each clan had rites of passage and other customs relating to the well-being of its members.

The major summer ceremonial was the Medicine Dance, which included a secret ceremony for members of the Medicine Dance Society (a religious society open to both men and women) as well as public rituals. The winter feast was a clan ceremonial intended to increase war and hunting powers. The spring Buffalo Dance was a magical ceremonial for calling the bison herds.

In response to the fur trade, the Ho-Chunk began a westerly expansion during the mid-17th century. By the early 19th century they claimed most of what are now southwestern Wisconsin and the northwestern corner of Illinois. This land was ceded to the U.S. government in a series of treaties. The Ho-Chunk were involved in the Black Hawk War of 1832, after which most members of the tribe were removed by the U.S. government to Iowa and later to Missouri and to South Dakota. In 1865 about 1,200 of the Ho-Chunk settled in Nebraska near their friends and allies the Omaha. The larger body of Ho-Chunk later moved

Ha-zah-zoch-kah ("Branching Horns"), a Winnebago Indian. Library of Congress, Washington, D.C. (neg. no. LC-USZ62-50347)

back to Wisconsin, where, from 1875, they remained.

Early 21st-century population estimates indicated some 10,000 individuals of Ho-Chunk descent.

SAUK

The Sauk, an Algonquian-speaking tribe closely related to the Fox and the Kickapoo, lived in the region of what is now Green Bay, Wis., when first encountered by the French in 1667.

In summer the Sauk (also spelled Sac) lived in permanent bark-house villages near fields where women raised corn and other crops. After the harvest the village separated into family groups that erected winter houses of poles covered with reed mats; in spring the tribe gathered on the Iowa prairies to hunt bison. Patrilineal clans regulated the inheritance of personal names and controlled certain religious ceremonies. Other ceremonies were sponsored by secret societies, such as the Midewiwin, or medicine society, whose members were believed to be able to heal the sick and to enlist supernatural aid for the tribe. Many rituals involved the use of sacred medicine bundles, which were collections of holy objects. The Sauk were governed by a tribal council and hereditary chiefs. When war broke out, these were temporarily replaced by war chiefs selected for their military ability.

By the 19th century the Sauk had settled along the Mississippi River between what are now Rock Island, Ill.,

Tah-Col-O-Quoit ("Rising Cloud"), a Sauk Warrior, lithograph by J.T. Brown, c. 1842. Library of Congress, Washington, D.C.

and St. Louis, Mo. In 1804 some of their minor chiefs ceded most of the tribal lands to the United States. Although the Sauk protested that this treaty was illegal, they were unable to prevent its enforcement. The resulting unrest led to the Black Hawk War (1832), after which the Sauk were forced to relinquish more territory. They moved to Iowa, then Kansas, and finally settled in Indian Territory (Oklahoma) at the end of the 19th century.

Early 21st-century population estimates indicated some 7,000 individuals of Sauk descent.

FOX

When the Fox first met French traders in 1667, the tribe lived in the forest zone of what is now northeastern Wisconsin. Tribes to their east referred to them as "foxes," a custom the colonial French and British continued. They called themselves Meshkwakihug, the "Red-Earth People." An Algonquian-speaking tribe, they are also known as the Meskwaki or Mesquakie.

Traditionally, the Fox moved with the seasons. Their permanent villages—located near fields in which women cultivated corn, beans, and squash—were occupied during the planting, growing, and harvest seasons. Most people left the villages after the harvest to participate in communal winter bison hunts on the prairies.

Fox social and political organization was centred upon a peace chief and council of elders who administered tribal affairs. Important issues were discussed by the entire tribe until consensus was reached. War parties rallied about men whose skill and reputation made them leaders. Families were grouped into

Fox men in traditional clothing, photograph by C.M. Bell, c. 1890. Library of Congress, Washington, D.C. (neg. no. LC-USZ62-92960)

clans that were mainly ceremonial organizations; members traced their descent from a mythical founder through the male line. A major religious organization was the Midewiwin, or Medicine Society, a group whose members were devoted to healing the sick and enlisting supernatural aid to ensure tribal welfare. Many Midewiwin ceremonies involved the use of medicine bundles, which were collections of sacred objects.

In the 18th century the Fox joined with the Sauk (Sac) in resisting colonization by the French and later by the English. The two tribes eventually retreated from the colonial front by moving from what is now Wisconsin to Illinois and then Iowa. They moved to Kansas in 1842, and in 1857 some returned to Iowa.

Early 21st-century population estimates indicated more than 6,500 Fox descendants, most living in Iowa, Kansas, and Oklahoma.

ILLINOIS

The Illinois were a confederation of small Algonquian-speaking tribes originally spread over what are now southern Wisconsin and northern Illinois and parts of Missouri and Iowa. The best-known of the Illinois tribes were the Cahokia, Kaskaskia, Michigamea, Peoria, and Tamaroa.

Like other Northeast Indians, the Illinois traditionally lived in villages, their dwellings covered with rush mats and housing several families each. The Illinois economy combined agriculture with foraging. Women cultivated corn and other plant foods, small parties took forest mammals and wild plants throughout the year, and most members of a given village participated in one or more winter bison hunts on the prairie. Little is known of Illinois social organization, but it was probably similar to that of the Miami, with a civil chief elected from among a village council and a war chief chosen according to his ability to lead raids.

By the middle of the 17th century, most of the Illinois people were living along the Illinois River from Starved Rock to the Mississippi, having moved there because of harassment by the Dakota Sioux, Fox, and other northern tribes. Iroquois raids greatly reduced their numbers, and the introduction of liquor by French traders further weakened the tribe. The murder of the Ottawa chief Pontiac by an Illinois individual provoked the vengeance of several northern Algonquian tribes, further reducing the Illinois population. The survivors took refuge with French settlers in Kaskaskia, while the Sauk, Fox, Kickapoo, and Potawatomi took most of the remaining Illinois territory. In 1832 the Illinois sold the lands they had retained, moving to Kansas and then to Indian Territory (present-day Oklahoma).

Early 21st-century population estimates indicated more than 1,500 individuals of Illinois descent.

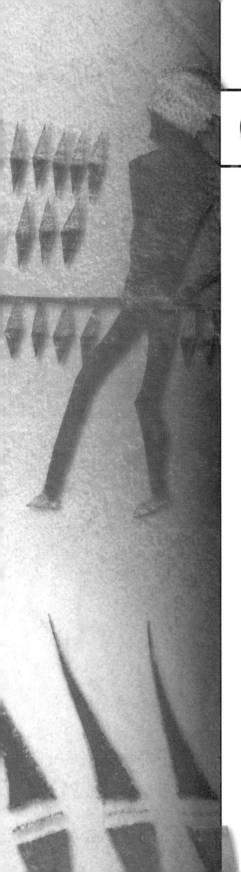

CHAPTER 4

THE SOUTHEAST

The Southeast region reaches from the southern edge of the Northeast culture area to the Gulf of Mexico; from east to west it stretches from the Atlantic Ocean to somewhat west of the Mississippi valley. The climate is warm temperate in the north and grades to subtropical in the south. The topography includes coastal plains, rolling uplands known as the Piedmont, and a portion of the Appalachian Mountains. Of these, the Piedmont was most densely populated. The predominant ecosystems were coastal scrub, wetlands, and deciduous forests.

Perhaps the best-known indigenous peoples originally from this region are the Cherokee, Choctaw, Chickasaw, Creek, and Seminole, sometimes referred to as the Five Civilized Tribes. Other prominent tribes included the Natchez, Caddo, Apalachee, Timucua, and Guale. Traditionally, most tribes in the Southeast spoke Muskogean languages. There were also some Siouan language speakers and one Iroquoian-speaking group, the Cherokee.

The region's economy was primarily agricultural and often supported social stratification. As chiefdoms, most cultures were structured around hereditary classes of elites and commoners, although some groups used hierarchical systems that had additional status levels. Most people were commoners and lived in hamlets located along waterways. Each hamlet was home to an extended family and typically included a few houses and auxiliary structures such as granaries and summer kitchens. These were surrounded by agricultural plots or fields. Hamlets were usually associated with a town that served as the area's ceremonial and market centre. Towns often included large earthen mounds on which religious structures and the homes of the ruling classes or families were placed. Together, each town and its associated hamlets constituted an autonomous political entity. In times of need these could unite into confederacies, such as those of the Creek and Choctaw.

People grew corn, beans, squash, tobacco, and other crops; they also gathered wild plant foods and shellfish, hunted deer and other animals, and fished. House forms varied extensively across the region, including wickiups (wigwams), earth-berm dwellings, and, in the 19th century, chickees (thatched roofs with open walls). The Southeast was also known for its religious iconography, which often included bird themes, and for the use of the "black drink," an emetic used in ritual contexts.

CHEROKEE

The Cherokee were the North American Indians of Iroquoian lineage who constituted one of the largest politically integrated tribes at the time of European colonization of the Americas. Their name is derived from a Creek word meaning "people of different speech"; many prefer

to be known as Keetoowah or Tsalagi. They are believed to have numbered some 22,500 individuals in 1650, and they controlled approximately 40,000 square miles (100,000 square km) of the Appalachian Mountains in parts of present-day Georgia, eastern Tennessee, and the western Carolinas at that time.

Traditional Cherokee life and culture greatly resembled that of the Creek and other tribes of the Southeast. The Cherokee nation was composed of a confederacy of symbolically red (war) and white (peace) towns. The chiefs of individual red towns were subordinated to a supreme war chief, while the officials of individual white towns were under the supreme peace chief. The peace towns provided sanctuary for wrongdoers. War ceremonies were conducted in red towns.

When encountered by Spanish explorers in the mid-16th century, the Cherokee possessed a variety of stone implements including knives, axes, and chisels. They wove baskets, made pottery, and cultivated corn, beans, and squash. Deer, bear, and elk furnished meat and clothing. Cherokee dwellings were bark-roofed, windowless log cabins, with one door and a smoke hole in the roof. A typical Cherokee town had between 30 and 60 such houses and a council house, where general meetings were held and a sacred fire burned. An important religious observance was the Busk, or Green Corn Festival, a first-fruits and new-fires celebration.

The Spanish, French, and English all attempted to colonize parts of the Southeast, including Cherokee territory. By the early 18th century the tribe had chosen alliance with the British in both trading and military affairs. During the French and Indian War (1754–63) they had allied themselves with the British, while the French had allied themselves with several Iroquoian tribes that were the Cherokee's traditional enemies. By 1759 the British had begun to engage in a scorched-earth policy that led to the indiscriminate destruction of native towns, including those of the Cherokee and other British-allied tribes. Tribal economies were seriously disrupted by British actions. In 1773 the Cherokee and Creek had to exchange a portion of their land to relieve the resulting indebtedness, ceding more than two million acres in Georgia through the Treaty of Augusta.

In 1775 the Overhill Cherokee were persuaded at the Treaty of Sycamore Shoals to sell an enormous tract of land in central Kentucky to the privately owned Transylvania Land Company. Although land sales to private companies violated British law, the treaty nevertheless became the basis for the colonial settlement of that area. As the American War of Independence loomed, the Transylvania Land Company declared its support of the revolutionaries; the Cherokee became convinced that the British were more likely to enforce boundary laws than a new government and announced their determination to support the crown. Despite

British attempts to restrain them, a force of 700 Cherokee under Chief Dragging Canoe attacked the colonist-held forts of Eaton's Station and Fort Watauga (in what is now North Carolina) in July 1776.

Both assaults failed, and the tribe retreated in disgrace. These raids were the first in a series of attacks by the Cherokee, Creek, and Choctaw on frontier towns, eliciting a vigorous response by militia and regulars of the Southern colonies during September and October. At the end of this time, Cherokee power was broken, their crops and villages destroyed, and their warriors dispersed. The defeated tribes sued for peace; in order to obtain it, they were forced to surrender vast tracts of territory in North and South Carolina at the Treaty of DeWitt's Corner (May 20, 1777) and the Treaty of Long Island of Holston (July 20, 1777).

Peace reigned for the next two years. When Cherokee raids flared up in 1780 during the American preoccupation with British armed forces elsewhere, punitive action led by Col. Arthur Campbell and Col. John Sevier subdued the tribe again. The second Treaty of Long Island of Holston (July 26, 1781) confirmed previous land cessions and caused the Cherokee to yield additional territory.

After 1800 the Cherokee were remarkable for their assimilation of American settler culture. The tribe formed a government modeled on that of the United States. Under Chief Junaluska they aided Andrew Jackson against the Creek in the Creek War, particularly in the Battle of

Horseshoe Bend. They adopted colonial methods of farming, weaving, and home building. Perhaps most remarkable of all was the syllabary of the Cherokee language, developed in 1821 by Sequoyah, a Cherokee who had served with the U.S. Army in the Creek War. The syllabary—a system of writing in which each symbol represents a syllable—was so successful that almost the entire tribe became literate within a short time. A written constitution was adopted, and religious literature flourished, including translations from the Christian Scriptures. Native Americans' first newspaper, the *Cherokee Phoenix*, began publication in February 1828.

The Cherokee's rapid acquisition of settler culture did not protect them against the land hunger of those they emulated. When gold was discovered on Cherokee land in Georgia, agitation for the removal of the tribe increased. In December 1835 the Treaty of New Echota, signed by a small minority of the Cherokee, ceded to the United States all Cherokee land east of the Mississippi River for $5 million. The overwhelming majority of tribal members repudiated the treaty and took their case to the U.S. Supreme Court. The court rendered a decision favourable to the tribe, declaring that Georgia had no jurisdiction over the Cherokee and no claim to their land.

Georgia officials ignored the court's decision, President Andrew Jackson refused to enforce it, and Congress passed the Indian Removal Act of 1830 to facilitate the eviction of tribal members from their homes and territory. Removal was implemented by 7,000 troops commanded by Gen. Winfield Scott. Scott's men moved through Cherokee territory, forcing many people from their homes at gunpoint; as many as 15,000 Cherokee were thus gathered into camps while their homes were plundered and burned by local residents. Subsequently these refugees were sent west in groups of about 1,000, the majority on foot.

The eviction and forced march, which came to be known as the Trail of Tears, took place during the fall and winter of 1838–39. Although Congress had allocated funds for the operation, it was badly mismanaged, and inadequate food supplies, shelter, and clothing led to terrible suffering, especially after frigid weather arrived. About 4,000 Cherokee died on the 116-day journey, many because the escorting troops refused to slow or stop so that the ill and exhausted could recover.

When the main body had finally reached its new home in what is now northeastern Oklahoma, new controversies began with the settlers already there. Feuds and murders rent the tribe as reprisals were made on those who had signed the Treaty of New Echota.

In Oklahoma the Cherokee joined four other tribes—the Creek, Chickasaw, Choctaw, and Seminole—all of which had been forcibly removed from the Southeast by the U.S. government in the 1830s. For three-quarters of a century, each tribe had a land allotment and a quasi-autonomous government modeled on that of the United States. In preparation for Oklahoma statehood (1907), some of this land was allotted to individual tribal members. The rest was opened up to homesteaders, held in trust by the federal government, or allotted to freed slaves. Tribal governments were effectively dissolved in 1906 but have continued to exist in a limited form.

At the time of removal in 1838, a few hundred individuals escaped to the mountains and furnished the nucleus for the several thousand Cherokee who were living in western North Carolina in the 21st century. Early 21st-century population estimates indicated more than 730,000 individuals of Cherokee descent living across the United States.

CHOCTAW

The Choctaw, a tribe of Muskogean linguistic stock, traditionally lived in what is now southeastern Mississippi. The Choctaw dialect is very similar to that of the Chickasaw, and there is evidence that they are a branch of the latter tribe.

In the mid-18th century, there were 20,000 Choctaw living in 60 or 70 settlements along the Pearl, Chickasawhay, and Pascagoula rivers. Their dwellings were thatched-roof cabins of logs or bark plastered over with mud. Among the southeastern agriculturalists the Choctaw were perhaps the most skillful farmers, producing surplus crops to sell and trade. They planted corn, beans, and pumpkins;

fished; gathered nuts and wild fruits; and hunted deer and bear. Their most important community ritual was the Busk, or Green Corn, festival, a first-fruits and new-fire rite celebrated at midsummer. A notable funerary custom involved the ritual removal of the bones of the deceased from the body. Subsequently, the bones were placed in an ossuary. This ritual was performed by spiritually powerful men and women known as bone-gatherers or bone-pickers, with the departed's family members in attendance. Bone-gatherers were notable for their distinctive tattooing and long fingernails.

In the power struggles that took place after colonization, the Choctaw were generally allied with the French against the English, the Chickasaw, and other Native American tribes. After the French defeat in the French and Indian War (1754–63), some Choctaw land was ceded to the United States and some tribal members began moving west across the Mississippi. In the 19th century the growth of the European market for cotton increased the pressure for the acquisition of Choctaw land, and in 1820 they ceded 5 million acres in west central Mississippi to the United States. In the 1830s the Choctaw were forced to move to what is now Oklahoma, as were the other members of the Five Civilized Tribes—the Creek, Cherokee, Chickasaw, and Seminole.

For three-quarters of a century each tribe had a communal land allotment and a quasi-autonomous government modelled on that of the United States. In preparation for Oklahoma statehood (1907), some of this land was allotted to individuals from the Five Civilized Tribes. The rest was opened up to white homesteaders, held in trust by the federal government, or allotted to freed slaves. Tribal governments were effectively dissolved in 1906 but have continued to exist in a limited form.

Choctaw descendants numbered more than 159,000 in the early 21st century.

CHICKASAW

The Chickasaw, a tribe of Muskogean linguistic stock, originally inhabited what is now northern Mississippi and Alabama. In their earlier history the Chickasaw and the Choctaw may have been a single tribe. Traditionally, the Chickasaw were a seminomadic people who patrolled the immense territory that they claimed for themselves and raided tribes far to the north; like many conquering peoples, they integrated the remnants of these tribes into their culture.

Prior to the 1830s, Chickasaw dwellings were organized along streams and rivers rather than clustered in villages. Descent was traced through the maternal line. The supreme deity was associated with the sky, sun, and fire, and a harvest and new-fire rite similar to the Green Corn ceremony of the Creek was celebrated annually.

Probably the earliest contact between Europeans and the Chickasaw was Hernando de Soto's expedition in 1540–41. In the 18th century the Chickasaw became involved in the power struggles between the British and French, siding with the British against the French and the Choctaw. They also gave refuge to the Natchez in their wars with the French. Relations with the United States began in 1786, when their northern territorial boundary was fixed at the Ohio River. In the 1830s they were forcibly removed to Indian Territory (present-day Oklahoma) where, with the Creek, Cherokee, Choctaw, and Seminole, they were among the Five Civilized Tribes. For three-quarters of a century each tribe had a land allotment and a quasi-autonomous government modeled on that of the United States. In preparation for Oklahoma statehood (1907), some of this land was allotted to individuals from the Five Civilized Tribes; the rest was opened up to non-Native homesteaders, held in trust by the federal government, or allotted to freed slaves. Tribal governments were effectively dissolved in 1906 but have continued to exist in a limited form. Some Chickasaw now live on tribal landholdings that are informally called reservations.

Early estimates placed the tribe's population at 3,000–4,000. At the time of their removal to Indian Territory they numbered about 5,000. Chickasaw descendants numbered more than 38,000 in the early 21st century.

CREEK

The Creek, a Muskogean-speaking tribe, originally occupied a huge expanse of

Ben Perryman, a Creek Indian, painting by George Catlin, 1836; in the Smithsonian American Art Museum, Washington, D.C. National Museum of American Art (formerly National Collection of Fine Arts), Smithsonian Institution, Washington, D.C., gift of Mrs. Sarah Harrison

the flatlands of what are now Georgia and Alabama. There were two divisions of Creeks: the Muskogee (or Upper Creeks), settlers of the northern Creek territory; and the Hitchiti and Alabama, who had the same general traditions as the Upper Creeks but spoke a slightly different dialect and were known as the Lower Creeks.

Traditional Creek economy was based largely on the cultivation of corn, beans, and squash. Most of the farming was done by women, while the men of the tribe were responsible for hunting and

defense. The Creek achieved status based on individual merit rather than by inheriting it. Like most Indians of the Southeast, they commonly tattooed their entire bodies.

Before colonization, Creek towns were symbolically grouped into white and red categories, set apart for peace ceremonials and war ceremonials, respectively. Each town had a plaza or community square, around which were grouped the houses—rectangular structures with four vertical walls of poles plastered over with mud to form wattle. The roofs were pitched and covered with either bark or thatch, with smoke holes left open at the gables. If the town had a temple, it was a thatched dome-shaped edifice set upon an eight-foot mound into which stairs were cut to the temple door. The plaza was the gathering point for such important religious observances as the Busk, or Green Corn, ceremony, an annual first-fruits and new-fire rite. A distinctive feature of this midsummer festival was that every wrongdoing, grievance, or crime—short of murder—was forgiven.

The Creeks' first contact with Europeans occurred in 1538 when Hernando de Soto invaded their territory. Subsequently, the Creeks allied themselves with the English colonists in a succession of wars (beginning about 1703) against the Apalachee and the Spanish. During the 18th century, a Creek Confederacy was organized in an attempt to present a united front against both Native and white enemies. It comprised not only the dominant Creeks but also speakers of other Muskogean languages (Hitchiti, Alabama-Koasati) and of non-Muskogean languages (Yuchi, some Natchez and Shawnee). The Seminole of Florida and Oklahoma are a branch of the Creek Confederacy of the 18th and early 19th centuries.

Ultimately, the confederacy did not succeed, in part because the Creek towns (about 50 with a total population of perhaps 20,000) were not able to coordinate the contribution of warriors to a common battle. In 1813–14, when the Creek War with the United States took place, some towns fought with the white colonizers and some (the Red Sticks) against them. Upon defeat, the Creeks ceded 23,000,000 acres of land (half of Alabama and part of southern Georgia); they were forcibly removed to Indian Territory (now Oklahoma) in the 1830s. There with the Cherokee, Chickasaw, Choctaw, and Seminole, they constituted one of the Five Civilized Tribes.

Creek descendants numbered more than 71,000 in the early 21st century.

SEMINOLE

In the last half of the 18th century, migrants from the Creek towns of southern Georgia moved into northern Florida, the former territory of the Apalachee and Timucua. By about 1775 these migrants had begun to be known under the name Seminole, probably derived from the Creek word *simanó-li*, meaning "separatist," or "runaway." The name may also have derived from the Spanish *cimarrón*, "wild."

The Seminoles located their new villages in the Everglades, a patchwork of dense thickets and wetlands that provided protective isolation from outsiders. There they were almost immediately joined by African, African American, and American Indian individuals who had escaped from slavery, as well as others attempting to avoid the bloody power struggles between European colonizers and other Southeast Indians. The tribe generally welcomed these newcomers. The Seminole economy emphasized hunting, fishing, and gathering wild foods. They also grew corn and other produce on high ground within the wetlands. Homes included substantial log cabins and, later, thatched-roof shelters with open sides known as chickees. People typically wore long tunics. By the late 19th century, Seminole clothing was often decorated with brightly coloured strips of cloth.

In an effort to stem further colonial encroachment and to avoid forced removal to the west, the Seminoles fought a succession of wars in 1817–18, 1835–42, and 1855–58. As a result of the First Seminole War, Spain ceded its Florida holdings to the United States. In 1832 a treaty proposal that would have obligated the Seminoles to move west of the Mississippi River was rejected by a large portion of the tribe. The Second Seminole War was one of the most costly of the U.S.–Indian wars, with military expenditures exceeding $20 million. In 1838 Osceola and other tribal leaders agreed to meet the U.S. military under a flag of truce; the American forces broke the truce by imprisoning the men, and Osceola died in custody some three months later. Fighting continued sporadically for another four years, but the tribe eventually surrendered. The people were required to move to Indian Territory (Oklahoma) and were resettled in the western part of the Creek reservation there. A few Seminoles remained in Florida. In Oklahoma the Seminoles became one of the Five Civilized Tribes, which also included the Cherokee, Chickasaw, Creek, and Choctaw, all of whom had been forcibly removed from the southeastern United States by the federal government in the 1830s.

Federal policies effectively dissolved the Oklahoma tribal governments in 1906. Changes in these federal policies resulted in the revitalization of the tribal governments in the mid-20th century.

For some 40 years, those Seminole who stayed in Florida endured hardships related to their resistance to removal. By the close of the 19th century, however, relations with neighbouring Euro-Americans had improved. During the first half of the 20th century, tribal members regained some 80,000 acres of land from the U.S. government. In 1957, a century after the end of the Seminole Wars, the Seminole tribe of Florida regained federal recognition. Over the next 50 years the tribe developed economic programs ranging from citrus production to tourist attractions and infrastructure, including an ecotourism park, a tribal museum, a casino, and a private airstrip.

Early 21st-century population estimates indicated some 27,000 individuals of Seminole descent.

NATCHEZ

The Natchez, a tribe of the Macro-Algonquian linguistic phylum, inhabited the east side of the lower Mississippi River. When French colonizers first interacted with the Natchez in the early 18th century, the tribal population comprised about 6,000 individuals living in nine villages between the Yazoo and Pearl rivers near the site of the present-day city of Natchez, Miss.

The traditional Natchez economy relied primarily on corn agriculture. They made clothes by weaving a fabric from the inner bark of the mulberry and excelled in pottery production. Like several other groups of Southeast Indians, the Natchez built substantial earthen mounds as foundations for large wattle-and-daub temple structures. Their dwellings—built in precise rows around a plaza or common ground—were also constructed of wattle and daub and had arched cane roofs.

Traditional Natchez religion venerated the Sun, which was represented by a perpetual fire kept burning in a temple. All fires in a village, including the sacred fire, were allowed to die once a year on the eve of the midsummer Green Corn ceremony, or Busk. The sacred fire was remade at dawn of the festival day, and all the village hearths were then lit anew from the sacred flames.

Natchez social organization was notable for its caste system; the system drew from and supported Natchez religious beliefs and classified individuals as suns, nobles, honoured people, and commoners. Persons of the sun caste were required to marry commoners; the offspring of female suns and commoners were suns, while the children of male suns and commoners belonged to the caste of honoured people. The heads of villages also claimed descent from the Sun, and the monarch was referred to as the Great Sun. He was entitled to marry several wives and to maintain servants. Upon his death, his wives and some servants, along with any others who wished to join him in the afterlife, were ritually sacrificed.

Relations between the French and the Natchez were friendly at first, but three French-Natchez wars—in 1716, 1723, and 1729—resulted in the French, with the aid of the Choctaw, driving the Natchez from their villages. In 1731 some 400 Natchez were captured and sold into the West Indian slave trade. The remainder took refuge with the Chickasaw and later with the Upper Creeks and Cherokee. When the latter tribes were forced to move west into Indian Territory (Oklahoma), the Natchez went with them.

Early 21st-century population estimates indicated some 500 individuals of Natchez descent.

CADDO

The Caddo were one tribe within a confederacy of North American Indian tribes comprising the Caddoan linguistic family. Their name derives from a French truncation of *kadohadacho*, meaning "real chief" in Caddo. The Caddo proper originally occupied the lower Red River area in what are now Louisiana and Arkansas. In the late 17th century they numbered approximately 8,000 persons living in villages scattered along the Red River and its tributaries. This is also the region of the Caddoan archaeological complex, where many striking examples of workmanship have been found. Archaeological research shows the Caddoan tenancy of the area to be ancient.

When first encountered by French and Spanish explorers, the Caddo were a semisedentary agricultural people. They lived in conical dwellings constructed of poles covered with a thatch of grass, which were grouped around ceremonial

Incised redware cat effigy bowl, Caddoan from Louisiana; in the National Museum of the American Indian, New York City. Courtesy of the National Museum of the American Indian, New York City

centres of temple mounds. The Caddo were skillful potters and basket makers. They wove cloth of vegetable fibres and, on special occasions, wore mantles decorated with feathers. They also wore nose rings and, like many other southeastern tribes, adorned their bodies with tattoos.

Traditional Caddo descent was matrilineal, and a hereditary upper group, marked by head flattening and other status symbols, directed political and religious activities. There are scattered reports of ceremonial human sacrifice and cannibalism. These and other traits probably indicate trade or other links between the Caddo and the centres of Aztec or Mayan cultures in Mexico and Yucatán.

During the 18th century the French and Spanish disputed over Caddo territory; the tribe was initially friendly to the French. By the close of the 18th century, colonial pressures had broken up Caddo tribal life and turned many of them into wanderers in their own land. When the vast territory of French Louisiana was purchased by the United States, the number of colonial settlers increased, and the tribe was pushed farther south. Under the treaty of 1835 the Caddo ceded all their land to the United States. The Louisiana Caddo moved southwest to join others of the tribe in Texas. There they lived peaceably for a time, but in 1859 threats of a massacre by a vigilante anti-Indian group forced them to flee to east-central Oklahoma, where they settled on a reservation on the banks of the Washita River.

Early 21st-century population estimates indicated more than 4,000 individuals of Caddo ancestry.

APALACHEE

The Apalachee were a tribe whose members spoke a Muskogean language and inhabited the area in northwestern Florida between the Aucilla and Apalachicola rivers above Apalachee Bay. In the 16th century the Spanish explorers Pánfilo de Narváez (in 1528) and Hernando de Soto (in 1539) led expeditions to Apalachee territory.

Traditionally, the tribe was divided into clans that traced descent through the maternal line; chieftainship and office were hereditary, probably in the lineage within the clan. An agricultural people who cultivated corn and squash, the Apalachee were also noted warriors. They were ultimately subdued about 1600 and missionized by Spanish Franciscans. They continued to prosper (in 1655, 6,000–8,000 Apalachee occupied eight towns, each with a Franciscan mission) until early in the 18th century when Creek tribes to the north, incited by the British, began a series of raids on Apalachee settlements. These attacks culminated in 1703 when an army made up of a few hundred Englishmen and several thousand Creek warriors defeated the combined Spanish and Apalachee. The tribe was almost totally destroyed, and 1,400 Apalachee were removed to Carolina where some of them merged with the

Creek. The remnants of the Florida tribe sought the protection of the French at Mobile and in Louisiana.

TIMUCUA

The Timucua inhabited the northeast coast of what is now Florida. This name is also used for the language they spoke. The estimated population of Timucua speakers was 13,000 in 1650, with 8,000 speaking Timucua proper and the remainder speaking various sister tongues. Their first European contact was probably with the expedition of Ponce de León in the 16th century. They were later missionized by the Franciscans, who compiled a grammar of their language.

In the early 1700s Timucua territory was invaded by the Creek Indians and the English. As a result of these incursions, many Timucua died in armed conflict, perished from deprivation, or succumbed to Old World diseases to which they had no immunity. Sometime after 1736 the remnants of the tribe moved to the area near the present Mosquito Lagoon in Florida. It is likely that the remaining Timucua were eventually absorbed into Seminole culture.

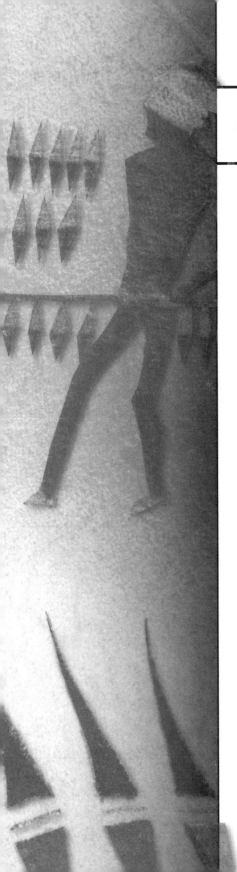

CHAPTER 5

PEOPLES OF THE PLAINS

The Plains lie in the centre of North America, spanning the area between the western mountains and the Mississippi River valley and from the southern edge of the subarctic to the Rio Grande in present-day Texas. The climate is of the continental type, with warm summers and cold winters. Relatively flat short-grass prairies with little precipitation are found west of the Missouri River and rolling tallgrass prairies with more moisture are found to its east. Tree-lined river valleys form a series of linear oases throughout the region.

The indigenous peoples of the Plains include speakers of Siouan, Algonquian, Uto-Aztecan, Caddoan, Athabaskan, Kiowa-Tanoan, and Michif languages. Plains peoples also invented a sign language to represent common objects or concepts such as "buffalo" or "exchange."

Earth-lodge villages were the only settlements on the Plains until the late 16th century; they were found along major waterways that provided fertile soil for growing corn, beans, squash, sunflowers, and tobacco. The groups who built these communities divided their time between village-based crop production and hunting expeditions, which often lasted for several weeks and involved travel over a considerable area. Plains villagers include the Mandan, Hidatsa, Omaha, Pawnee, and Arikara.

By 1750 horses from the Spanish colonies in present-day New Mexico had become common in the Plains and had revolutionized the hunting of bison. This new economic opportunity caused some local villagers to become dedicated nomads, as with the Crow (who retained close ties with their Hidatsa kin), and also drew agricultural tribes from surrounding areas into a nomadic lifestyle, including the Sioux, Blackfoot, Cheyenne, Comanche, Arapaho, and Kiowa.

Groups throughout the region had in common several forms of material culture, including the tepee, tailored leather clothing, a variety of battle regalia (such as feathered headdresses), and large drums used in ritual contexts. The Sun Dance, a ritual that demanded a high degree of piety and self-sacrifice from its participants, was also found throughout most of the Plains.

The Plains is perhaps the culture area in which tribal and band classifications were most conflated. Depictions of indigenous Americans in popular culture have often been loosely based on Plains peoples, encouraging many to view them as the "typical" American Indians.

MANDAN

The Mandan were Plains Indians who traditionally lived in semipermanent villages along the Missouri River in what is now North Dakota. They spoke a Siouan language, and their oral traditions suggest that they once lived in eastern North America. According to 19th-century anthropologist Washington Matthews, the self-name Numakiki means "people."

In the 19th century the Mandan lived in dome-shaped earth lodges clustered in stockaded villages. Their economy centred on raising corn, beans, pumpkins, sunflowers, and tobacco and on hunting buffalo, fishing, and trading with nomadic Plains tribes. The Mandan also made a variety of utilitarian and decorative items, including pottery, baskets, and painted buffalo robes depicting the heroic deeds of the tribe or of individuals. At this time Mandan culture was one of the richest of the Plains. The tribe hosted many prominent European and American travelers, including American explorers Lewis and Clark, Prussian scientist Prince Maximilian of Wied-Neuwied, and artists Karl Bodmer and George Catlin.

Traditional Mandan villages consisted of 12 to 100 or more earth lodges. Each village generally had three chiefs: one for war, one for peace, and one as the day-to-day village leader. Mandan social organization was built upon the ties of kinship and of age sets. It included a wide variety of age- and gender-based societies in which membership was obtained by apprenticeship or purchase. These included social, shamanistic, warrior, harvest, and other groups.

Mandan religion included many ceremonies and rituals that were performed by the various societies. The Okipa was the most complex of these; a four-day ritual requiring lengthy preparation and self-sacrifice by participants, it was an elaboration of the Sun Dance common to many Plains tribes. The Okipa had at least three equally important purposes: to commemorate the tribe's divine salvation from a primordial flood, to call the

Bird's-Eye View of the Mandan Village, 1800 Miles Above St. Louis, *detail of painting by George Catlin, 1837–39; in the National Museum of American Art, Washington, D.C.* National Museum of American Art, Washington, D.C., gift of Mrs. Sarah Harrison

buffalo and other creatures through communication with their spirit avatars, and to provide a vehicle through which individuals could complete vows made to the Almighty (e.g., in thanks or exchange for curing the sick or preventing death in childbirth or battle). It emphasized community prayer and was punctuated by a series of performances (some ribald) to call powerful spirit-beings to the ritual locale, by self-sacrifice through fasting, exertion, and piercing, and by the giving of gifts from supplicants to their spiritual mentors.

In 1750 there were nine large Mandan villages, but recurrent epidemics of smallpox, pertussis, and other diseases introduced through colonization reduced the tribe to two villages by 1800. In 1837 another smallpox epidemic left only 100 to 150 Mandan survivors. Some of these accompanied the Hidatsa to a new settlement near Fort Berthold in 1845, while others followed later, as did members of the Arikara tribe. The Mandan, Hidatsa, and Arikara eventually became known as the Three Affiliated Tribes.

In the mid-20th century, the Three Affiliated Tribes lost a considerable portion of their reservation to the waters of Lake Sakakawea, which rose behind the newly built Garrison Dam. With the flooding of the river bottoms, on which had been the best agricultural land, many tribal members shifted from agriculture to ranching or off-reservation pursuits.

Population estimates indicated approximately 1,300 Mandan descendants in the early 21st century.

HIDATSA

The Hidatsa, also called the Minitari or the Gros Ventres of the Missouri, once lived in semipermanent villages on the upper Missouri River between the Heart and the Little Missouri rivers in what is now North Dakota. The Hidatsa language is a member of the Siouan language family. The word *Hidatsa* in the Hidatsa language means "people of the willow."

Until the reservation period began in the late 19th century and limited the tribe's access to its traditional territory, the Hidatsa were a semisedentary people who lived in dome-shaped earth-berm lodges. They raised corn, beans, squash, and tobacco and made pottery. Hidatsa

Earth lodge dwelling of the Plains tribes of North America, photograph by Edward S. Curtis, c. 1908. Edward S. Curtis Collection/Library of Congress, Washington, D.C. (neg. no. LC-USZ62-114582)

women raised all the food crops, while tobacco was grown and traded by men. Men also hunted bison and other large game and engaged in warfare.

Traditional Hidatsa social organization was structured around clan lineages, age sets, and other groups, including several military societies for men and a variety of men's and women's religious societies. Descent was traced through the maternal line. As with other Plains Indians, the Sun Dance was the major religious ritual, involving long preparation, sacred vows, prayer, and self-sacrifice.

The Hidatsa language is most closely related to that of the Crow, with whom they were once united. After a dispute over the division of a buffalo carcass sometime between the late 17th and the early 18th centuries, the Crow chose to leave village life and become nomadic equestrians. The two tribes maintained close trading relations and frequently intermarried. In other areas of culture, the Hidatsa and the Mandan most closely resemble each other, a result of more than 400 years of continuous and peaceful association.

In the latter part of the 18th century, there were more than 2,000 Hidatsa who, with the Mandan, occupied a central position in the extensive trading network on the northern Plains. Horses, dressed hides, and buffalo robes, obtained from the nomadic tribes to the west, were exchanged with European traders to the east for guns, knives, and other manufactured goods.

In 1837 a smallpox epidemic so severely reduced Hidatsa and Mandan numbers that the two tribes consolidated into one village in order to mount an effective defense against their traditional enemy, the Sioux. Continual harassment by the Sioux and other enemies caused the Hidatsa and Mandan to move the village to a new location near Fort Berthold. Many Arikara joined them in 1862, also for purposes of defense. Since 1868 the Hidatsa, Mandan, and Arikara, collectively known as the Three Affiliated Tribes, have lived together on what is now the Fort Berthold Reservation in North Dakota.

In the mid-20th century the Three Affiliated Tribes lost more than one-fourth of their reservation to the waters rising behind the Garrison Dam on the Missouri River. Tribal members, who had been farming in the fertile river bottomlands, were relocated to the arid Plains uplands, deeply depressing the reservation economy. By the late 20th century the Three Affiliated Tribes had established buffalo ranching operations and a casino, returning a level of prosperity to their communities.

Early 21st-century population estimates indicated some 1,500 individuals of Hidatsa descent.

OMAHA

The Omaha were a people of the Dhegiha branch of the Siouan language stock. It is thought that Dhegiha speakers, which include the Osage, Ponca, Kansa, and

Quapaw as well as the Omaha, migrated westward from the Atlantic coast at some point in prehistory and that their early settlements were in the present U.S. states of Virginia and the Carolinas. After a time they moved to the Ozark Plateau and the prairies of what is now western Missouri. There the five tribes separated, with the Omaha and the Ponca moving north to present-day Minnesota, where they lived until the late 17th century. At that time the two tribes were driven farther west by the migrating Dakota Sioux. The Omaha and Ponca separated in present-day South Dakota, with the former moving on to Bow Creek in present-day Nebraska. In 1854, under the pressure of encroaching settlers, the Omaha sold most of their land to the U.S. government. In 1882 the government allotted land in Nebraska that prevented the removal of the tribe to Oklahoma; somewhat later they received U.S. citizenship.

As with many other Plains Indian tribes, the traditional Omaha economy combined corn agriculture with hunting and gathering. In spring and autumn the people lived in permanent villages of dome-shaped earth lodges, moving into portable tepees for the hunting seasons. Omaha social organization was elaborate, with a class system of chiefs, priests, physicians, and commoners. Rank was inherited through the male line, although individuals could raise their status by distributing horses and blankets or providing feasts.

Traditional Omaha kinship was organized into 10 clans within two larger groups, representing earth and sky. Earth clans had charge of ceremonies concerning war and food supply, while the ceremonies overseen by the sky clans were designed to secure supernatural aid. When the entire tribe camped together during the summer bison hunt or on migrations, tepees were arranged in a large circle symbolizing the tribal organization. The Omaha, like many other Plains peoples, awarded special insignia for such daring war exploits as touching an enemy in battle, touching a dead enemy surrounded by his tribesmen, and removing a trained horse from the enemy's camp. Killing the enemy was considered a lesser exploit.

Early 21st-century population estimates indicated more than 5,000 individuals of Omaha descent.

PAWNEE

The Pawnee, a people of Caddoan linguistic stock, lived on the Platte River in what is now Nebraska, U.S., from before the 16th century to the latter part of the 19th century. In the 19th century the Pawnee tribe was composed of relatively independent bands: the Kitkehahki, Chaui, Pitahauerat, and Skidi. Each of these bands occupied several villages, which were the basic social unit of the Pawnee people.

Like many other Plains Indians, the Pawnee traditionally lived in large, dome-shaped, earth-covered lodges during most of the year, opting for tepees while on bison hunts. Pawnee women raised corn, squash, and beans and were practiced in the art of pottery making. Horses were first introduced in the 17th and 18th centuries from Spanish settlements in the Southwest.

Pawnee class distinctions favoured chiefs, priests, and shamans. Each chief of a village or band had in his keeping a sacred bundle. Shamans were believed to possess special powers to treat illness and to ward off enemy raids and food shortages. Priests were trained in the performance of rituals and sacred songs. Along with shamanistic and hunt societies, the Pawnee also had military societies.

The traditional religion of the Pawnee was quite elaborate. They believed some of the stars to be gods and performed rituals to entreat their presence, and they also used astronomy in practical affairs (e.g., to determine when to plant corn). Corn was regarded as a symbolic mother through whom the sun god bestowed his blessing. Other important deities were the morning and evening stars and Tirawa, the supreme power who created all these. For a time Pawnee religion included the sacrifice of a captive adolescent girl to the morning star, but this practice ended in the 19th century.

Relations between the Pawnee and settlers were peaceful, and many Pawnee individuals served as scouts in the U.S. Army of the Frontier. The Pawnee nation ceded most of its land in Nebraska to the U.S. government by treaties in 1833, 1848, and 1857. In 1876 their last Nebraska holdings were given up, and they were moved to Oklahoma, where they remained.

Early 21st-century population estimates indicated some 4,500 individuals of Pawnee descent.

ARIKARA

The Arikara, or Sahnish, were a people of the Caddoan linguistic family. The cultural roots of Caddoan-speaking peoples lay in the prehistoric mound-building societies of the lower Mississippi River valley. The Arikara were culturally related to the Pawnee, from whom they broke away and moved gradually northward, becoming the northernmost Caddoan tribe. Before American colonization of the Plains, the Arikara lived along the Missouri River between the Cannonball and Cheyenne rivers in what are now North and South Dakota.

The Arikara traditionally lived in substantial semipermanent villages of earth lodges, domed earth-berm structures. Their economy relied heavily upon raising corn, beans, squash, sunflowers, and tobacco. Arikara households used these products and traded them with other tribes for meat and processed hides. Arikara women were responsible for farming, food preparation and preservation, clothing production, lodge building, and the rituals associated with their work. Arikara men hunted deer, elk, and buffalo, provided defense, and performed rituals related to these practices.

The most important items in Arikara material culture were the sacred bundles. These collections of objects were treated as living connections to the divine, and many village activities were organized around the perceived needs of the bundles and the sacred beings who communicated through them. Each bundle had a bundle-keeper, an office that tended to be the hereditary prerogative of a few leading families. Lower leadership positions were associated with organized military, dancing, and curing societies. The Arikara shared with other Plains tribes the practice of self-sacrifice in the Sun Dance.

The Arikara were seen as an obstacle by white trading parties moving up the Missouri River; in 1823 a battle with traders under the aegis of William H. Ashley's Rocky Mountain Fur Company resulted in the first U.S. Army campaign against a Plains tribe. In response, the Arikara left their villages and adopted a nomadic equestrian lifestyle for a period of years.

Although the Arikara had numbered between 3,000 and 4,000 individuals near the end of the 1700s, wars and epidemic disease had severely reduced their population by the middle of the 19th century. In the 1860s they joined the Mandan and Hidatsa tribes, which together were

Members of the Arikara Night Society dancing in a traditional ceremony, photograph by Edward S. Curtis, c. 1908. Library of Congress, Washington, D.C. (neg. no. LC-USZ62-101185)

known as the Three Affiliated Tribes, and a reservation was created for them at Fort Berthold, N.D. By 1885 the Arikara had taken up farming and livestock production on family farmsteads dispersed along the rich Missouri River bottomlands.

In the 1950s construction of the Garrison Dam flooded the Missouri River bottomlands, creating Lake Sakakawea. More than a quarter of the Fort Berthold reservation lands were permanently flooded by the rising waters. This and the discovery of oil in the Williston Basin forced another removal, this time to new homes on the arid North Dakota uplands, where farming was difficult. As a result, reservation communities suffered an economic depression; however, by the end of the 20th century, the Three Affiliated Tribes had regained a level of prosperity through buffalo ranching and other tribal businesses.

Early 21st-century population estimates indicated more than 1,000 individuals of Arikara descent.

CROW

The Crow, who were of Siouan linguistic stock, historically affiliated with the village-dwelling Hidatsa of the upper Missouri River. They occupied the area around the Yellowstone River and its tributaries, particularly the valleys of the Powder, Wind, and Bighorn rivers in what is now Montana.

Perhaps lured by the trade in horses, and putatively in response to a dispute over the distribution of meat from a slain buffalo, the Crow (also called the Absaroka or the Apsarokee) broke with the Hidatsa and moved westward sometime between the mid-17th and the early 18th century. Traditional Crow social organization included three bands, which were known as Mountain Crow, River Crow, and Kicked-in-Their-Bellies. The last was most likely an offshoot from the Mountain Crow and remained closely allied to that band.

Much of traditional Crow life revolved around the buffalo and the horse. From the former they made food, clothing, robes, tepee covers, sinew thread, containers, and shields. The latter provided transportation and, through horse racing and trading, a means of entertainment and exchange. By 1740 the Crow had emerged as middlemen engaged in the trading of horses, bows, shirts, and featherwork to the Plains Village tribes for guns and metal goods; these they traded in turn to the Shoshone in Idaho.

In Crow society women's responsibilities included the processing and preparation of food, housing, and clothing. Women also occasionally engaged in raiding parties, particularly when avenging the death of a close relative. Generally, however, warfare was carried on by men and was largely a matter of raiding for horses. For a man to be ranked as a chief, performance of four insults to the enemy, or coups, was required: leading a war party without losing a Crow life, taking a tethered horse from an enemy camp, striking an enemy with a coupstick (a

A Crow woman holding an infant in a decorated cradleboard, photograph by Edward S. Curtis, c. 1908. Library of Congress, Washington, D.C.

type of club), and wresting a weapon from an enemy. One man from among a camp's chiefs became the head of the camp.

A basic element in traditional Crow religious life was the vision quest. Through a process involving prayer, solemn vows, fasting in isolation, and, sometimes, piercing the body, a man who attained a vision was "adopted" by a supernatural guardian who instructed him in gathering objects into a medicine bundle. He was permitted to share part of his power with other men who had not received visions and to create replica bundles for them. Women also engaged in vision quests, though we know less about traditional women's rituals because few were recorded in the 19th and early 20th centuries.

The Crow grew tobacco for ritual use. According to their traditions, it had been given to them to overcome their enemies. Unlike other clubs and societies among the Crow, Tobacco Societies involved an entrance fee and an elaborate initiation rite, and they were joined by married couples rather than individuals.

The Crow began to suffer high losses from the Blackfoot and Dakota Sioux as the American colonial frontier expanded and drove those tribes into Crow country. In response to constant threats from these enemies, the Crow sided with the U.S. military in the Plains wars of the 1860s and '70s. In 1868 they accepted a reservation carved from former tribal lands in southern Montana.

In the early 21st century, population estimates indicated some 15,000 individuals of Crow descent.

SIOUX

The Sioux were a broad alliance of Indian peoples who spoke three related languages within the Siouan language family. The name Sioux is an abbreviation of Nadouessioux ("Adders"; i.e., "enemies"), a name originally applied to them by the Ojibwa. The Santee, also known as the Eastern Sioux, were Dakota speakers and comprised the Mdewkanton, Wahpeton, Wahpekute, and Sisseton. The Yankton, who spoke Nakota, included the Yankton and Yanktonai. The Teton, also referred to as the Western Sioux, spoke Lakota and had seven divisions: the Sihasapa, or Blackfoot; Brulé (Upper and Lower); Hunkpapa; Miniconjou; Oglala; Sans Arcs; and Oohenonpa, or Two-Kettle.

THE SIOUX WAY OF LIFE

Before the middle of the 17th century, the Santee Sioux lived in the area around Lake Superior, where they gathered wild rice and other foods, hunted deer and buffalo, and speared fish from canoes. Prolonged and continual warfare with the Ojibwa to their east drove the Santee into what is now southern and western Minnesota, at that time the territory of the agricultural Teton and Yankton. In turn, the Santee forced these two groups from Minnesota into what are now North and South Dakota. Horses were becoming common on the Plains during this period, and the Teton and Yankton abandoned agriculture in favour of an economy centred on the nomadic hunting of bison.

Traditionally the Teton and Yankton shared many cultural characteristics with other nomadic Plains Indian societies. They lived in tepees, wore clothing made from leather, suede, or fur, and traded buffalo products for corn produced by the farming tribes of the Plains. The Sioux also raided those tribes frequently, particularly the Mandan, Arikara, Hidatsa, and Pawnee, actions that eventually drove the agriculturists to ally themselves with the U.S. military against the Sioux tribes.

PRECONTACT SIOUX CULTURE

Sioux men acquired status by performing brave deeds in warfare; horses and scalps obtained in a raid were evidence of valour. Sioux women were skilled at porcupine-quill and bead embroidery, favouring geometric designs. They also produced prodigious numbers of processed bison hides during the 19th century, when the trade value of these "buffalo robes" increased dramatically. Community policing was performed by men's military societies, the most significant duty of which was to oversee the buffalo hunt. Women's societies generally focused on fertility, healing, and the overall well-being of the group. Other societies focused on ritual dance and shamanism.

Religion was an integral part of all aspects of Sioux life, as it was for all Native American peoples. The Sioux recognized four powers as presiding over the universe, and each power in turn was divided into hierarchies of four. The buffalo had a prominent place in all Sioux rituals. Among the Teton and Santee the bear was also a symbolically important animal; bear power obtained in a vision was regarded as curative, and some groups enacted a ceremonial bear hunt to protect warriors before their departure on a raid. Warfare and supernaturalism were closely connected, to the extent that designs suggested in mystical visions were painted on war shields to protect the bearers from their enemies. The annual Sun Dance was the most important religious event.

THE BEGINNING OF THE STRUGGLE FOR THE WEST

Having suffered from the encroachment of the Ojibwa, the Sioux were extremely resistant to incursions upon their new territory. Teton and Yankton territory included the vast area between the Missouri River and the Teton Mountains and between the Platte River on the south and the Yellowstone River on the north (e.g., all or parts of the present-day states of Montana, North Dakota, South Dakota, Nebraska, Colorado, and Wyoming); this territory was increasingly broached as the colonial frontier moved westward past the Mississippi River in the mid-19th century. The California Gold Rush of 1849 opened a floodgate of travelers, and many Sioux became incensed by the U.S. government's attempt to establish the

Bozeman Trail and other routes through the tribes' sovereign lands.

The United States sought to forestall strife by negotiating the First Treaty of Fort Laramie (1851) with the Sioux and other Plains peoples. The treaty assigned territories to each tribe throughout the northern Great Plains and set terms for the building of forts and roads within the region. In accordance with the treaty the Santee Sioux gave up most of their land in Minnesota in exchange for annuities and other considerations. They were restricted to a reservation and encouraged to take up agriculture, but government mismanagement of the annuities, depleted game reserves, and a general resistance to an agricultural lifestyle combined to precipitate starvation on the reservation by 1862. That year, with many settler men away fighting the Civil War, Santee warriors under the leadership of Chief Little Crow mounted a bloody attempt to clear their traditional territory of outsiders. U.S. troops soon pacified the region, but only after more than 400 settlers, 70 U.S. soldiers, and 30 Santee had been killed. More than 300 Santee were condemned to death for their roles in what had become known as the Sioux Uprising. Although President Lincoln commuted the sentences of most of these men, 38 Santee were ultimately hanged in the largest mass execution in U.S. history. After their defeat the Santee were relocated to reservations in Dakota Territory and Nebraska.

Although the Native peoples of the Plains had putatively accepted some development in the West by agreeing to the terms of the First Treaty of Fort Laramie, many were soon dissatisfied with the extent of encroachment on their land. In 1865–67 the Oglala chief Red Cloud led thousands of Sioux warriors in a campaign to halt construction of the Bozeman Trail. In December 1866 warriors under Chief High Backbone drew a U.S. military patrol from Fort Phil Kearny into an ambush. The patrol's commanding officer, Capt. William J. Fetterman, ignored warnings that the Sioux often used apparently injured riders as decoys to draw their enemies into poorly defensible locations. Fetterman led his men in chase of such a decoy, and the entire group of some 80 U.S. soldiers was killed. The decoy was Crazy Horse, already displaying the characteristics that later made him a major military leader among his people. The worst U.S. defeat on the Plains to that point, the so-called Fetterman Massacre reignited the anti-Indian sentiment that had flared in the eastern states after the Sioux Uprising of 1862.

The terms of the Second Treaty of Fort Laramie (1868) implicitly acknowledged that the West was proving a very expensive and difficult place to develop. The United States agreed to abandon the Bozeman Trail and guaranteed the Sioux peoples exclusive possession of the present state of South Dakota west of the Missouri River. When gold was discovered in the Black Hills of South Dakota in the mid-1870s, however, thousands of miners disregarded the treaty and

Sioux chiefs Red Cloud and American Horse. Library of Congress, Washington, D.C.

swarmed onto the Sioux reservation, thus precipitating another round of hostilities.

THE BATTLE OF THE LITTLE BIGHORN AND THE CESSATION OF WAR

At the Battle of the Little Bighorn in June 1876 a large contingent of Sioux and Cheyenne warriors again took advantage of the hubris of U.S. officers, overwhelming Lieut. Col. George A. Custer and 200 men of his 7th Cavalry. This definitive indigenous victory essentially sealed the fate of the tribes by instigating such shock and horror among American citizens that they demanded unequivocal revenge. The so-called Plains Wars essentially ended later in 1876, when American troops trapped 3,000 Sioux at the Tongue River valley. The tribes formally surrendered in October, after which the majority of members returned to their reservations.

In spite of the surrender of most Sioux bands, the chiefs Sitting Bull, Crazy Horse, and Gall refused to take their people to the reservations. Crazy Horse surrendered in 1877 only to be killed later that year while resisting arrest for leaving the reservation without authorization; he was reportedly transporting his ill wife to her parents' home. Sitting Bull and Gall escaped to Canada for several years, returning to the United States in 1881 and surrendering without incident.

In 1890–91 the Ghost Dance religion began to take a strong hold among the Sioux people, promising the coming of a messiah, the disappearance of all people of European descent from North America, the return of large buffalo herds and the lifestyle they supported, and reunion with the dead. The new religion held great appeal, as most of the Sioux bands had suffered harsh privations while confined to reservations. Game had all but disappeared, the supplies and annuities promised in treaties were frequently stolen by corrupt officials, and many people lived almost continuously on the verge of starvation. Believing that the Ghost Dance religion threatened an already uneasy peace, U.S. government agents set out to arrest its leaders.

In 1890 Sitting Bull was ordered to stay away from Ghost Dance gatherings. He stated that he intended to defy the order and was killed as Lakota policemen attempted to take him into custody. When the revitalized U.S. 7th Cavalry—Custer's former regiment—massacred more than 200 Sioux men, women, and children at Wounded Knee Creek later that year, the Sioux ceased military resistance.

The warrior ethic continued among the Siouan tribes throughout the 20th century, with many people—women as well as men—serving in the U.S. military. However, Sioux individuals did not take up arms against the U.S. government again until 1973, when a small group of American Indian Movement members occupied the community of Wounded Knee, exchanging gunfire with federal marshals who demanded their surrender.

Early 21st-century population estimates indicated some 160,000 individuals of Sioux descent.

BLACKFOOT

The Blackfoot were a group of three closely related Algonquian-speaking tribes comprising the Piegan, or Pikuni, the Blood, or Kainah, and the Siksika, or Blackfoot-proper (often referred to as the Northern Blackfoot). The three groups traditionally lived in what is now Alberta, Can., and Montana, U.S.

Among the first Algonquians to move westward from timberland to open grassland, the Blackfoot probably migrated on foot using wooden travois drawn by dogs to transport their goods. In the early 18th century they were pedestrian buffalo hunters living in the Saskatchewan valley about 400 miles (645 km) east of the Rocky Mountains. They acquired horses and firearms before 1750. Driving weaker tribes before them, the Blackfoot pushed westward to the Rockies and southward into what is now Montana. At the height of their power, in the first half of the 19th century, they held a vast territory extending from northern Saskatchewan to the southernmost headwaters of the Missouri River.

The Blackfoot were known as one of the strongest and most aggressive military powers on the northwestern Plains. For a quarter of a century after 1806, they prevented British, French, and American fur traders, whom they regarded as poachers, from trapping in the rich beaver country of the upper tributaries of the Missouri. At the same time, they warred upon neighbouring tribes, capturing horses and taking captives.

Each Blackfoot tribe was divided into several hunting bands led by one or more chiefs. These bands wintered separately in sheltered river valleys. In summer they gathered in a great encampment to observe the Sun Dance, the principal tribal religious ceremony. Many individuals owned elaborate medicine bundles—collections of sacred objects that, when properly venerated, were said to bring success in war and hunting and protection against sickness and misfortune.

For three decades after their first treaty with the United States in 1855, the Blackfoot declined to forsake hunting in favour of farming. When the buffalo were almost exterminated in the early 1880s, nearly one-quarter of the Piegan died of starvation. Thereafter the Blackfoot took up farming and ranching.

Early 21st-century population estimates indicated some 90,000 individuals of Blackfoot descent in Canada and the United States.

CHEYENNE

The Cheyenne spoke an Algonquian language and inhabited the regions around the Platte and Arkansas rivers during the 19th century. Before 1700 the Cheyenne lived in what is now central Minnesota, where they farmed, hunted, gathered wild rice, and made pottery. They later

SITTING BULL

Born in 1831 near Grand River, Dakota Territory (now in South Dakota), Sitting Bull (Indian name Tatanka Iyotake) was a Teton Dakota Indian chief under whom the Sioux tribes united in their struggle for survival on the North American Great Plains. He is remembered for his lifelong distrust of white men and his stubborn determination to resist their domination.

Respected for his courage and wisdom, Sitting Bull was made principal chief of the entire Sioux nation about 1867. In 1868 the Sioux accepted peace with the U.S. government on the basis of the Second Treaty of Fort Laramie, which guaranteed the Sioux a reservation in what is now southwestern South Dakota. But when gold was discovered in the Black Hills in the mid-1870s, a rush of white prospectors invaded lands guaranteed to the Indians by the treaty. Late in 1875 those Sioux who had been resisting the whites' incursions were ordered to return to their reservations by Jan. 31, 1876, or be considered hostile to the United States.

Sitting Bull. Library of Congress, Washington, D.C. (neg. no. LC-USZ62-12277)

After further conflict with the U.S. Army, the Sioux, Cheyenne, and certain Arapaho under Sitting Bull then moved their encampment into the valley of the Little Bighorn River. At this point Sitting Bull performed the Sun Dance, and when he emerged from a trance induced by self-torture, he reported that he had seen soldiers falling into his camp like grasshoppers from the sky. His prophecy was fulfilled on June 25, when Lieut. Col. George Armstrong Custer rode into the valley and he and all the men under his immediate command were annihilated in the Battle of the Little Bighorn.

Strong public reaction among whites to the Battle of the Little Bighorn resulted in stepped-up military action. The Sioux emerged the victors in their battles with U.S. troops, but though they might win battle after battle, they could never win the war. The Sioux depended on the buffalo for their livelihood, and the buffalo, under the steady encroachment of whites, were rapidly becoming extinct. Hunger led more and more Sioux to surrender, and in May 1877 Sitting Bull led his remaining followers across the border into Canada. But the Canadian government could not acknowledge responsibility for feeding a people whose reservation was south of the border, and after four years, during which his following dwindled steadily, famine forced Sitting Bull to surrender. After 1883 he lived at the Standing Rock Agency, where he vainly opposed the sale of tribal lands. In 1885, partly to get rid of him, the Indian agent allowed him to join Buffalo Bill's Wild West show, in which he gained international fame.

occupied a village of earth lodges on the Cheyenne River in North Dakota; it was probably during this period that they acquired horses and became more dependent on the buffalo for food.

After their town was destroyed by the Ojibwa (Chippewa), the Cheyenne settled along the Missouri River near the Mandan and Arikara tribes. Toward the close of the 18th century, smallpox and the aggression of the Dakota Sioux decimated the village tribes at the same time that the horse and gun were becoming generally available in the northeastern Plains. The Cheyenne moved farther west to the area of the Black Hills, where they developed a unique version of nomadic Plains culture and gave up agriculture and pottery. During the early 19th century they migrated to the headwaters of the Platte River in what is now Colorado. In 1832 a large segment of the tribe established itself along the Arkansas River, thus dividing the tribe into northern and southern branches. This division was recognized in the First Treaty of Fort Laramie with the United States in 1851.

Traditional Cheyenne religion focused upon two principal deities, the Wise One Above and a god who lived

In a Piegan Lodge, photograph by Edward S. Curtis, c. 1910. Courtesy of the Edward E. Ayer Collection, The Newberry Library, Chicago

beneath the ground. In addition, four spirits lived at the points of the compass. The Cheyenne performed the Sun Dance in a very elaborate form. They placed heavy emphasis on visions in which a guardian spirit adopted the individual and bestowed special powers upon him or her so long as certain prescribed laws or practices were observed. Their most-venerated objects, contained in a sacred bundle, were a hat made from the skin and hair of a buffalo cow and four arrows—two painted for hunting and two for battle. These objects were carried in war to ensure success over the enemy.

Traditional Cheyenne society was organized into 10 major bands governed by a council of 44 chiefs and seven military societies. The Dog Soldiers were the most powerful and aggressive of the military groups. There were also social, dance, medicine, and shamanistic societies. A given society was generally open to either male or female members, but not to both.

The Cheyenne fought constantly with the Kiowa until 1840, when a lasting peace was established between them. From 1857 to 1879 the Cheyenne were embroiled in raids and wars with U.S. military troops. The conflicts often caused suffering for civilians, including Cheyenne and settler women, children, and elders. The tribe began raiding emigrant settlements and military and trading posts on a wide front after the Sand Creek Massacre (1864), in which a peaceful Cheyenne village was destroyed by the U.S. cavalry. In the Treaty of Medicine Lodge (1867), the Southern

Cheyenne were assigned a reservation in Oklahoma, but they settled there only after 1875. After George Armstrong Custer's attack on their Washita River village in 1868, the Southern Cheyenne were fairly peaceful until 1874–75, when they joined in the general uprisings of the southern Plains tribes. In 1876 the Northern Cheyenne joined the Dakota in the Battle of the Little Bighorn and there defeated Custer.

Early 21st-century population estimates indicated more than 20,000 Cheyenne descendants.

COMANCHE

The Comanche were a tribe of equestrian nomads whose 18th- and 19th-century territory comprised the southern Great Plains. The name Comanche is derived from a Ute word meaning "anyone who wants to fight me all the time."

The Comanche (also called the Padouca) had previously been part of the Wyoming Shoshone. They moved south in successive stages, attacking and displacing other tribes, notably the Apache, whom they drove from the southern Plains. By the early 1800s the Comanche were very powerful, with a population estimated at 7,000 to 10,000 individuals. Their language, of the Shoshonean branch of the Uto-Aztecan linguistic stock, became a lingua franca for much of the area.

Like most other tribes of Plains Indians, the Comanche were organized into autonomous bands, local groups formed on the basis of kinship and other social relationships. Buffalo products formed the core of the Comanche economy and included robes, tepee covers, sinew thread, water carriers made of the animal's stomach, and a wide variety of other goods.

The Comanche were one of the first tribes to acquire horses from the Spanish and one of the few to breed them to any extent. Highly skilled Comanche horsemen set the pattern of nomadic equestrian life that became characteristic of the Plains tribes in the 18th and 19th centuries. Comanche raids for material goods, horses, and captives carried them as far south as Durango in present-day Mexico.

In the mid-19th century the Penateka, or southern branch of the Comanche, were settled on a reservation in Indian Territory (now Oklahoma). The northern segment of the tribe, however, continued the struggle to protect their realm from settlers. In 1864 Col. Christopher ("Kit") Carson led U.S. forces in an unsuccessful

Comanche Village, Women Dressing Robes and Drying Meat, *oil on canvas, detail of a painting by George Catlin, 1834–35; in the Smithsonian American Art Museum, Washington, D.C.* National Museum of American Art/Art Resource, New York

campaign against the Comanche. In 1865 the Comanche and their allies the Kiowa signed a treaty with the United States, which granted them what is now western Oklahoma, from the Red River north to the Cimarron. Upon the failure of the United States to abide by the terms of the treaty, hostilities resumed until 1867, when, in agreements made at Medicine Lodge Creek in Kansas, the Comanche, Kiowa, and Kiowa Apache undertook to settle on a reservation in Oklahoma. The government was unable to keep squatters off the land promised to the tribes, and it was after this date that some of the most violent encounters between U.S. forces and the Comanche took place.

Early 21st-century population estimates indicated some 20,000 individuals of Comanche descent.

ARAPAHO

The Arapaho, a tribe of Algonquian linguistic stock, lived during the 19th century along the Platte and Arkansas rivers of what are now the U.S. states of Wyoming, Colorado, Nebraska, and Kansas. Their oral traditions suggest that they once had permanent villages in the Eastern Woodlands, where they engaged in agriculture. Because of pressure from tribes to the east, the Arapaho gradually moved westward, abandoning farming and settled life during the process. They split into northern (Platte River) and southern (Arkansas River) groups after 1830.

Like many other tribes that moved from the East to the Plains, the Arapaho became nomadic equestrians, living in tepees and depending on buffalo hunting for subsistence. They also gathered wild plant foods and traded buffalo products for corn, beans, squash, and European manufactured goods; their main trading partners were the farming Mandan and Arikara tribes in what are now North and South Dakota and the Spanish in the Southwest.

Traditionally, the Arapaho were a highly religious people for whom everyday actions and objects (e.g., beadwork designs) had symbolic meanings. Their chief object of veneration was a flat pipe that was kept in a sacred bundle with a hoop or wheel. The Arapaho practiced the Sun Dance, and their social organization included age-graded military and religious societies.

From early times the Arapaho were continually at war with the Shoshone, the Ute, and the Pawnee. The southern Arapaho were for a long period closely associated with the southern Cheyenne; some Arapaho fought with the Cheyenne against Lt. Col. George Armstrong Custer at the Little Bighorn in 1876. In the Treaty of Medicine Lodge in 1867, the southern Arapaho were assigned a reservation in Oklahoma together with the Cheyenne, while the northern Arapaho were assigned a reservation in Wyoming with the Shoshone.

Early 21st-century population estimates indicated some 15,000 individuals of Arapaho descent.

Runs Medicine, an Arapaho man wearing traditional regalia, c. 1899. Library of Congress, Washington, D.C. (neg. no. LC-USZ62-101281)

Kiowa tribal members A-ke-a (left) and her father, Elk Tongue, modeling traditional regalia, photograph by H.P. Robinson, c. 1891. Library of Congress, Washington, D.C. (neg. no. LC-USZ62-126696) Library of Congress, Washington, D.C. (neg. no. LC-USZ62-126696)

KIOWA

The Kiowa, a people of Kiowa-Tanoan linguistic stock, are believed to have migrated from what is now southwestern Montana into the southern Great Plains in the 18th century. Numbering some 3,000 at the time, they were accompanied on the migration by Kiowa Apache, a small southern Apache band that became closely associated with the Kiowa.

Guided by the Crow, the Kiowa learned the technologies and customs of the Plains Indians and eventually formed a lasting peace with the Comanche, Arapaho, and Southern Cheyenne. The name Kiowa may be a variant of their name for themselves, Kai-i-gwu, meaning "principal people."

The Kiowa and their confederates were among the last of the Plains tribes to capitulate to the U.S. Cavalry. Since 1868 they have shared a reservation with the Comanche between the Washita and Red rivers, centring on Anadarko, Okla. Before their surrender, Kiowa culture was typical of nomadic Plains Indians. After they acquired horses from the Spanish, their economy focused on equestrian bison hunting. They lived in large tepees and moved camp frequently in pursuit of game. Kiowa warriors attained rank according to their exploits in war, including killing an enemy or touching his body during combat.

Traditional Kiowa religion included the belief that dreams and visions gave individuals supernatural power in war, hunting, and healing. Ten medicine bundles, believed to protect the tribe, became central in the Kiowan Sun Dance. The Kiowa and the Comanche were instrumental in spreading peyotism.

The Kiowa were also notable for their pictographic histories of tribal events, recorded twice each year. Each summer and winter from 1832 to 1939, one or more Kiowa artists created a sketch or drawing that depicted the events of

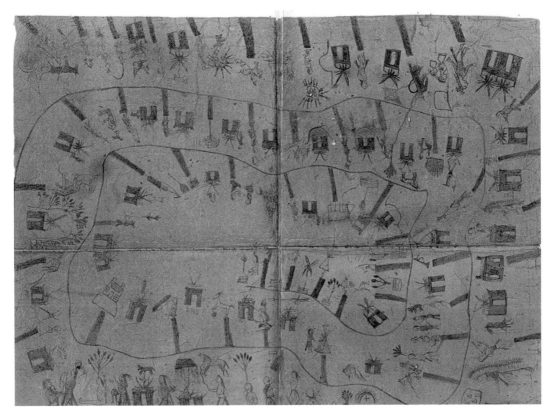

Kiowa calendar painting of the years 1833–92 on buffalo hide, photograph by James Mooney, 1895. "Seventeenth Annual Report of the Bureau of American Ethnology to the Smithsonian Institution, 1895-96," by James Mooney.

the past six months; in the early years of this practice, the drawings were made on dressed skins, while artists working later in the period drew on ledger paper. The National Anthropological Archives of the Smithsonian Institution contain a number of these extraordinary drawings.

Early 21st-century population estimates indicated more than 12,000 individuals of Kiowa descent.

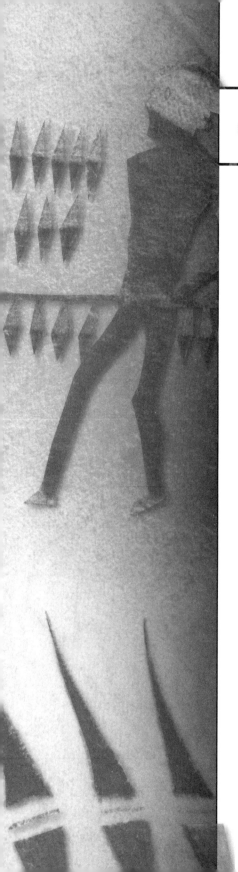

CHAPTER 6

THE SOUTHWEST

The Southwest culture area lies between the Rocky Mountains and the Mexican Sierra Madre, mostly in present-day Arizona and New Mexico. The topography includes plateaus, basins, and ranges. The climate on the Colorado Plateau is temperate, while it is semitropical in most of the basin and range systems. There is little precipitation, and the major ecosystem is desert. The landscape includes several major river systems, notably those of the Colorado and the Rio Grande, that create linear oases in the region.

The Southwest is home to speakers of Hokan, Uto-Aztecan, Tanoan, Keresan, Kiowa-Tanoan, Penutian, and Athabaskan languages. The region was the home of both agricultural and hunting and gathering peoples, although the most common lifeway combined these two economic strategies. Best known among the agriculturists are the Pueblo Indians, including the Zuni and Hopi. The Yumans, Pima, and Tohono O'odham (Papago) engaged in both farming and foraging, relying on each to the extent the environment would allow. The Navajo and the many Apache groups usually engaged in some combination of agriculture, foraging, and the raiding of other groups.

The major agricultural products were corn, beans, squash, and cotton. Wild plant foods, deer, other game, and fish (for those groups living near rivers) were the primary foraged foods. The Pueblo peoples built architecturally remarkable apartment houses of adobe and stone masonry and were known for their complex kinship structures, kachina (*katsina*) dances and dolls, and fine pottery, textiles, and kiva and sand paintings. The Navajo built round houses ("hogans") and were known for their complex clan system, healing rituals, and fine textiles and jewelry. The Apaches, Yumans, Pima, and Tohono O'odham generally built thatched houses or brush shelters and focused their expressive culture on oral traditions. Stone channels and check dams (low walls that slowed the runoff from the sporadic but heavy rains) were common throughout the Southwest, as were basketry and digging sticks.

PUEBLO INDIANS

Pueblo Indians are known for living in compact permanent settlements known as pueblos. Representative of the Southwest Indian culture area, most live in northeastern Arizona and northwestern New Mexico.

Pueblo peoples are thought to be the descendants of the prehistoric Ancestral Pueblo (Anasazi) culture. Just as there was considerable regional diversity among the Ancestral Pueblo, there is similar diversity, both cultural and linguistic, among the Pueblo. Contemporary Puebloans are customarily described as belonging to either the eastern or the western division. The eastern Pueblo villages are in New Mexico along the Rio Grande and comprise groups who speak Tanoan and Keresan languages. Tanoan languages such as Tewa are distantly related to Uto-Aztecan, but Keresan has no known affinities. The western Pueblos include the Hopi villages of northern Arizona and the Zuni, Acoma, and Laguna villages, all in western New Mexico. Of the western Pueblos, Acoma and Laguna speak Keresan; the Zuni

Pueblo Indian pottery: (left) Acoma water jar, c. 1890, (centre) Santa Clara vase, c. 1880, (right) San Ildefonso water jar, c. 1906; in the Denver Art Museum. Courtesy of the Denver Art Museum, Denver, Colorado

speak Zuni, a language of Penutian affiliation; and the Hopi Pueblos, with one exception, speak Hopi, a Uto-Aztecan language. The exception is the village of Hano, composed of Tewa refugees from the Rio Grande.

Each of the 70 or more Pueblo villages extant before Spanish colonization was politically autonomous, governed by a council composed of the heads of religious societies. These societies were centred in the kivas, subterranean ceremonial chambers that also functioned as private clubs and lounging rooms for men. Traditionally, Pueblo peoples were farmers, with the types of farming and associated traditions of property ownership varying among the groups. Along the Rio Grande and its tributaries corn and cotton were cultivated in irrigated fields in river bottoms. Among the western Pueblos, especially the Hopi, farming was less reliable because there were few permanent water sources. Traditionally women did most of the farming, but as hunting diminished in importance, men also became responsible for agricultural work. Many of the Rio Grande Pueblos had special hunting societies that hunted deer and antelope in the mountains, and easterly Pueblos such as the Taos and Picuris sometimes sent hunters to the Plains for bison. Among all Pueblos communal rabbit hunts were held, and women gathered wild plants to eat.

In 1539 a Franciscan friar, Marcos de Niza, claimed the Pueblo region for Spain. Explorer Francisco Vázquez de Coronado followed in 1540, quickly and brutally pacifying all indigenous resistance. In 1680 a Tewa man, Popé, led the Pueblo Rebellion against the Spanish. The colonizers retreated from the region for several years but completed a reconquest in 1691. Subsequently, most villages adapted to colonial rule through syncretism, adopting and incorporating those aspects of the dominant culture necessary for survival under its regime, while maintaining the basic fabric of traditional culture. Historical examples of Pueblo syncretism include the addition of sheep and shepherding to the agricultural economy and the adoption of some Christian religious practices.

Contemporary Pueblo peoples continue to use syncretic strategies; they have adopted a variety of modern convenience products, yet extensively retain their traditional kinship systems, religions, and crafts. Social life centres on the village, which is also the primary political unit. Kinship plays a fundamental role in social and religious life in 21st-century Pueblo communities. It may delimit an individual's potential marriage partners and often determines eligibility for membership in religious societies and a wide variety of social and economic obligations.

Kinship is typically reckoned through the lineage, a group that shares a common ancestor; several lineages together form a clan. Early 20th-century kinship studies indicated that some pueblos may have had more than 30 clans at one time, which were often grouped into two larger units, or moieties. The clans of the eastern Pueblos are organized into complementary moieties, known respectively as the Summer people and the Winter people (Tanoans) or as the Turquoise people and the Squash people. These groups alternate responsibility for pueblo activities, and their secret societies deal primarily with curing rituals. In contrast, the western Pueblos are organized into several matrilineal lineages and clans; secret societies, each controlled by a particular clan, perform a calendrical cycle of rituals to ensure rain and tribal welfare. Many Pueblo peoples continue to practice the kachina (*katsina*) religion, a complex belief system in which hundreds of divine beings act as intermediaries between humans and God.

Early 21st-century population estimates indicated approximately 75,000 individuals of Pueblo descent.

ZUNI

The Zuni—a tribe of what is now west-central New Mexico, on the Arizona border—are a Pueblo Indian group and

Zuni Potter, photograph by Edward S. Curtis, c. 1903. Edward S. Curtis Collection/Library of Congress, Washington, D.C. (neg. no. LC-USZ62-112233)

KACHINAS

In traditional religions of the Pueblo Indians of North America, a kachina (Hopi: katsina) is any of more than 500 divine and ancestral spirit beings who interact with humans. Each Pueblo culture has distinct forms and variations of kachinas.

Kachinas are believed to reside with the tribe for half of each year. They will allow themselves to be seen by a community if its men properly perform a traditional ritual while wearing kachina masks and other regalia. The spirit-being depicted on the mask is thought to be actually present with or within the performer, temporarily transforming him.

Kachinas are also depicted in small, heavily ornamented carved-wood dolls, which are traditionally made by the men of a tribe and presented to girls; boys receive bows and arrows. These wooden dolls are used to teach the identities of the kachinas and the symbolism of their regalia. The identity of the spirit is depicted not by the form of the doll's body, which is usually simple and flat, but primarily by the applied colour and elaborate feather, leather, and, occasionally, fabric ornamentation of its mask.

Mask of the Zuni kachina Sekya; painted leather, trimmed with feathers and hair. Courtesy of the Museum of the American Indian, New York City

speak a Penutian language. Zuni traditions depict a past in which their ancestors emerged from underground and eventually settled at the tribe's present location.

When Pueblo tribes first encountered Spanish colonizers in the 16th century, the Zuni were living in Hawikuh and five or six other towns. Collectively these towns came to be called the Seven Cities of Cibola, host to a rumoured empire of gold that was sought in vain by Francisco Vázquez de Coronado and other conquistadors. In 1680 the Zuni and other Pueblo tribes defeated the Spanish through the Pueblo Rebellion. The tribes retained their independence until 1691, when the Spanish reconquered the area.

Zuni society is organized through kinship and includes 13 matrilineal clans. Like other Pueblo peoples, the Zuni are deeply religious and have a complex ceremonial organization. Religious life centres on gods or spirit-beings called kachinas.

Most Zunis farm, raising corn, squash, and beans. Since the early 19th century the Zuni have been known for making silver and turquoise jewelry, baskets, beadwork, animal fetishes, and pottery, all of very high quality. Many Zuni have chosen to adopt only some parts of modern American life and to maintain much of their traditional culture.

In the early 21st century the population of Zuni Pueblo was some 10,000 individuals.

HOPI

The Hopi are the westernmost group of Pueblo Indians, situated in what is now northeastern Arizona, on the edge of the Painted Desert. Also called the Moki or Moqui, they speak a Shoshonean language of Uto-Aztecan stock.

The precise origin of the Hopi is unknown, although it is thought that they and other Pueblo peoples descended from the Ancestral Pueblo (Anasazi), whom the Hopi call Hisatsinom, "Ancient People." Archaeology has revealed that some abandoned pueblos, such as Sikyatki and Awatovi, were once occupied by Hopi people. Hopi origin

traditions tell that their ancestors climbed upward through underground chambers called kivas and lived in many places before reaching their present settlements in this, the Fourth World.

Traditional Hopi culture emphasized monogamy and matrilineal descent. Hopi people also practiced matrilocal

Hopi kachina of Laqán, the squirrel spirit, c. 1950; in the National Museum of the American Indian, New York, N.Y. Courtesy of the Museum of the American Indian, Heye Foundation, New York City

residence, in which a new husband becomes part of his mother-in-law's household. A given pueblo, or town, might include two dozen or more matrilineal clans, which were grouped into several larger social units, or phratries.

The traditional Hopi economy centred on farming and, after Spanish colonization, on herding sheep. The chief crop was corn, and the Hopi also grew beans, squash, melons, and a variety of other vegetables and fruits. Men farmed and herded, in addition to building houses, performing most of the ceremonies, making moccasins, and weaving garments and blankets. Women made baskets and pottery, gardened, raised children, cared for the elderly, and were responsible for the strenuous tasks of providing their families with hand-drawn water and hand-ground cornmeal.

Girls and boys began their ceremonial careers soon after reaching six years of age by being inducted into the kachina (Hopi: *katsina*) religious tradition. Hopi kachinas represented a wide variety of gods, spirits, departed ancestors, and clouds; during certain ceremonies they were impersonated by men in elaborate regalia. Women generally took the role of observers during the public aspects of ceremonies, except in events involving one or more of the three women's societies. Men also had the option of joining a number of societies, including those that conducted a strenuous tribal initiation and staged an annual winter solstice celebration, or soyal. So important was the soyal that its

leadership was always entrusted to a high official, usually the town's chief.

The most widely publicized of Hopi rituals was the snake dance, held annually in late August, during which the performers danced with live snakes in their mouths. Although part of the snake dance was performed in public, visitors saw only a brief, though exciting, portion of a lengthy ceremony, most of which was conducted privately in kivas.

Some aspects of Hopi life have been considerably affected as a result of Spanish, and later American, colonization. Foremost among these are land disputes between the Hopi and the neighbouring Navajo. However, many aspects of traditional Hopi life persisted into the early 21st century. At that time, terraced pueblo structures of stone and adobe continued to dominate the architecture of a number of independent Hopi towns. Kachina religion remained vibrant, and a strong craft tradition persisted in Hopi communities.

Early 21st-century population estimates indicated more than 15,000 individuals of Hopi descent.

YUMAN

The Yumans traditionally lived in the lower Colorado River valley and adjacent areas in what are now western Arizona and southern California, U.S., and northern Baja California and northwestern Sonora, Mex. They spoke related languages of the Hokan language stock.

Two major divisions of Yumans are recognized: the river Yumans, who lived along the lower Colorado and middle Gila rivers and whose major groups included, from north to south, the Mojave, Halchidhoma, Yuma, and Cocopa, together with the Maricopa in the middle Gila; and the upland Yumans, who inhabited what is now western Arizona south of the Grand Canyon and whose major groups included the Hualapai (Walapai), Havasupai, and Yavapai. Two other groups of Yuman-speaking people, the Diegueño and the Kamia (now known as the Tipai and Ipai), lived in what are now southern California and northern Baja California. The Kiliwa and Paipai still live in northern Baja California.

Traditionally, the river Yumans were primarily farmers who lived in the Colorado and Gila river valleys. By placing their fields near the rivers, the Yumans took advantage of the annual floods that deposited rich burdens of silt on the flood plain; these locations also made irrigation unnecessary in what was otherwise an arid environment. The Maricopa were somewhat influenced by their neighbours, the Pima, and frequently allied with the Pima against other river Yumans such as the Mojave and the Yuma.

The upland Yumans traditionally engaged in some farming, but a major part of subsistence was based on hunting and on gathering wild foods. The Havasupai were exceptions, partly because of contacts with the Hopi and partly because of their location in

Cataract Canyon, a side canyon of the Grand Canyon. The creek flowing through this canyon made extensive farming possible through irrigation. Unlike other Yumans, the Havasupai were very peaceful. The Yavapai, on the other hand, frequently allied themselves with bands of western Apache for raiding and were sometimes called Yavapai-Apache.

All Yuman peoples were similar in choosing to live in dispersed settlements or hamlets rather than in villages, in adopting loose forms of political organization rather than a centralized authority, and in their material culture, which included pottery. Yuman religion was characterized by belief in a supreme creator, faith in dreams, and use of song narratives in ritual and ceremony.

Early 21st-century population estimates indicated some 9,000 individuals who identified themselves as Yumans.

PIMA

The Pima traditionally lived along the Gila and Salt rivers in Arizona, U.S., in what was the core area of the prehistoric Hohokam culture. The Pima, who speak a Uto-Aztecan language and call themselves the River People, are usually considered to be the descendants of the Hohokam. Like their presumed ancestors, the Pima were traditionally sedentary farmers who lived in one-room houses and utilized the rivers for irrigation. Some hunting and gathering were done to supplement their diet, and in drought years, which occurred on the average of one year in five, crop failure made hunting and gathering the sole mode of subsistence. During these dry years jackrabbits and mesquite beans became the group's dietary staples.

The intensive farming of the Pima made possible larger villages than were feasible for their neighbours and relatives, the Tohono O'odham (Papago). With larger communities came a stronger and more complex political organization. In the early Spanish colonial period the Pima possessed a strong tribal organization, with a tribal chief elected by the chiefs of the various villages. The tribal and local chiefs attained their status through their personal qualities rather than through birth. The village chief, aided by a council of all adult males, had the responsibilities of directing the communal irrigation projects and of protecting the village against alien tribes, notably the Apache. Planting and harvesting crops were handled as a cooperative venture.

From the time of their earliest recorded contacts with European and American colonizers, the Pima have been regarded as a friendly people. During the California Gold Rush (1849–50), the Pima often gave or sold food to emigrant settlers and gold seekers and provided them with an escort through Apache territory. During the Apache wars (1861–86), Pimas served as scouts for the U.S. Army.

In the early 21st century Pima descendants numbered some 11,000.

TOHONO O'ODHAM

The Tohono O'odham, or Papago, traditionally inhabited the desert regions of present-day Arizona, U.S., and northern Sonora, Mex. They speak a Uto-Aztecan language, a dialectal variant of Piman, and culturally they are similar to the Pima living to the north. There are, however, certain dissimilarities. The drier territory of the Tohono O'odham made farming difficult and increased the tribe's reliance on wild foods. They moved seasonally because of the arid climate, spending the summer in "field villages" and the winter in "well villages."

Traditionally, unlike the Pima, the Tohono O'odham did not store water to irrigate their fields, instead practicing a form of flash-flood farming. After the first rains, they planted seeds in the alluvial fans at the mouths of washes that marked the maximum reach of the water after flash floods. Because the floods could be heavy, it was necessary for the seeds to be planted deeply, usually 4 to 6 inches (10–15 cm) into the soil. Reservoirs, ditches, and dikes were constructed by Tohono O'odham men to slow and impound runoff waters along the flood channels. Women were responsible for gathering wild foods.

With a shifting residential pattern and the wide dispersal of the Tohono O'odham fields, the people had no compelling need to create large villages or a unified tribal political organization and so chose not to do so. The largest organizational unit appears to have been a

Tohono O'odham (Papago) woman wearing a basket tray headpiece, photograph by Edward S. Curtis, c. 1907. Edward S. Curtis Collection/Library of Congress, Washington, D.C. (neg. no. LC-USZ62-105389)

group of related villages. Villages tended to be composed of several families related through the male line. The Tohono O'odham had much less contact with settlers than the Pima and retained more of their traditional culture.

Early 21st-century population estimates indicated more than 20,000 individuals of Tohono O'odham descent.

NAVAJO

The Navajo are the most populous of all North American Indian peoples in the United States, with some 300,000 individuals in the early 21st century, most of them living in New Mexico, Arizona, and Utah.

The Navajo speak an Apachean language which is classified in the Athabaskan language family. At some point in prehistory the Navajo and Apache migrated to the Southwest from Canada, where most other Athabaskan-speaking peoples still live. Although the exact timing of the relocation is unknown, it is thought to have been between AD 1100 and 1500. These early Navajo were mobile hunters and gatherers; after moving to the Southwest, however, they adopted many of the practices of the sedentary, farming Pueblo Indians near whom they settled.

Navajo interactions with Pueblo tribes were recorded at least as early as the 17th century, when refugees from some of the Rio Grande pueblos came to the Navajo after the Spanish suppression of the Pueblo Revolt. During the 18th century, some Hopi tribal members left their mesas because of drought and famine and joined with the Navajo, particularly in Canyon de Chelly in northeast Arizona. Pueblo artistic influences drew Navajo people to adopt painted pottery and weaving; Navajo rugs are particularly fine examples of this art form. Elements of Navajo ceremonialism such as dry-sand painting are also products of these contacts. Another important Navajo artistic tradition, the creation of silver jewelry, dates from the middle of the 19th century and was probably first learned from Mexican smiths.

Navajo religion is widely practiced and notable for its intricacy. Some of its many traditions relate the emergence of the first people from various worlds beneath the surface of the earth. Other stories explain the origins and purposes of numerous rites and ceremonies. Some of these are simple rituals carried out by individuals or families for luck in travel and trade or for the protection of crops and herds. More-complex rites involve a specialist who is paid according to the complexity and length of the ceremonial. Traditionally, most rites were primarily for curing physical and mental illness. In other ceremonies there were simply prayers or songs, and dry paintings might be made of pollen and flower petals. In some cases there were public dances and exhibitions at which hundreds or thousands of Navajo gathered. Many of these rites are still performed.

Although the Navajo never raided as extensively as the Apache, their raiding was serious enough to cause the U.S.

government in 1863 to order Col. Kit Carson to subdue them. The ensuing campaign resulted in the destruction of large amounts of crops and herds and the incarceration of about 8,000 Navajo, along with 400 Mescalero Apache, at Bosque Redondo, 180 miles (290 km) south of Santa Fe, N.M. This four-year (1864–68) captivity left a legacy of bitterness and distrust that has still not entirely disappeared.

The Navajo resemble other Apachean peoples in their general preference for limiting centralized tribal or political organization, although they have adopted pan-tribal governmental and legal systems in order to maintain tribal sovereignty. Traditional Navajo society was organized through matrilineal kinship; small, independent bands of related kin generally made decisions on a consensus basis. Similar groups still exist but tend to be based on locality of residence as well as kinship; many of these local groups have elected leaders. A local group is not a village or town but rather a collection of dwellings or hamlets distributed over a wide area.

In the early 21st century many Navajo continued to live a predominantly traditional lifestyle, speaking the Navajo language, practicing the religion, and organizing through traditional forms of social structure. Navajo men and women also continued the tradition of volunteering for the armed services at a high rate, perhaps as an expression of a cultural ethic that emphasizes both personal competence and community. In maintaining these disparate traditions, the Navajo have been cultural innovators. For example, the Navajo code talkers of World War II—Marines who used their native language to foil enemy monitoring of vital communications—played a definitive role in winning the war (and saved countless lives) by maintaining crucial radio contact on the battlefield.

Many Navajo continue to live in the area they settled centuries ago; in the early 21st century their reservation and government-allotted lands in New Mexico, Arizona, and Utah totaled more than 24,000 square miles (64,000 square km). The region is mainly arid, however, and generally will not support enough agriculture and livestock to provide a livelihood for all of its residents. Thousands earn their living away from the Navajo country, and appreciable numbers have settled on irrigated lands along the lower Colorado River and in such places as Los Angeles, Calif., and Kansas City, Mo.

APACHE

The Apache, under such leaders as Cochise, Mangas Coloradas, Geronimo, and Victorio, figured largely in the history of the Southwest during the latter half of the 19th century. Their name is probably derived from a Spanish transliteration of *ápachu*, the term for "enemy" in Zuñi.

Before Spanish colonization, Apache domain extended over what are now (in the United States) east-central and southeastern Arizona, southeastern Colorado, southwestern and eastern New Mexico, and western Texas and (in Mexico) northern Chihuahua and Sonora states. However, the ancestral Apache probably did not reach the Southwest until at least AD 1100. They apparently migrated to the area from the far north, for the Apachean languages are clearly a subgroup of the Athabaskan language family. With the exception of the Navajo, all other Athabaskan-speaking tribes were originally located in what is now western Canada.

Although the Apache eventually chose to adopt a nomadic way of life that relied heavily on horse transport, semisedentary Plains Apache farmers were living along the Dismal River in what is now Kansas as recently as 1700. When the horse and gun trades converged in the central Plains about 1750, guerrilla-style raiding by previously nomadic groups such as the Comanche greatly increased. The remaining Plains Apache were severely pressured and retreated to the south and west.

Culturally, the Apache are divided into Eastern Apache, which include the Mescalero, Jicarilla, Chiricahua, Lipan, and Kiowa Apache, and Western Apache, which include the Cibecue, Mimbreño, Coyotero, and Northern and Southern Tonto or Mogollon Apache. With the exception of the Kiowa Apache, who joined the Kiowa tribal circle (adopting Kiowa customs and allegiance), the Apache traditionally functioned without a centralized tribal organization. Instead,

the band, an autonomous small group within a given locality, was the primary political unit as well as the primary raiding unit. The strongest headman of a band was recognized as an informal chief, and several bands might be united under one leader. Chieftainship was thus an earned privilege rather than a hereditary one.

Once the Apache had moved to the Southwest, they developed a flexible subsistence economy that included hunting and gathering wild foods, farming, and obtaining food and other items from Pueblo villages via trade, livestock hunts, and raiding. The proportion of each activity varied greatly from tribe to tribe. The Jicarilla farmed fairly extensively, growing corn and other vegetables, and also hunted bison extensively. The Lipan of Texas, who were probably originally a band of Jicarilla, had largely given up farming for a more mobile lifestyle. The Mescalero were influenced by the Plains tribes' corn- and bison-based economies, but their chief food staple was the mescal plant (hence the name Mescalero). The Chiricahua were perhaps the most nomadic and aggressive of the Apache west of the Rio Grande, raiding into northern Mexico, Arizona, and New Mexico from their strongholds in the Dragoon Mountains. The Western Apache appear to have been more settled than their Eastern relatives. Although their economy emphasized farming, they did raid fully sedentary tribes frequently. One of the Western Apache tribes, the Navajo, traded extensively with the

GERONIMO

Geronimo. Library of Congress, Washington, D.C. (neg. no. LC-USZ62-124428)

Born in 1829 in No-Doyohn Canyon, Mex., Geronimo, a Bedonkohe Apache whose Indian name was Goyathlay ("One Who Yawns"), led the Chiricahua Apache in defense of their homeland against the military might of the United States.

For generations the Apaches had resisted white colonization of their homeland in the Southwest by both Spaniards and North Americans. Geronimo continued the tradition of his ancestors from the day he was admitted to the warriors' council in 1846, participating in raids into Sonora and Chihuahua in Mexico. He was further embittered by the death of his mother, wife, and children at the hands of Mexicans in 1858. He then rose to the leadership of a band of warriors after successive raids of vengeance upon Mexicans.

In 1874 some 4,000 Apaches were forcibly moved by U.S. authorities to a reservation at San Carlos, a barren wasteland in east-central Arizona. Deprived of traditional tribal rights, short on rations, and homesick, they turned to Geronimo and others who led them in depredations that plunged the region into turmoil and bloodshed.

In the early 1870s Lieut. Col. George F. Crook, commander of the Department of Arizona, had succeeded in establishing relative peace in the territory. The management of his successors, however, was disastrous, and spurred by Geronimo, hundreds of Apaches left the reservation to resume their war against the whites. Geronimo surrendered in January 1884, only to take flight from the San Carlos reservation in May 1885. Ten months later he again surrendered, at Cañón de Los Embudos in Sonora, but, fearing that they would be murdered once they crossed into U.S. territory, he and a small band escaped. During this final campaign no fewer than 5,000 white soldiers and 500 Indian auxiliaries were employed at various times in the apprehension of Geronimo's small band.

Five months and 1,645 miles later, Geronimo was tracked to his camp in the Sonora mountains. At a conference (Sept. 3, 1886) at Skeleton Canyon in Arizona, Geronimo was induced to surrender once again, with the promise that, after an indefinite exile in Florida, he and his followers would be permitted to return to Arizona. The promise was not kept. Geronimo and his fellow prisoners were put at hard labour, and it was May 1887 before he saw his family.

Moved to Fort Sill, in Oklahoma Territory, in 1894, he at first attempted to "take the white man's road." He farmed and joined the Dutch Reformed Church, which expelled him because of his gambling. He never saw Arizona again, but, by special permission of the War Department, he was allowed to sell photographs of himself and his handiwork at expositions.

Pueblo tribes and was heavily influenced by these firmly agriculturist cultures.

Although they were among the fiercest groups on the colonial frontiers of Mexico and the United States, and perhaps because of their confidence in their own military prowess, the Apache initially attempted to be friends of the Spanish, Mexicans, and Americans. As early as the 17th century, however, Apache bands were raiding Spanish missions. The Spanish failure to protect missionized Pueblo villages from Apache raids during a five-year drought in the late 17th century may have helped to instigate the Pueblo Rebellion of 1680. During the Spanish retaliation immediately following the revolt, many Pueblo individuals took shelter with the Navajo.

In 1858 a meeting at Apache Pass in the Dragoon Mountains between the Americans and the Chiricahua Apache resulted in a peace that lasted until 1861, when Cochise went on the warpath. This marked the beginning of 25 years of confrontation between U.S. military forces and the native peoples of the Southwest. The causes of the conflict included the Apache disinclination toward reservation life and incursions onto Apache lands that were related to the development of gold, silver, and coal mining operations in the region. The latter often took place with the consent of corrupt Office of Indian Affairs staff.

Despite their adept use of swift horses and their knowledge of the terrain, the Apache were eventually outmatched by the superior arms of American troops. The Navajo surrendered in 1865 and agreed to settle on a reservation in New Mexico. Other Apache groups ostensibly followed suit in 1871–73, but large numbers of warriors refused to yield their nomadic ways and accept permanent confinement. Thus, intermittent raids continued to be led by such Apache leaders as Geronimo and Victorio, evoking federal action once more.

The last of the Apache wars ended in 1886 with the surrender of Geronimo and his few remaining followers. The Chiricahua tribe was evacuated from the West and held as prisoners of war successively in Florida, in Alabama, and at Fort Sill, Okla., for a total of 27 years. In 1913 the members of the tribe were given the choice of taking allotments of land in Oklahoma or living in New Mexico on the Mescalero Reservation. Approximately one-third chose the former and two-thirds the latter.

Apache descendants totaled some 100,000 individuals in the early 21st century.

CHAPTER 7

THE GREAT BASIN AND PLATEAU

The Great Basin culture area is centred in the intermontane deserts of present-day Nevada and includes adjacent areas in California, Oregon, Idaho, Montana, Wyoming, Colorado, Utah, and Arizona. It is so named because the surrounding mountains create a bowl-like landscape that prevented water from flowing out of the region. The most common topographic features are basin and range systems; these gradually transition to high intermontane plateaus in the north. The climate is temperate in the north and becomes subtropical to the south. Higher elevations tend to receive ample moisture but other areas average as little as 2 inches (50 millimetres) per year. Much of the region's surface water, such as the Great Salt Lake, is brackish. The predominant ecosystem is desert.

Lying at the crossroads of five culture areas (the subarctic, Plains, Great Basin, California, and Northwest Coast), the Plateau is surrounded by mountains and drained by two great river systems, the Fraser and the Columbia. It is located in present-day Montana, Idaho, Oregon, Washington, and British Columbia. Topographically, the area is characterized by rolling hills, high flatlands, gorges, and mountain slopes. The climate is temperate although milder than the adjacent Plains, because the surrounding mountain systems provide protection from continental air masses. The mountains also create a substantial rain shadow; most precipitation in this region falls at higher elevations, leaving other areas rather

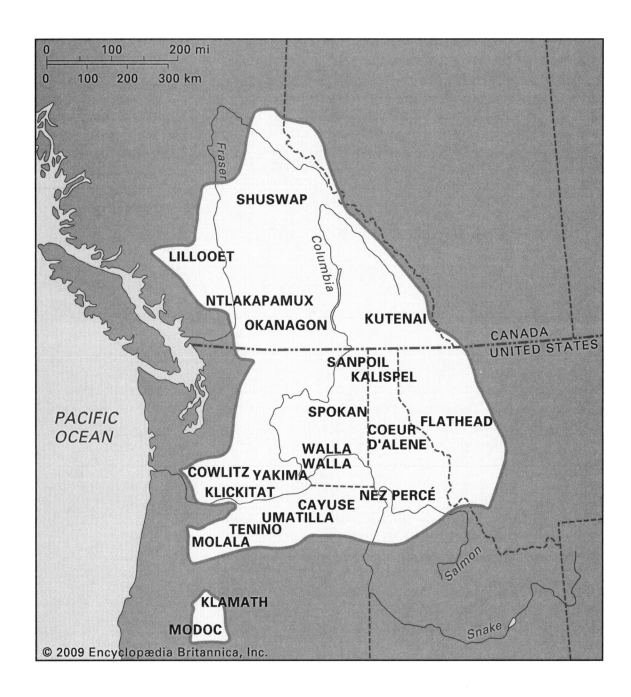

Distribution of North American Plateau Indians.

dry. The predominant ecosystems are grassland and high desert, although substantial forested areas are found at altitude.

THE GREAT BASIN

The Great Basin is home to the Washoe, speakers of a Hokan language, and a number of tribes speaking Numic languages (a division of the Uto-Aztecan language family). These include the Mono, Paiute, Bannock, Shoshone, Ute, and Gosiute.

The peoples of this region were hunters and gatherers and generally organized themselves in mobile, kin-based bands. Seeds, piñon nuts, and small game formed the bulk of the diet for most groups, although those occupying northern and eastern locales readily adopted horses and equestrian bison hunting after Spanish mounts became available. Some of these latter groups also replaced wickiups and brush shelters, the common house forms until that time, with Plains-style tepees; peoples in the west and south, however, continued to use traditional house forms well into the 19th century. Other common forms of material culture included digging sticks, nets, basketry, grinding stones for processing seeds, and rock art

MONO

The Mono (or Monachi) were originally from what is now central California, U.S. They spoke a language belonging to the Numic group of the Uto-Aztecan family and were related to the Northern Paiute. The Western Mono, who resided in the pine belt of the Sierra Nevada mountains, had a culture similar to that of the nearby Yokuts. The Owens Valley Paiute (previously called the Eastern Mono) were more similar to their neighbours from the Great Basin culture area.

Historically, the two divisions traded with each other, the Owens Valley Paiute exchanging salt, piñon nuts, baskets, and poison in return for acorn flour, baskets, and shafts for arrows.

Traditional Mono social organization consisted of small villages of as many as 50 to 75 people, organized in patrilineal families and ranging over loosely defined hunting areas. Although the power of the chief was far from absolute, his consent was required for all major religious or warlike undertakings. His greatest responsibilities were the settlement of disputes and the sanctioning of punishment.

Early 21st-century population estimates indicated some 3,000 Mono descendants.

PAIUTE

The two distinct groups that constitute the Paiute (self-name: Numa) speak languages of the Numic group of the Uto-Aztecan family. The Southern Paiute, who speak Ute, at one time occupied what are now southern Utah, northwestern Arizona, southern Nevada, and southeastern California, the latter group being

Paiute woman making a basket, photograph by Charles C. Pierce, c. 1902. Library of Congress, Washington, D.C.; photograph, Charles C. Pierce (neg. no. LC-USZ62-104705)

known as the Chemehuevi. Although encroached upon and directed into reservations by the U.S. government in the 19th century, the Southern Paiute had comparatively little friction with settlers and the U.S. military. Many found ways to stay on their traditional lands, usually by working on ranches or living on the fringes of the new towns.

The Northern Paiute (called Paviotso in Nevada) are related to the Mono of California. Like a number of other California and Southwest Indians, the Northern Paiute have been known derogatorily as Diggers because some of the wild foods they collected required digging. They occupied east-central California, western Nevada, and eastern Oregon. A related group, the Bannock, lived with the Shoshone in southern Idaho, where they were bison hunters. After 1840 a rush of prospectors and farmers despoiled the arid environment's meagre supply of food plants, after which the Northern Paiute acquired guns and horses and fought at intervals with the trespassers until 1874, when the last Paiute lands were appropriated by the U.S. government.

The Northern and Southern Paiute were traditionally hunting and gathering cultures that subsisted primarily on seed, pine nuts, and small game, although many Southern Paiute also planted small gardens. Given the warm climate of the area, they chose to live in temporary brush shelters, wore little or no clothing except rabbit-skin blankets, and made a variety of baskets for gathering and cooking food. Families were affiliated through intermarriage, but there were no formal bands or territorial organizations except in the more fertile areas such as the Owens River valley in California.

Population estimates in the early 21st century indicated approximately 17,000 individuals of Paiute descent.

BANNOCK

The Bannock lived in what is now southern Idaho, especially along the Snake River and its tributaries, and joined with the Shoshone tribe in the second half of the 19th century. Linguistically, they were most closely related to the Northern Paiute of what is now eastern Oregon, from whom they were separated by approximately 200 miles (320 km).

According to both Paiute and Bannock legend, the Bannock moved eastward to Idaho to live among the Shoshone and hunt buffalo. Traditional Bannock and Shoshone cultures emphasized equestrian buffalo hunting and a seminomadic life. The Bannock also engaged in summer migrations westward to the Shoshone Falls, where they gathered salmon, small game, and berries. They traveled into the Rockies each fall to hunt buffalo in the Yellowstone area of what are now Wyoming and Montana.

Bannock social organization was based upon independent bands, and the autumn hunting expeditions allowed band chiefs to acquire power over one sector of hunting and subsistence activities. These trips traversed Shoshone territory, requiring a good deal of cooperation with that tribe. Much of the Bannocks' eastern territory was contiguous with the Shoshone's western lands. As close and friendly neighbours, they often camped side by side, and intermarriage was common. The two tribes also shared a common enemy in the fierce Blackfoot, who controlled the buffalo-hunting grounds in Montana. The Fort Hall reservation in Idaho was established for the Shoshone in the 1860s, and many Bannock soon joined them. Very close interaction and continued intermarriage blended the two cultures, and the tribes began to use the combined name Shoshone-Bannock.

Before colonization the Bannock were not numerous, probably never reaching more than 2,000. However, they had considerable influence in inciting their more pacific neighbours to revolts and raids against the U.S. settlers in the area. Famine, frustration over the disappearance of the buffalo, and insensitive reservation policy by the U.S. government led to the Bannock War in 1878, which was suppressed with a massacre of about 140 Bannock men, women, and children at Charles's Ford in what is now Wyoming.

Early 21st-century population estimates indicated more than 5,000 individuals of Shoshone and Bannock descent.

SHOSHONE

The Shoshone occupied the territory from what is now southeastern California across central and eastern Nevada and northwestern Utah into southern Idaho and western Wyoming. The Shoshone (also called the Snake) of historic times were organized into four groups: Western, or unmounted, Shoshone, centred in Nevada; Northern, or horse, Shoshone of northern Utah and Idaho; Wind River Shoshone in western Wyoming; and Comanche in western Texas, a comparatively recent offshoot of the Wind River group. The Shoshone language is a Central Numic language of the Uto-Aztecan family. Shoshone dialects were so similar that speakers from the extreme ends of Shoshone territory were mutually intelligible.

The Western Shoshone were organized into loosely affiliated family bands that subsisted on wild plants, small mammals, fish, and insects. Each family was independently nomadic during most of the year and joined other families only briefly for activities such as rabbit drives, antelope hunts, or dancing. Like other Great Basin Indians, they were sometimes referred to by the derogatory name Diggers, taken from their practice of digging tubers and roots for food. A few Western Shoshone obtained horses after the colonial settlement of Nevada and Utah.

The Wind River Shoshone and Northern Shoshone probably acquired horses as early as 1680, before Spanish occupation of their lands. They formed loosely organized bands of mounted buffalo hunters and warriors and adopted many Plains Indian cultural traits such as

Heebe-tee-tse, Shoshone Indian, photograph by Rose & Hopkins, c. 1899. Library of Congress, Washington, D.C.; photograph, Rose & Hopkins (neg. no. LC-USZ62-102137)

the use of tepees and the importance of counting coup (striking or touching an enemy in warfare in a prescribed way) as a war honour. Sacagawea, the Shoshone woman who acted as interpreter and guide for the Lewis and Clark expedition of 1804–06, is thought to have been a member of either the Wind River or the Northern group.

After acquiring horses, the Comanche split off from the Wind River Shoshone and moved south into Texas. Comanche bands were feared by the Spaniards of the Southwest because they subsisted as much by plunder as by buffalo hunting.

Early 21st-century population estimates indicated some 41,000 descendants of the four Shoshone groups.

UTE

The Ute, a Numic-speaking group, originally lived in what is now western Colorado and eastern Utah; the latter state is named after them. When the Spanish Father Silvestre Vélez de Escalante traversed their territory in 1776 while seeking a route from Santa Fe (now in New Mexico) to the California missions, the Ute had no horses and lived in small family clusters. At that time there was no clear distinction between the Ute and the Southern Paiute, both of whom spoke Ute.

Like many other desert peoples, the Ute traditionally subsisted by collecting wild foods. After acquiring horses in the early 19th century, the Ute of western Colorado and later of northern Utah organized into loose bands of hunters. The area had been settled by some 30,000 Hispanic mestizos under the aegis of the Spanish colonial government, and soon Ute bands began to prey on the settlers' livestock. In the southern regions of Utah, Nevada, and California, however, the Ute and Chemehuevi remained afoot; there the Ute came to be called Southern Paiute. After the Indian wars (1864–70) most of the Colorado Ute were settled on a reservation in southwestern Colorado; those of Utah were placed on the Uintah and Ouray Reservation. Ute descendants numbered more than 10,300 in the early 21st century.

GOSIUTE

The Gosiute were an ethnolinguistic group of Western Shoshone Indians formerly living west of the Great Salt Lake in the arid region of the North American Great Basin. They were often reported in the 19th century to have lived wretched lives, subsisting with difficulty in the desert wasteland; the reports were probably exaggerated, however, and some later reports told of their cultivation of crops and employment by settlers. Gosiute descendants numbered more than 300 in the early 21st century.

THE PLATEAU

Most of the languages spoken in the Plateau culture area belong to the

Salishan, Sahaptin, Kutenai, and Modoc and Klamath families. Tribes include the Salish, Flathead, Nez Percé, Yakima, Kutenai, Modoc and Klamath, Spokan, Kalispel, Pend d'Oreille, Coeur d'Alene, Wallawalla, and Umatilla. "Flathead" is incorrectly used in some early works to denote all Salishan-speaking peoples, only some of whom moulded infants' heads so as to achieve a uniform slope from brow to crown; notably, the people presently referred to as the Flathead did not engage in this practice.

The primary political unit was the village. Among some groups a sense of larger tribal and cultural unity led to the creation of representative governments, tribal chieftainships, and confederations of tribes. This was possible in part because the Columbia and Fraser rivers provided enough salmon and other fish to support a relatively dense population. However, this region was never as heavily populated or as rigidly stratified as the Northwest Coast.

Efficient hunters and gatherers, Plateau groups supplemented fish with terrestrial animals and wild plant foods, especially certain varieties of camas (*Camassia*). Most groups resided in permanent riverside villages and traveled to upland locales during fair-weather foraging excursions. However, some groups subsequently shifted to nomadic buffalo hunting when horses were available. These groups quickly adopted tepees and many other Plains cultural forms. They became particularly respected for their equine breeding programs and fine herds.

Plateau fishing villages were characterized by their multifamily A-frame dwellings, while smaller conical structures were used in the uplands; both house forms were covered with grass, although canvas became a popular covering once available. In terms of portable culture, the Plateau peoples were most characterized by the wide variety of substances and technologies they used; continuously exposed to new items and ideas through trade with surrounding culture areas, they excelled at material innovation and at adapting others' technologies to their own purposes.

SALISH

The term *Salish* refers to a linguistic grouping of tribes speaking related languages and living in the upper basins of the Columbia and Fraser rivers and their tributaries in what are now the province of British Columbia, Can., and the U.S. states of Washington, Idaho, and Montana. These tribes are commonly called the Interior Salish to distinguish them from their neighbours, the Coast Salish tribes who resided on the Northwest Pacific Coast. The Salish tribes comprised mainly the Coeur d'Alene, Columbia, Cowlitz, Flathead, Kalispel, Lake, Lillooet, Nespelem, Okanagon, Sanpoil, Shuswap, Sinkaietk (southern Okanagon), Spokan, Thompson, and Wenatchee peoples, all of whom spoke various Salishian languages. Salish was formerly a native name for the Flathead alone; by the mid-20th century, however, it was more often broadly applied to the entire group.

As Plateau Indians, the Salish had an unusually reliable food supply for desert dwellers. Most Salish tribes were divided into autonomous, loosely organized bands of related families, each with its own chief and local territory. In winter a band would occupy a river village; in summer it would travel, living at camp-sites, fishing, and gathering wild plant foods. Tribes toward the centre of the culture area, such as the Sanpoil, avoided complex social and political organiza-tion; warfare in that area was almost unknown, and external trade was not an important part of the local economy.

On the fringes of the Plateau culture area, however, conditions were different. The westernmost Salish groups, such as the Lillooet and western Shuswap, traded with the Northwest Coast Indians and adopted some of their customs. The Lillooet, for instance, had a well-orga-nized clan system similar to those used by Coast Salish peoples, and the western Shuswap had both clans and castes of nobles, commoners, and slaves, forms of social organization similar to those found on the coast. The easternmost Salish, such as the Flathead, who were horsemen, bison hunters, and warriors, had a relatively well-developed system of tribal chiefs and councils, much in the manner of the Plains Indians with whom they traded.

Although a typical Salish group had either dugout or bark canoes, the rivers were so full of rapids that traveling was more often accomplished on foot. The typical dwelling was an earth- or mat-cov-ered lodge, sometimes semisubterranean. As with other customs, however, the Flathead used a Plains architectural form, the tepee, and the Lillooet built coastal-style houses of poles and planks. Most Salish wore clothing made of dressed skins: breechclouts (breechcloths) for men, tunics for women, and leggings and moccasins for all.

Traditional Salish religious beliefs focused chiefly on guardian spirits. In the years just prior to puberty, boys undertook isolated nightly vigils, hop-ing for visions that would reveal their spirit-guide; some girls did likewise. Shamanism was also important, and shamans and medicine men and women could cure, and in some cases cause, dis-ease or social strife. The winter guardian spirit dance, involving dances, feasts, and prayers in propitiation of guardian spirits, was the most important commu-nity ritual for the Salish.

Early 21st-century population esti-mates indicated more than 25,000 individuals of Salish descent.

FLATHEAD

The original territory of the Flathead, a Salish-speaking North American Indian tribe of what is now western Montana, U.S., extended from the crest of the Bitterroot Range to the Continental

Divide of the Rocky Mountains and centred on the upper reaches of the Clark Fork of the Columbia River. Although early accounts referred to all Salish-speaking tribes as Flathead, the people now known by this name never engaged in head flattening.

The Flatheads were the easternmost of the Plateau Indians; like other tribes that regularly traversed the Rocky Mountains, they shared many traits with nomadic Plains Indians. The Flatheads acquired horses in great numbers and mounted annual fall expeditions to hunt bison on the Plains, often warring with tribes that were permanent residents of the area. Traditional Flathead culture also emphasized Plains-type warfare and its honours, including staging war dances, killing enemies, counting coups (touching enemies to shame or insult them), kidnapping women and children, and stealing horses.

Before colonization, the Flathead usually lived in tepees; the A-framed mat-covered lodge, a typical Plateau structure,

Chief Charlot of the Flathead, photograph by Norman A. Forsyth, c.. 1908. Library of Congress, Washington, D.C. (neg. no. LC-USZ62-112331)

was also used. Western Flathead groups had bark canoes, while eastern groups used the bison-skin tubs known as bull-boats that were typical of the Plains. Fishing was important among the Flathead, as it was among other Plateau tribes.

Traditional Flathead religion centred on guardian spirits, with whom individuals communicated in visions. A spirit could bring good fortune and health to the person it guarded or disease and misfortune to others. Shamanism was also important to traditional religious and healing practices.

Early 21st-century population estimates indicated more than 4,000 Flathead descendants.

NEZ PERCÉ

The Nez Percé were a Sahaptin-speaking people centring on the lower Snake River and such tributaries as the Salmon and Clearwater rivers in what is now northeastern Oregon, southeastern Washington, and central Idaho, U.S. They were the largest, most powerful, and best-known of the Sahaptin peoples and were called by various names by other groups; the French name, Nez Percé ("Pierced Nose"), referred to the wearing of nose pendants, though the fashion does not seem to have been widespread among them.

The Nez Percé were considered to be Plateau Indians; as one of the Plateau's easternmost groups, however, they were influenced by the Plains Indians just east of the Rockies. Typical of the Plateau, Nez Percé domestic life traditionally centred on small villages located on streams having abundant salmon, which, dried, formed their main source of food. They also sought a variety of game, berries, and roots. Their dwellings were communal lodges, A-framed and mat-covered, varying in size and sometimes housing as many as 30 families.

After they acquired horses early in the 18th century, life for the Nez Percé began to change dramatically, at least among some groups. Horse transport enabled them to mount expeditions to the eastern slope of the Rockies, where they hunted bison and traded with Plains peoples. Always somewhat warlike, the Nez Percé became more so, adopting many war honours, war dances, and battle tactics common to the Plains, as well as other forms of equestrian material culture such as the tepee. The Nez Percé built up one of the largest horse herds on the continent; they were almost unique among Native Americans in conducting a selective breeding program, and they were instrumental in creating the Appaloosa breed.

As the 18th century progressed, the Nez Percé's increased mobility fostered their enrichment and expansionism, and they began to dominate negotiations with other tribes in the region. The 19th century was a period of increasing change in Nez Percé life. Just six years after the explorers Meriwether Lewis and William Clark visited the Nez Percé in 1805, fur traders and trappers began penetrating the area. They were followed later by missionaries. By the 1840s emigrant settlers were moving through the area on the Oregon Trail. In 1855 the Nez Percé agreed to a treaty with the United States that created a large reservation encompassing most of their traditional land. The 1860 discovery of gold on the Salmon and Clearwater rivers, which generated an influx of thousands of miners and settlers, led U.S. commissioners in 1863 to force renegotiation of the treaty. The new treaty reduced the size of the reservation by three-fourths, and continued pressure from homesteaders and squatters reduced the area even more.

Many Nez Percé, perhaps a majority, had never accepted either treaty, and hostile actions and raids by both settlers and Native Americans eventually evolved into the Nez Percé War of 1877. For five months a small band of 250 Nez Percé warriors, under the leadership of Chief Joseph, held off a U.S. force of 5,000 troops led by Gen. O.O. Howard, who tracked them through Idaho, Yellowstone Park, and Montana before they surrendered to Gen. Nelson A. Miles. In the campaign Chief Joseph lost 239 persons, including women and children, and the U.S. military lost 266. The tribe was then assigned to malarial country in Oklahoma rather than being returned to the Northwest as promised.

Early 21st-century population estimates indicated approximately 6,500 individuals of Nez Percé descent.

YAKIMA

The Yakima were a Sahaptin-speaking tribe that lived along the Columbia, Yakima, and Wenatchee rivers in what is now the south-central region of the state of Washington. As with many other Sahaptin Plateau Indians, they were primarily salmon fishers before colonization.

The Yakima acquired historical distinction in the Yakima Indian Wars (1855–58), an attempt by the tribe to resist U.S. forces intent upon clearing the Washington Territory for prospectors and settlers. The conflict stemmed from a treaty that had been negotiated in 1855, according to which the Yakima and 13 other tribes were to be placed on a reservation and confederated as the Yakima Nation. Before the treaty could be ratified, however, a force united under the leadership of Yakima chief Kamaiakan, who declared his intention to drive all nonnatives from the region. After initial Yakima successes the uprising spread to other tribes in Washington and Oregon. Three years of raids, ambushes, and engagements followed, until September 1858, when the Native American forces were decisively defeated at the Battle of Four Lakes on a tributary of the Spokane River.

In 1859 the treaty of 1855 was effected, with the Yakima and most of the other tribes confined to reservations and their fertile ancestral lands opened to colonial appropriation. Since that time, all of the residents of the Yakima Reservation have been referred to as members of the Yakima Nation.

Early 21st-century population estimates indicated some 11,000 individuals of Yakima Nation ancestry.

Kutenai

The Kutenai are a tribe that traditionally lived in what are now southeastern British Columbia, northern Idaho, and northwestern Montana. Their language is of uncertain classification, some authorities placing it in the Wakashan family and some classifying it independently. The tribe, whose name is also rendered as Kootenay, is thought to be descended from an ancient Blackfoot group that migrated westward from the Great Plains to the drainage of the Kootenai River, a tributary of the upper Columbia. Plentiful streams and lakes, adequate rainfall, and abundant game and fish made this area the most favourable part of the plateau between the Rockies and the Pacific Coast ranges.

Kutenai people modeling traditional dress, photograph by J.R. White, c. 1907. Library of Congress, Washington, D.C. (neg. no. LC-USZ61-119219)

Kutenai culture combines some traits of the Plains Indians with others of the Plateau Indians. After acquiring horses, they engaged in annual bison hunts beyond the Rockies and into the Plains. The advent of horse transport also increased the importance and frequency of military activities. Formalized war honours became a means of social advancement, and increasing numbers of war captives (women and children, mostly Blackfoot) made slavery, adoption, and intermarriage more common. The Kutenai dressed in clothing made of antelope, deer, or buffalo hide (breechcloths for men, tunics for women), lived in conical tepees, and painted their garments, tents, and bodies much in the manner of the Plains tribes. Like other Plateau peoples, however, they engaged in communal fishing, built great bark and dugout canoes, and acknowledged a supreme chief only when undertaking special expeditions.

Among the Kutenai there were no clans, classes, or secret societies; they were divided loosely into bands, each with a nominal leader and an informal council of elders. They deified the sun and, like most other indigenous North American peoples, practiced animism, the belief that a multitude of spirits pervades all things in nature. Shamanism also had considerable influence within Kutenai culture.

Early 21st-century population estimates indicated more than 5,000 individuals of Kutenai descent.

MODOC AND KLAMATH

The Modoc and Klamath were two neighbouring North American Indian tribes who lived in what are now south-central Oregon and northern California, spoke related languages (or dialects) of Penutian stock, and shared many cultural traits. Their traditional territory lay in the southern Cascade Range and was some 100 miles (160 km) long and 25 miles (40 km) wide, dotted with marshes, lakes, rivers, and streams. The Klamath, in the northern sectors, were primarily fishers and hunters of waterfowl. The Modoc, in the southern sectors, were also fishers but relied more on gathering edible roots, seeds, and berries and on hunting various game. Both tribes are considered to be Plateau Indians, though they were influenced by neighbouring California Indians as well as those from the Pacific Northwest and Great Basin.

The Modoc and Klamath were organized into relatively autonomous villages, each with its own leaders, shamans, and medicine men. Although functioning independently in most situations, the villages would ally for war, and members of different villages often married. During winter, when snowdrifts could reach six feet (two metres) or more, most village families lived in semisubterranean earth-covered lodges, usually one family to a lodge. Poorer families lived in simpler mat-covered houses. In summer the usual dwelling was either a domed house of poles and matting or a lean-to of brush.

Klamath woman preparing food on a stone slab, photograph by Edward S. Curtis, c. 1923.
Edward S. Curtis Collection/Library of Congress, Washington, D.C. (neg. no. LC-USZ62-115814)

Sweat houses, used by both men and women, doubled as community centres for prayer and other religious activities. Religious belief focused largely on guardian spirits, whose aid was sought for all manner of human accomplishments.

In 1864 the U.S. government pressed the two tribes to relinquish most of their territory and take up residence on a reservation around Upper Klamath Lake. The land was traditionally Klamath, however, and that tribe treated the Modoc as intruders; the U.S. government, moreover, failed in its treaty obligations to supply rations to the Modoc. Hence, in 1870 an insurgent band of Modocs under Kintpuash, a subchief known to the American military as Captain Jack, left the reservation.

Federal efforts to induce this group's return precipitated the Modoc War of 1872–73, in which about 80 warriors and their families retreated to the California Lava Beds, a land of complex ravines and caves. There they mounted an effective resistance. After the murder of Brig. Gen. Edward Canby, who headed a peace commission in April 1873, U.S. troops prosecuted the war more vigorously. Betrayed by four of his followers, Captain Jack surrendered and was hanged. His followers were removed to Indian Territory (Oklahoma) and were not allowed to return to Oregon until 1909, after spending more than 30 years away from the region in which they sought to stay.

In the mid-20th century the U.S. government instituted a movement known as termination, in which tribes lost federal recognition and the benefits and protections associated with that status. In 1954 the federal government terminated its relationship with the inhabitants of the Klamath reservation. The reservation land was condemned and sold, and the proceeds were distributed among the former residents. Most of the land was incorporated into the Winema National Forest. The Modoc and Klamath people regained federal recognition in 1986, but they did not regain their former reservation lands.

Population estimates indicated some 5,500 Modoc and Klamath descendants in the early 21st century.

CHAPTER 8

THE NORTHWEST COAST AND CALIFORNIA

The Northwest Coast culture area is bounded on the west by the Pacific Ocean and on the east by the Coast Range, the Sierra Nevada, and the Rocky Mountains; it reaches from the area around Yakutat Bay in the north to the Klamath River area in the south. It includes the coasts of present-day Oregon, Washington, British Columbia, much of southern Alaska, and a small area of northern California. The topography is steep and in many places the coastal hills or mountains fall abruptly to a beach or riverbank. There is an abundance of precipitation—in many areas more than 160 inches (406 cm) annually, but rarely less than 30 inches (76 cm). The predominant ecosystems are temperate rainforests, intertidal zones, and the ocean.

The California culture area approximates the present states of California (U.S.) and northern Baja (Mex.). Other than the Pacific coast, the region's dominant topographic features are the Coast Range and the Sierra Nevada. These north-south ranges are interspersed with high plateaus and basins. An extraordinary diversity of local conditions created microenvironments such as coasts, tidewaters, coastal redwood forests, grasslands, wetlands, high deserts, and mountains.

THE NORTHWEST COAST

The Northwest Coast culture area is home to peoples speaking Athabaskan, Tshimshianic, Salishan, and other languages.

Prominent tribes include the Tlingit, Haida, Tsimshian, Kwakiutl, Bella Coola, Nuu-chah-nulth (Nootka), Coast Salish, and Chinook.

The peoples of the Northwest Coast had abundant and reliable supplies of salmon and other fish, sea mammals, shellfish, birds, and a variety of wild food plants. The resource base was so rich that they are unique among nonagricultural peoples in having created highly stratified societies of hereditary elites, commoners, and slaves. Tribes often organized themselves into corporate "houses"—groups of a few dozen to 100 or more related people that held in common the rights to particular resources. As with the house societies of medieval Japan and Europe, social stratification operated at every level of many Northwest Coast societies. Villages, houses, and house members each had their designated rank, which was reflected in nearly every social interaction.

Most groups built villages near waterways or the coast. Each village also had rights to an upland territory from which the residents could obtain terrestrial foods. Dwellings were rectilinear structures built of timbers or planks and were usually quite large, as the members of a corporate "house" typically lived together in one building. Northwest Coast cultures are known for their fine wood and stone carvings, large and seaworthy watercraft, memorial or totem poles, and basketry. The potlatch, a feast associated with the bestowal of lavish gifts, was also characteristic of this culture area.

TLINGIT

The Tlingit, the northernmost of the Northwest Coast Indians of North America, lived on the islands and coastal lands of southern Alaska from Yakutat Bay to Cape Fox. They spoke the Tlingit language, which is related to Athabaskan. According to their traditions, some of their ancestors came from the south and others migrated to the coast from the Canadian interior.

Traditional Tlingit society included three levels of kinship organization. Every individual belonged to one of two moieties, the largest kin group. Each moiety comprised several clans, and the members of a given clan attributed their origin to a common legendary ancestor. The most basic and important organizational level was the lineage, an extended family group related through maternal descent. Each lineage that was essentially self-sufficient, owned a specific territory, could conduct ceremonies, was politically independent, and had its own leaders. There was rarely a leader or authority over the entire tribe; lineages might cooperate during periods of war and choose a temporary leader for that purpose, but there was no compulsion to join such alliances. During the historic period there was a tendency for two or more lineages to consolidate into unified villages, but before contact with Europeans each lineage probably had its own village.

The traditional Tlingit economy was based on fishing; salmon was the main source of food. The Tlingit also hunted sea, and sometimes land, mammals. Wood was the primary material for manufacture and was used for houses, memorial (totem) poles, canoes, dishes, utensils, and other objects. Large permanent houses were built near good fishing grounds and safe landing places for canoes, often along the beaches of a bay sheltered from the tides. These houses were winter residences; during the summer, inhabitants dispersed to take advantage of more-distant fishing and hunting grounds. Potlatches, or ceremonial distributions of gifts, marked a cycle of rituals mourning the death of a lineage chief.

Early 21st-century population estimates indicated some 22,000 individuals of Tlingit descent.

HAIDA

The Haida were a Haida-speaking people of what are now the Queen Charlotte Islands, British Columbia, Can., and the southern part of Prince of Wales Island, Alaska, U.S. The Alaskan Haida are called Kaigani. Haida culture is related to the cultures of the neighbouring Tlingit and Tsimshian.

Traditional Haida social organization was built around two major subdivisions, or moieties; moiety membership was assigned at birth and based on maternal affiliation. Each moiety consisted of many local segments or lineages which owned rights to economically important lands, occupied separate villages, and

had their own primary chiefs (a village's highest ranking member) and lesser house chiefs. Each lineage functioned independently of the others in matters of war, peace, religion, and economics.

Traditional Haida economics were based on fishing (especially of salmon, halibut, and cod) and hunting; the annual salmon run offered the Haida and other Northwest Coast Indians a very productive and reliable resource that required relatively little investment on their part,

Wooden thunderbird of the Haida tribe, northwest coast of North America, 19th century; in the British Museum, London. Courtesy of the trustees of the British Museum

thus supporting the tribe's artistic and ceremonial pursuits. The Haida were widely known for their art and architecture, both of which focused on the creative embellishment of wood. They decorated utilitarian objects with depictions of supernatural and other beings in a highly conventionalized style. They also produced elaborate totem poles with carved and painted crests. These poles were used for a variety of symbolic functions ranging from mortuary markers to records of family histories; carved from big tree trunks, they could function as particularly large-scale ornaments or as structural supports outside, and sometimes inside, the house. Fine examples of traditional Haida arts and architecture may be seen at the Haida Heritage Centre at Kaay Llnagaay, near the town of Skidegate in the Queen Charlotte Islands.

Haida ceremonial culture was most fully expressed in the potlatch, or ceremonial distribution of goods. Potlatches were held to confer, validate, or uphold political rank, such as chieftainship, or social status. Potlatches were also given to mark events such as house building, totem-pole raising, and funerals and for purposes such as saving face.

Early 21st-century population estimates indicated more than 20,000 Haida descendants.

TSIMSHIAN

The Tsimshian traditionally lived on the mainland and islands around the Skeena and Nass rivers and Milbanke Sound in what is now British Columbia, Can., and Alaska, U.S. They speak any of three Tsimshian dialects: Niska, spoken along the Nass River; coastal Tsimshian, along the lower Skeena and the coast; and Kitksan (or Gitksan), along the upper Skeena. Tsimshian is classified as a Penutian language.

The traditional economy of the Tsimshian (also spelled Chimmesyan) was based on fishing. They passed the summer months trapping migrating salmon and eulachon (candlefish), a species of smelt. Eulachon were particularly valuable for their oil, which was made into a food highly regarded by many peoples of the area. Large permanent winter houses, made of wood and often carved and painted, symbolized the wealth of Tsimshian families. During the winter months, some land animals were also hunted.

The coastal Tsimshian and the Niska were divided into four major clans, or kin groups; the Kitksan into three. These were further divided into local segments or lineages, descent being traced through the maternal line. Each lineage was generally an independent social and ceremonial unit with its own fishing and hunting areas, berry grounds, house or houses, and heraldic crests representing events in the family history, as well as its own chiefs. Local groupings, or tribes, were composed of several lineages. Each lineage was ranked relative to the others, and the chief of the highest-ranked lineage was recognized as chief of the tribe. The tribe as a whole held properties such as the winter village site and participated in ceremonies and warfare.

The Tsimshian were known for their highly conventionalized applied art. Carved and painted columns (popularly known as totem poles) were erected, primarily as memorials to deceased chiefs. The major Tsimshian potlatches, or ceremonial distributions of gifts, had as their purpose the announcement and validation of the position of the new chief. Potlatches could also mark a series of events several years apart, such as house building, totem-pole raising, and dramatizations of privileges and crests.

Early 21st-century population estimates indicated some 5,000 Tsimshian descendants.

Kwakiutl

The Kwakiutl were North American Indians who traditionally lived in what is now British Columbia, Can., along the shores of the waterways between Vancouver Island and the mainland. Their self-name, Kwakwaka'wakw, means "those who speak Kwakwala." They speak a Wakashan language that included three major dialects: Haisla, spoken on the Gardner Canal and Douglas Channel; Heiltsuq, spoken from Gardner Canal to Rivers Inlet; and southern Kwakiutl, spoken from Rivers Inlet to Cape Mudge on the mainland and on the northern end of Vancouver Island. The Kwakiutl are culturally and linguistically related to the Nootka.

The Kwakiutl contributed extensively to the early development of anthropology as the subjects of ethnographic studies by pioneering scholar Franz Boas. In more than 5,000 pages written over almost half a century, Boas described and analyzed nearly every aspect of Kwakiutl culture and its relationships to other Northwest Coast Indians with whom the tribe shared general features of technology, economy, art, myths, and religion.

Traditionally, the Kwakiutl subsisted mainly by fishing and had a technology based on woodworking. Their society was stratified by rank, which was determined primarily by the inheritance of names and privileges. The latter could include the right to sing certain songs, use certain crests, and wear particular ceremonial masks.

The potlatch, a ceremonial distribution of property and gifts unique to Northwest Coast peoples, was elaborately developed by the southern Kwakiutl. Their potlatches were often combined with performances by dancing societies, each society having a series of dances that dramatized ancestral interactions with supernatural beings. These beings were portrayed as giving gifts of ceremonial prerogatives such as songs, dances, and names, which became hereditary property.

Early 21st-century population estimates indicated approximately 700 individuals of Kwakiutl descent.

Kwakiutl man wearing traditional regalia, photograph by Edward S. Curtis, c. 1914. Edward S. Curtis Collection/Library of Congress, Washington, D.C. (neg. no. LC-USZ62-52212)

BELLA COOLA

The villages of the Bella Coola were located in what is now the central British Columbia coast, along the upper Dean and Burke channels and the lower parts of the Bella Coola River valley. They spoke a Salishan language related to that of the Coast Salish to the south. Their ancestors probably separated from the main body of Salish and migrated northward. Although their material culture, ceremonials, and mythology resembled those of their Heiltsuq neighbours, their social organization was similar to that of the more distant Salish.

Traditionally, the Bella Coola (also called the Nuxalk) lived in permanent villages of large plank-built houses occupied by a number of families. They used wood for houses, canoes, and watertight boxes that served a variety of domestic purposes. Cedar bark provided fibres for clothing, baskets were made of cedar and spruce, and alder and cedar were carved into masks and other ceremonial objects,

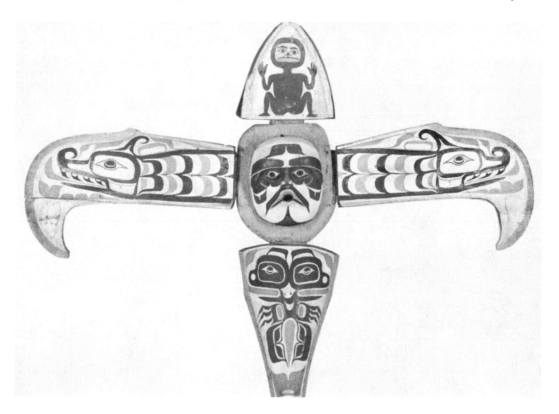

Thunderbird mask of the Kwakiutl Indians, shown with beak and wings open to reveal a human face, painted wood; in the Brooklyn Museum, New York. Courtesy of the Brooklyn Museum, New York

including spectacular totem poles. Fish was their basic food source, supplemented by hunting and by collecting wild plant foods. Salmon, taken in the summer, were eaten fresh or smoked; oil extracted from eulachon (candlefish) was used as a condiment. Life was organized on a village basis, with status dependent on both hereditary rank and wealth, measured by ostentatious giving at potlatches. There was no formal political structure connecting Bella Coola communities to one another but rather a strong feeling of shared identity based on common language, common origin, and cultural pride. Secret societies were important, with an unusually well-developed pantheon of deities and great emphasis on numerous oral traditions.

The Bella Coola probably numbered about 5,000 at the time of their first contacts with Europeans but were reduced by disease in the 19th century to less than 1,000 people, most living in a single village. Bella Coola and other Salish descendants numbered more than 21,000 in the early 21st century.

NUU-CHAH-NULTH

The Nuu-chah-nulth (or Nootka) live on what are now the southwest coast of Vancouver Island, Can., and on Cape Flattery, the northwest tip of the state of Washington, U.S. The groups on the southeast end of the island were the Nitinat, those on Cape Flattery the Makah. The Nuu-chah-nulth are culturally related to the Kwakiutl. Their name means "along the mountains." They speak a Wakashan language.

Local groups in the central and southern Nuu-chah-nulth regions were traditionally socially and politically independent; in northern areas they usually formed larger tribes with large winter villages. There were also several confederacies of tribes, dating to prehistoric times, that shared summer villages and fishing and hunting grounds near the coast. The Nuu-chah-nulth moved seasonally to areas of economic importance, returning to their principal villages during the winter when subsistence activity slowed.

Like several other Northwest Coast Indians, the Nuu-chah-nulth were whale hunters, employing special equipment such as large dugout canoes and harpoons with long lines and sealskin floats. The whale harpooner was a person of high rank, and families passed down the magical and practical secrets that made for successful hunting. There was also a whale ritualist who, by appropriate ceremonial procedures, caused whales that had died of natural causes to drift ashore. Many features of this whaling complex suggest ancient ties with Eskimo and Aleut cultures.

Before the Nuu-chah-nulth were colonized by Russia, England, Canada, and the United States, their religion centred on shamanism and animism. The most important Nuu-chah-nulth ceremony was the shamans' dance, a reenactment of the kidnapping of an ancestor by supernatural beings who later gave him supernatural gifts and released him. The ceremony served to define each individual's place in the social order. The public performance ended with a potlatch, a ceremonial distribution of property.

Early 21st-century population estimates indicated some 8,500 individuals of Nuu-chah-nulth descent.

COAST SALISH

The Coast Salish, a Salish-speaking people, lived around what are now the Strait of Georgia, Puget Sound, southern Vancouver Island, much of the Olympic Peninsula, and most of western Washington state. One Salishan group, the Tillamook, lived south of the Columbia River in Oregon. The Bella Coola, a group living farther to the north in British Columbia, probably migrated from the main body of Coast Salish. The Coast Salish probably migrated to the coast from the interior, where other Salish-speakers lived. They were culturally similar to the Chinook.

Like other Northwest Coast Indians before colonial contact, the Coast Salish lived principally on fish, although some groups living along the upper rivers relied more heavily on hunting. They built permanent winter houses of wood and used mat lodges for temporary camps.

Traditionally, the tribe's basic social unit was the local group consisting of close relatives. Each extended family usually lived in one large house, and groups of houses formed a winter village. People dispersed during the summer for fishing, hunting, and berrying.

One of the most important Coast Salish events was the ceremonial distribution of gifts in the potlatch. Elaborate ceremonies held during the winter included dances inspired by spirits in dreams or trances. Many other forms of performance art were treated as property to which individuals or groups acquired exclusive rights by inheritance, marriage, or purchase.

Early 21st-century population estimates indicated more than 25,000 Coast Salish descendants in Canada and the United States.

CHINOOK

The Chinook traditionally lived in what are now Washington and Oregon, from the mouth of the Columbia River to The Dalles. They spoke Chinookan languages.

The Chinook were famous as traders, with connections stretching as far as the Great Plains. The Columbia was a major indigenous thoroughfare, and the Chinooks' location facilitated contact with northern and southern coastal peoples as well as with interior groups. The river was a rich source of salmon, the basis of the regional economy, and many groups traded with the Chinook for dried fish. Other important trade items were slaves from California, Nuu-chah-nulth canoes, and dentalium shells, which were highly valued as hair and clothing ornaments. Chinook Jargon, the trade language of the Northwest Coast, was a combination of Chinook with Nuu-chah-nulth and other Native American, English, and French terms. Chinook Jargon may have originated before European contact. It was used across a very broad territory reaching from California to Alaska.

The Chinook were first described ethnographically by the American explorers Lewis and Clark in 1805. Because American colonialism severely disrupted Chinook culture, ultimately removing the people to reservations, most information about traditional Chinook life is based on the records of these and other traders and explorers, together with what is known of neighbouring groups.

The tribe's basic social unit was probably a local group consisting of close relatives and headed by a senior member. Traditional Chinook religion focused on the first-salmon rite, a ritual in which each group welcomed the annual salmon run. Another important ritual was the individual vision quest, an ordeal undertaken by all male and some female adolescents to acquire a guardian spirit that would give them hunting, curing, or other powers, bring them good luck, or teach them songs and dances. Singing ceremonies were public demonstrations of these gifts. The Chinook also had potlatches, which were ceremonial distributions of property.

Early 21st-century population estimates indicated more than 1,500 Chinook descendants.

CALIFORNIA

The California culture area includes representatives of some 20 language families, including Uto-Aztecan, Penutian, Yokutsan, and Athabaskan. American linguist Edward Sapir described California's languages as being more diverse than those found in all of Europe. Prominent tribes, many with a language named for them, include the Hupa, Yurok, Pomo, Yuki, Wintun, Maidu, and Yana.

Many California peoples eschewed centralized political structures and instead organized themselves into tribelets, groups of a few hundred to a few thousand people that recognized cultural ties with others but maintained their political independence. Some tribelets comprised just one village and others included several villages; in the latter cases, one village was usually recognized as more important than the others. The relatively few groups that lived in areas with sparse natural resources preferred to live in small mobile bands.

Agriculture was practiced only along the Colorado River; elsewhere hunting and gathering provided a relatively easy living. Acorns were the most important of the wild food sources. California peoples devised a method of leaching the toxins from acorn pulp and converting it into flour, thus ensuring abundant and constant food. Fishing, hunting, and gathering shellfish and other wild foods were also highly productive. Housing varied from wood-framed single-family dwellings to communal apartment-style buildings; ceremonial structures were very important and could often hold several hundred people. The California peoples were also known for their fine basketry, ritualized trade fairs, and the Kuksu and Toloache religions.

HUPA

The Hupa lived along the lower Trinity River in what is now the state of California and spoke Hupa, an Athabaskan language. Culturally, they combined aspects of the Pacific Northwest Indians and the California Indians.

Hupa villages were traditionally located on the riverbank and included dwellings for women and children, separate semisubterranean buildings where men slept and took sweat baths, and small menstrual lodges for women. The Hupa economy was based on elk, deer, salmon, and acorns, all of which were readily available in the region. Fine basketry was made by twining segments of certain roots, leaves, and stems around prepared shoots. As an inland group, the Hupa often exchanged acorns and other local foods with the coast-dwelling Yurok, who reciprocated with redwood canoes, saltwater fish, mussels, and seaweed. Members of the two tribes attended each other's ceremonies and sometimes intermarried.

Hupa people traditionally measured wealth in terms of the ownership of woodpecker scalps and dentalium shells, the

latter of which were probably received in trade from the Yurok. The village's richest man was its headman. His power and his property passed to his son, but anyone who acquired more property might obtain the dignity and power of that office. Personal insult, injury, or homicide were usually settled through the payment of blood money.

The recitation of magical formulas was an important part of traditional Hupa religion. Shamanism was also common; shamans' fees were paid in dentalium shells or deerskin blankets. Three major dances were held annually for the benefit of the community, as were spring and fall ceremonial feasts.

Early 21st-century population estimates indicated more than 3,000 Hupa descendants.

YUROK

The Yurok lived in what is now California along the lower Klamath River and the Pacific coast. They spoke a Macro-Algonquian language and were culturally and linguistically related to the Wiyot. As their traditional territory lay on the border between divergent cultural and ecological areas, the Yurok combined the typical subsistence practices of Northwest Coast Indians with many religious and organizational features common to California Indians.

Traditional Yurok villages were small collections of independent houses owned by individual families. Avoiding unified communities and an overall political authority, village residents sometimes shared rights to general subsistence areas and to the performance of certain rituals. Other rights, such as the right to use specific areas for fishing, hunting, and gathering, generally belonged to particular houses. These rights were acquired by inheritance or dowry, as part of blood money settlements, or by sale. In addition to dwellings, villages had sweat houses, each of which served as a gathering places for the men of an extended patrilineal family. There were also separate shelters to which women retired during menstruation.

The traditional Yurok economy focused on salmon and acorns. The people also produced excellent basketry and made canoes from redwood trees, selling them to inland tribes. Wealth was counted in strings of dentalium shells, obsidian blades, woodpecker scalps, and albino deerskins. Acquiring wealth was an important goal in Yurok culture. Feuds were common, and payments of blood money were precisely defined according to the seriousness of the offense; the value of a man's life depended on his social status.

Traditional Yurok religion was concerned with an individual's effort to elicit supernatural aid, especially through ritual cleanliness, and with rituals for the public welfare. The tribe did not practice the potlatch, masked dances, representative carving, and other features typical of their Northwest Coast

neighbours. The major ceremonies were those of the World Renewal cycle, which ensured an abundance of food, riches, and general well-being. This cycle included the recitation of magical formulas, repeating the words of an ancient spirit race, and other acts. The spiritual power to cure disease was granted only to women, giving these shamans prestige and a source of wealth.

Early 21st-century population estimates indicated some 6,000 individuals of Yurok descent.

POMO

The territory of the Pomo, a Hokan-speaking people, was centred in the Russian River valley some 50 to 100 miles (80 to 160 km) north of what is now San Francisco. The Pomo's territory also included the adjacent coastlands and the interior highlands near Clear Lake. A small detached group lived in the Sacramento River valley surrounded by Wintun people.

Traditionally the Pomo were a comparatively wealthy people, well supplied with food and other natural resources. Fish, waterfowl, deer, acorns, bulb plants, seeds, and other wild foods were plentiful. Northeastern Pomo settlements held a lucrative salt deposit, and southeastern settlements had magnesite, a substance that was combined with ground shells and made into the beads that were used as standard currency in north-central California. Pomo basketry, considered by

A Pomo woman demonstrates traditional seed-gathering techniques, photograph by Edward S. Curtis, c. 1924. Edward S. Curtis Collection/Library of Congress, Washington, D.C. (neg. no. LC-USZ62-116525)

some to be the finest in California, was exceptionally well twined and intricately ornamented, using various woody materials, beads, and coloured feathers. Pomo housing varied with the locale. Coastal residents constructed dwellings of heavy timber and bark, and inland peoples built various types of dwellings out of such materials as poles, brush, grass, and tule mats. Traditional Pomo religion involved the Kuksu cult, a set of beliefs and practices involving private ceremonies, esoteric dances and rituals, and impersonations of spirits. There were also ceremonies for such things as ghosts, coyotes, and thunder.

Early 21st-century population estimates indicated approximately 8,000 individuals of Pomo descent.

YUKI

The Yuki consisted of four groups of North American Indians who lived in the Coast Ranges and along the coast of what is now northwestern California, U.S. They spoke distinctive languages that are unaffiliated with any other known language. The four Yuki groups were the Yuki-proper, who lived along the upper reaches of the Eel River and its tributaries; the Huchnom of Redwood Valley to the west; the Coast Yuki, who were distributed farther westward along the redwood coast; and the Wappo, who occupied an enclave among the Pomo, some 40 miles (65 km) southward in the Russian River valley.

Only the linguistic identification links the Wappo with other Yuki; Wappo cultural traditions were otherwise like those of the Pomo. The other Yuki groups were traditionally organized into tribelets, communities composed of several scattered settlements or villages occupying a particular area. Each settlement had its own chief, and there was also a head chief for the community as a whole. There was also a war leader, a person in charge of religious dances, and a shaman, or medicine man or woman. Warfare was apparently frequent between certain communities, between the different Yuki groups, and with other California Indians. The Coast Yuki were an exception, usually maintaining friendly relations with their neighbours. Trade was prevalent among all groups, inland people trading such items as furs with coastal groups, who in turn plied a variety of seafood and shells. Clamshell beads were used as currency.

The Yuki economy was based on gathering acorns, fishing, mostly for salmon, and hunting such animals as bear and deer. The Coast Yuki relied somewhat more on seafood than the other groups. Interior groups lived in domed earth-covered houses; Coast Yuki had conical houses covered with bark. All had large dance houses and sweat houses.

Traditional Yuki religious beliefs centred generally on two contrasting deities—a creator, whose actions were essentially well intended, and another deity, sometimes associated with thunder, who might help but might also blunder or do evil. Usually the creator was the supreme god of the two, but among the Coast Yuki he had disappeared and only Thunder remained. All Yuki had a great array of ceremonies, rituals, and initiations.

Early 21st-century population estimates indicated some 600 Yuki descendants.

WINTUN

The term *Wintun* embraces a number of groups of Penutian-speaking North American Indians originally inhabiting the west side of the Sacramento Valley in what is today California. Traditional Wintun territory was some 250 miles (400 km) from north to south and included stretches of the flanking foothills. Four primary linguistic groupings, each including a number of dialects, made up the Wintun population: the northern Wintun (Wintu), the central Wintun (Nomlaki), and the two subdivisions of the southern Wintun, the Hill and River Patwin. The Patwin are sometimes classified as a group separate from the Wintun.

The elongated shape of Wintun territory made for considerable cultural diversity; before colonization by the Spanish, contacts with close neighbours to the east and west were more frequent for most communities than were those with other Wintun at the extremities of the territory. In the north, for instance, basketry was twined in the fashion of the Oregon Indians. In the centre it was intricately ornamented like that of the Pomo, and in the south it had mixed characteristics. Similarly, Wintun houses varied by region. River Patwin houses were earth-covered domes, while Hill Patwin used conical bark structures and simpler thatched dwellings. The nature of the northern groups' houses is unknown. Wintun economies relied upon wild foods, including acorns, fish, and waterfowl. Not much is known of Wintun social or political organization, although the Patwin are known to have had a community chief with near-absolute power.

Wintun religion was based on the belief in a single creator. The southern Wintun greatly influenced the development of the Kuksu cult, a religion of secret societies and rituals that spread to a number of California tribes. The cult's main purposes were to bring strength to young male initiates, to bring fertility to natural crops, and to ward off natural disasters.

There were at least 12,000 Wintun before the Spanish colonization of California. Epidemics of Old World diseases (to which the Wintun had no immunity) greatly reduced their numbers, as did violence resulting from California's mid-19th century gold rush. Wintun descendants numbered more than 3,800 in the early 21st century.

MAIDU

The Maidu spoke a language of Penutian stock and originally lived in a territory extending eastward from the Sacramento River to the crest of the Sierra Nevada mountains and centring chiefly in the drainage of the Feather and American rivers in California, U.S.

As with other tribes of California Indians, the Maidu ate seeds and acorns and hunted elk, deer, bears, rabbits, ducks, and geese. They also fished for salmon, lamprey eel, and other river life. Before Spanish colonization, each Maidu group resided in one of three habitats: the inland valleys, the Sierra Nevada foothills, or the mountains themselves. The valley people were prosperous, but poverty was more common in the higher habitats. Ironically, those Maidu who were the least exposed to inclement conditions had the most-sophisticated technology and were able to construct the most-protective shelter. Thus, the valley people built large earth-covered communal dwellings, whereas the foothill dwellers and mountaineers made more-fragile brush or bark lean-tos.

Traditional Maidu social organization was built around autonomous, yet allied, settlements; each claimed a communal territory and acted as a single political unit. Among southern groups the chiefs were hereditary, but among northern groups they could be deposed and probably achieved their position through wealth and popularity.

Like many other central California tribes, the Maidu practiced the Kuksu religion, involving male secret societies, rites, masks and disguises, and special earth-roofed ceremonial chambers. Some of the purposes of the rituals were naturalistic—to ensure good crops or plentiful game or to ward off floods and other natural disasters such as disease.

Population estimates indicated more than 4,000 individuals of Maidu descent in the early 21st century.

YANA

The Yana, a Hokan-speaking people, formerly lived along the eastern tributaries of the upper Sacramento River, from the Pit River to southwest of Lassen Peak, in what is now California. Traditional Yana territory comprised myriad foothills and narrow, rugged canyons, which were partly wooded but mostly brush-covered and rocky.

Before colonization there were four Yana divisions—Northern, Central, and Southern Yana, as well as Yahi—speaking mutually intelligible dialects. A significant characteristic of Yana speech was its use of separate forms for men and women. The differences were small, but women used their word forms exclusively, whereas men used the male forms among themselves and the so-called female forms when addressing women.

Life generally was very difficult in the harsh, barren environment. The Yana lived in earth-covered winter lodges and thatch-covered summer dwellings, hunted various game, and fished for salmon. Little is known of their social organization, except that it probably comprised small bands and contained classes or rankings. Before colonization the Yana had relatively frequent skirmishes with their neighbours, an unusual trait for California Indians.

In 1864 the tribe was the victim of particularly brutal attacks by nearby miners. The miners launched an overt campaign of extermination, and over the course of several days they killed all but about 50 of the estimated 3,000 tribal members; the survivors subsequently avoided contact with Euro-Americans by living in isolated canyons. From 1911 until his death in 1916, the last known survivor of the Yahi band, Ishi, worked to record his memories of traditional culture with anthropologist A.L. Kroeber.

Early 21st-century population estimates indicated some 100 Yana descendants.

CHAPTER 9

PREHISTORY

A sia and North America remained connected until about 12,000 years ago. Although most of the routes used by the Paleo-Indians are difficult to investigate because they are now underwater or deeply buried or have been destroyed by erosion and other geological processes, research has divulged a variety of information about their lives and cultures.

PALEO-INDIAN CULTURES

Archaeological discoveries in the first half of the 20th century indicated that the migration had occurred by about 9500 BC, and subsequent finds pushed this boundary to even earlier dates. Scholars group Paleo-Indians into two distinct traditions: the Clovis, Folsom, and related cultures of the North American interior; and the pre-Clovis cultures, whose distribution is emerging through current research.

All the Paleo-Indian groups lived in a relatively dynamic landscape that they shared with Pleistocene flora and fauna, most notably with megafauna such as mammoths, mastodons, giant bison, giant ground sloths, sabre-toothed cats, and short-faced bears. Paleo-Indian sites often include the remains of megafauna, sometimes leading to the mistaken impression that these peoples were solely dedicated to the capture of big game.

For a time this impression was sustained by a variety of preservation and identification issues such as the rapid degeneration of small mammal, fish, and vegetal remains in the archaeological record and the use of recovery techniques that neglected or ignored such materials. By the turn of the 21st century, however, excavations at sites such as Gault (Texas) and Jake Bluff (Oklahoma) had clearly demonstrated that at least some Paleo-Indians used a variety of wild animal and plant foods and so are better characterized as generalized hunter-gatherers than as people who limited themselves to the pursuit of big game.

THE CLOVIS AND FOLSOM CULTURES

In 1908 George McJunkin, ranch foreman and former slave, reported that the bones of an extinct form of giant bison (*Bison antiquus*) were eroding out of a wash near Folsom, N.M. An ancient spear point was later found embedded in the animal's skeleton. In 1929 teenager Ridgley Whiteman found a similar site near Clovis, N.M., albeit with mammoth rather than bison remains. The Folsom

Clovis points exhibiting characteristic channels, or flutes, that extend from mid-blade to the base of the implement. Courtesy, Robert N. Converse, The Archaeological Society of Ohio

and Clovis sites yielded the first indisputable evidence that ancient Americans had coexisted with and hunted the megafauna, a possibility that most scholars had previously met with skepticism.

The Clovis culture proved to be the earlier of the two. Clovis projectile points are thin, lanceolate (leaf-shaped), and made of stone; one or more longitudinal flakes, or flutes, were removed from the base of each of the point's two flat faces. Clovis points were affixed to spear handles and are often found on mammoth kill sites, usually accompanied by side scrapers (used to flense the hide) and other artifacts used to process meat. Clovis culture was long believed to have lasted from approximately 9500 to 9000 BC, although early 21st-century analyses suggest it may have been of shorter duration, from approximately 9050 to 8800 BC.

Folsom culture seems to have developed from Clovis culture. Also lanceolate, Folsom points were more carefully manufactured and include much larger flutes

Three end scrapers and a uniface blade. Courtesy, Robert R. Converse, the Archaeological Soceity of Ohio

than those made by the Clovis people. The Lindenmeier site, a Folsom campsite in northeastern Colorado, has yielded a wide variety of end and side scrapers, gravers (used to engrave bone or wood), and bone artifacts. The Folsom culture is thought to have lasted from approximately 9000 to 8000 BC. Related Paleo-Indian groups, such as the Plano culture, persisted until sometime between 6000 and 4000 BC.

Pre-Clovis Cultures

The long-standing belief that Clovis people were the first Americans was challenged in the late 20th century by the discovery of several sites antedating those of the Clovis culture. Although many scholars were initially skeptical of the evidence from these sites, the late 1990s saw general agreement that humans had arrived in North and South America by at least 11,000 BC, some 1,500 years before the appearance of Clovis culture.

Dating to about 10,500 BC, Monte Verde, a site in Chile's Llanquihue province, is the oldest confirmed human habitation site in the Americas. First excavated in the 1970s, the site did not seem to concord with findings that placed the earliest humans in northeastern Asia no earlier than c. 11,500 BC; it seemed extremely unlikely that people could have meandered from Siberia to Chile in just 1,000 years. However, excavations at the Yana Rhinoceros Horn site in Siberia subsequently determined that humans

were present on the western side of the Bering land bridge as early as 25,000 BC, providing ample time for such a migration.

A number of other sites may be as early or earlier than Monte Verde. Excavations of note include those at the Topper site (South Carolina), Cactus Hill (Virginia), Schaefer and Hebior (Wisconsin), and others. Further investigations will continue to clarify the patterns of Paleo-Indian migration.

ARCHAIC CULTURES

Beginning about 6000 BC, what had been a relatively cool and moist climate gradually became warmer and drier. A number of cultural changes are associated with this environmental shift. Most notably, bands became larger and somewhat more sedentary, tending to forage from seasonal camps rather than roaming across the entire landscape. Fish, fowl, and wild plant foods (especially seeds) also become more apparent in the archaeological record, although this may be a result of differential preservation rather than changes in ancient subsistence strategies. Finally, various forms of evidence indicate that humans were influencing the growth patterns and reproduction of plants through practices such as the setting of controlled fires to clear forest underbrush, thereby increasing the number and productivity of nut-bearing trees. In aggregate, these changes mark the transition from Paleo-Indian to Archaic cultures.

The duration of the Archaic Period varied considerably in Northern America: in some areas it may have begun as long ago as 8000 BC, in others as recently as 4000 BC. Between 6000 and 4000 BC the wild squash seeds found at archaeological sites slowly increased in size, a sign of incipient domestication. Similar changes are apparent by about 5000 BC in the seeds of wild sunflowers and certain "weedy" plants (defined as those that prefer disturbed soils and bear plentiful seeds) such as sumpweed (*Iva annua*) and lamb's-quarters (*Chenopodium album*). Northern Americans independently domesticated several kinds of flora, including a variety of squash (*c.* 3000 BC) unrelated to the those of Mesoamerica or South America, sunflowers *Helianthus annuus* (*c.* 3000 BC), and goosefoot *Chenopodium berlandieri* (*c.* 2500 BC).

Many prehistoric Native American peoples eventually adopted some degree of agriculture; they are said to have transitioned from the Archaic to subsequent culture periods when evidence indicates that they began to rely substantively upon domesticated foods and in most cases to make pottery. Archaeologists typically place the end of the North American Archaic at or near 1000 BC, although there is substantial regional variation from this date. For instance, the Plains Archaic continued until approximately the beginning of the Common Era, and other groups maintained an essentially Archaic lifestyle well into the 19th century, particularly in the diverse microenvironments of the Pacific Coast, the arid Great Basin, and the cold boreal forests, tundras, and coasts of Alaska and Canada.

PACIFIC COAST ARCHAIC CULTURES

Archaic peoples living along the Pacific Coast and in neighbouring inland areas found a number of innovative uses for the rich microenvironments of that region. Groups living in arid inland locales made rough flint tools, grinding stones, and, eventually, arrowheads and subsisted upon plant seeds and small game. Where there was more precipitation the food supply included elk, deer, acorns, fish, and birds. People on the coast itself depended upon the sea for their food supply, some subsisting mainly on shellfish, some on sea mammals, others on fish, and still others on a mixture of all three.

In contrast to the larger projectile points found elsewhere in North America, many Pacific Coast Archaic groups preferred to use tools made of microblades. Sometimes these were set into handles to make knives composed of a series of small individually set teeth rather than a long, continuous cutting edge. However, in the Northwest Coast culture area, the people of the Old Cordilleran culture (sometimes called the Paleoplateau or Northwest Riverine culture; *c.* 9000/8500–5000 BC) preferred lanceolate points, long blades, and roughly finished choppers.

During the postglacial warming period that culminated between 3000

DOMESTICATION

Domestication is the process of hereditary reorganization of wild animals and plants into domestic and cultivated forms according to the interests of people. In its strictest sense, it refers to the initial stage of human mastery of wild animals and plants. The fundamental distinction of domesticated animals and plants from their wild ancestors is that they are created by human labour to meet specific requirements or whims and are adapted to the conditions of continuous care and solicitude people maintain for them.

Domestication has played an enormous part in the development of humankind and material culture. It has resulted in the appearance of agriculture as a special form of animal and plant production. It is precisely those animals and plants that became objects of agricultural activity that have undergone the greatest changes when compared with their wild ancestors.

and 2000 BC, the inhabitants of the drier areas without permanent streams took on many of the traits of the Desert Archaic cultures, while others turned increasingly toward river and marsh resources. In the 1st millennium BC the Marpole complex, a distinctive toolmaking tradition focusing on ground slate, appeared in the Fraser River area. Marpole people shared a basic resemblance to historic Northwest Coast groups in terms of their maritime emphasis, woodworking, large houses, and substantial villages.

DESERT ARCHAIC CULTURES

Ancient peoples in the present-day Plateau and Great Basin culture areas created distinctive cultural adaptations to the dry, relatively impoverished environments of these regions. The Cochise or Desert Archaic culture began by about 7000 BC and persisted until the beginning of the Common Era.

Desert Archaic people lived in small nomadic bands and followed a seasonal round. They ate a wide variety of animal and plant foods and developed techniques for small-seed harvesting and processing; an essential component of the Desert Archaic tool kit was the milling stone, used to grind wild seeds into meal or flour. These groups are known for having lived in caves and rock shelters; they also made twined basketry, nets, mats, cordage, fur cloaks, sandals, wooden clubs, digging sticks, spear-throwers, and dart shafts tipped with pointed hardwood, flint, or obsidian. Their chopping and scraping tools often have a rough, relatively unsophisticated appearance, but their projectile points show excellent craftsmanship.

PLAINS ARCHAIC CULTURES

The Plains Archaic began by about 6000 BC and persisted until about the beginning of the Common Era. It is marked by a shift from just a few kinds of fluted Paleo-Indian points to a myriad of styles, including stemmed and side-notched points. The primary game animal of the Plains Archaic peoples was the bison, although as savvy foragers they also exploited a variety of other game and many wild plant foods.

As the climate became warmer, some groups followed grazing herds north into present-day Saskatchewan and Alberta; by 3000 BC these people had reached the Arctic tundra zone in the Northwest Territories and shifted their attention from bison to the local caribou. Other groups moved east to the Mississippi valley and western Great Lakes area.

EASTERN ARCHAIC CULTURES

The Eastern Archaic (c. 8000–1500 BC) included much of the eastern subarctic, the Northeast, and the Southeast culture areas; because of this very wide distribution, Eastern Archaic cultures show more diversity over time and space than Archaic cultures elsewhere in North America. Nonetheless, these cultures are characterized by a number of material similarities. The typical house was a small circular structure framed with wood; historical analogies suggest that the covering was probably bark. Cooking was accomplished by placing hot rocks into wood, bark, or hide containers of food, which caused the contents to warm or even boil; by baking in pits; or by roasting. Lists of mammal, fish, and bird remains from Eastern Archaic sites read like a catalog of the region's fauna at about the time of European contact. Game-gathering devices such as nets, traps, and pitfalls were used, as were spears, darts, and dart or spear throwers. Fishhooks, gorges, and net sinkers were also important, and in some areas fish weirs (underwater pens or corrals), were built. River, lake, and ocean mollusks were consumed, and a great many roots, berries, fruits, and tubers were part of the diet.

Over time, Eastern Archaic material culture reflects increasing levels of technological and economic sophistication. A large variety of chipped-flint projectiles, knives, scrapers, perforators, drills, and adzes appear. The era is also marked by the gradual development of ground and polished tools such as grooved stone axes, pestles, gouges, adzes, plummets (stones ground into a teardrop shape, used for unknown purposes), and bird stones and other weights that attached to spear throwers.

Eastern Archaic people in what are now the states of Michigan and Wisconsin began to work copper, which can be found in large nodules there. Using cold-hammer techniques, they created a variety of distinctive tools and art forms. Their aptly named Old Copper culture appeared about 3000 BC and lasted approximately 2,000 years. Its tools and weapons, particularly its adzes, gouges, and axes, clearly indicate an adaptation to the forest environment.

In the area south of James Bay to the upper St. Lawrence River about 4000 BC,

TOOLS OF ARCHAIC CULTURES

A spear-thrower—also called a throwing-stick, or atlatl—is a device for throwing a spear (or dart) usually consisting of a rod or board with a groove on the upper surface and a hook, thong, or projection at the rear end to hold the weapon in place until its release. Its purpose is to give greater velocity and force to the spear. In use from prehistoric times, the spear-thrower was used to efficiently fell animals as large as the mammoth.

Usually constructed of wood, bamboo, bone, or antler, the spear-thrower performs the function of an extra joint in the arm. The spear lies along the spear-thrower, with its butt resting against a projecting peg or in the slight socket made by the septum of the node (in the case of bamboo devices). Eskimo and Indian tribes of the northwest coast of North America used it for discharging harpoons and fish spears. It was also used in Central and South America, as among the Mayan and the Aztecs (who called it the atlatl).

Allied to these spear-throwers is the becket, a short length of cord that operates like a sling, causing the hurled spear to spin as it flies.

A bird stone, or atlatl weight, is an abstract stone carving, one of the most striking artifacts left by the prehistoric North American Indians who inhabited the area east of the Mississippi River in the United States and parts of eastern Canada. The stones resemble birds and rarely exceed 6 inches (15 cm) in length.

The great majority of these stones were carved from black, brown, or dark green slate, with a few examples carved from porphyry. The stone was evidently chipped away to a rough approximation of the finished form and then smoothed to a high polish with sand and other abrasives. A distinctive feature of all bird stones is a pair of conical holes running diagonally through the base.

There have been many theories about the function of bird stones, but none seems to have gained wide acceptance. Bird stones were probably not invested with ritual or ceremonial significance, for they are typically found not in burial mounds but dispersed in fields. The most credible theory is that the stone was used as a weight on a dart- or spear-thrower, or atlatl, a short hooked rod. The atlatl lent the user more speed and power than would be possible if the projectiles were thrown by hand alone. Most bird stones have been found in New York, Ohio, Indiana, Illinois, Michigan, Wisconsin, and Ontario, but others have been discovered in places as far from the Northeast as Georgia, Mississippi, and South Dakota.

Slate bird stone, approximately 3.5 inches (8.9 cm) long. Courtesy, Robert N. Converse, The Archaeological Society of Ohio

there was a regional variant called the Laurentian Boreal Archaic and, in the extreme east, the Maritime Boreal Archaic (c. 3000 BC). In this eastern area, slate was shaped into points and knives similar to those of the copper implements to the west. Trade between the eastern and western areas has been recognized; in addition, copper implements have been found as far south as Louisiana and Florida and southeastern marine shells have been found in the upper Mississippi–Great Lakes area. This suggests that transportation by canoe was known to Eastern Archaic peoples.

Along the southern border of the central and eastern boreal forest zone between 1500 and 500 BC there developed a distinctive burial complex, reflecting an increased attention to mortuary ceremonies. These burials, many including cremations, were often accompanied by red ochre, caches of triangular stone blanks (from which stone tools could be made), fire-making kits of iron pyrites and flint strikers, copper needles and awls, and polished stone forms. The triangular points of this complex may have represented the introduction of the bow and arrow from the prehistoric Arctic peoples east of Hudson Bay.

PREHISTORIC FARMERS

In much of North America, the shift from generalized foraging and horticultural experimentation to a way of life dependent on domesticated plants occurred about 1000 BC, although regional variation from this date is common.

Corn (maize), early forms of which had been grown in Mexico since at least 5000 BC, appeared among Archaic groups in the Southwest culture area by about 1200 BC and in the Eastern Woodlands by perhaps 100 BC; other Mesoamerican domesticates, such as chile peppers and cotton, did not appear in either region until approximately the beginning of the Common Era. Although the importance of these foreign domesticates increased over time, most Native American groups retained the use of locally domesticated plants for several centuries. For instance, improvements to sumpweed continued until about AD 1500, after which the plants abruptly returned to their wild state. It is unclear why sumpweed fell out of favour, although some have suggested that its tendency to cause hay fever and contact dermatitis may have contributed to the demise of its domesticated forms. Others believe that the timing of the event, coincident with the first wave of European conquest, suggests that cultural disruption initiated this change. Notably, many other indigenous American domesticates, including sunflowers, squashes, beans, and tobacco, have persisted as economically important crops into the 21st century.

Although prehistoric farming communities exhibited regional and temporal variation, they shared certain similarities. For the most part, farming groups were more sedentary than Archaic peoples, although the dearth of domesticated animals in Northern America (turkeys and dogs being the exception) meant that most households or communities continued to engage in hunting forays. Agriculturists' housing and settlements tended to be more substantial than those of Archaic groups, and their communities were often protected by walls or ditches. Many also developed hierarchical systems of social organization, wherein a priestly or chiefly class had authority over one or more classes of commoners.

SOUTHWESTERN CULTURES: THE ANCESTRAL PUEBLO, MOGOLLON, AND HOHOKAM

The first centuries of the Common Era saw the development of three major farming complexes in the Southwest, all of which relied to some extent on irrigation. The Ancestral Pueblo peoples (also known as the Anasazi; c. AD 100–1600) of the Four Corners area built low walls (check dams) to slow and divert the flow of water from seasonal rivulets to cultivated fields. The Mogollon (c. 200–1450) built their communities in the mountainous belt of southwestern New Mexico and southeastern Arizona and depended upon rainfall and stream diversion to water their crops. The Hohokam (c. 200–1400) lived in the desert area of the Gila basin of southern Arizona and built irrigation canals to water their fields.

These three cultures are known for their geographic expansion, population growth, and pueblo architecture, all of which reached their greatest levels of complexity between approximately 700 and 1300—a period that generally coincided with an unusually favourable distribution of rainfall over the entire Southwest (analogous climatic conditions elsewhere in North America supported cultural florescences in the Eastern Woodlands [c. 700–1200] and on the Plains [c. 1000–1250]). During this period the population and cultures of central and western Mexico expanded to the northwest; trade and cultural stimuli were thus moving from Mesoamerica into the Southwest culture area at a time when the climate in both regions was most favourable for population and cultural growth. Materials entering the Southwest from Mexico during this era included cast copper bells, parrots, ball courts, shell trumpets, and pottery with innovative vessel shapes and designs.

Between 750 and 1150 the Ancestral Pueblo expanded into the Virgin River valley of southeastern Nevada, north as far as the Great Salt Lake and northwestern Colorado, to the east into southeastern Colorado and to the Pecos and upper Canadian River valleys of New Mexico. They also developed priestly offices, rituals, and ceremonialism during this period.

Ancestral Pueblo achievements during 1150–1300, a period known as Pueblo III, included the construction of large cliff dwellings, such as those found at Mesa Verde National Park, and the apartmentlike "great houses" of Chaco Canyon and elsewhere. Dressed stones were used in many localities to bear the weight of these massive structures, which had from 20 to as many as 1,000 rooms and from one to four stories. Each of the larger buildings was in effect a single village. Windows and doors were quite small, and usually no openings were made in the lowest rooms, which were entered by ladder through the roof. Buildings had a stepped appearance because each level or floor was set back from the one below it; the resulting terraces were heavily used as outdoor living space. Roofs were constructed to carry great weights by using heavy beams, covering them with a mat of smaller poles and brush, then adding a coat of adobe 6 to 8 inches (15 to 20 cm) thick.

A number of new kivas (a type of subterranean ceremonial structure found at each settlement) were also built during this period, with some as large as 80 feet (25 metres) in diameter. Craftsmanship in pottery reached a high level; innovations included the use of three or more colours, and the techniques used by different communities—Chaco canyon, Mesa Verde, Kayenta, and a number of others—became so distinct that the vessels from each settlement can be recognized easily.

Ruins of a kiva at Aztec Ruins National Monument, N.M. Bob Harper

Cotton cloth, blankets, and bags were woven, and yucca fibre also entered into various articles of clothing and such utility objects as mats. Feather-cloth robes were worn in cold weather.

Between about 1300 and 1600, increasing aridity and the arrival of hostile outsiders accelerated the pace of change. Armed conflict and drought redirected Ancestral Pueblo efforts from artistic development to survival. Rituals designed to ensure rain increased in importance and elaboration and are portrayed in wall paintings and pottery. This period was also characterized by a general movement southward and eastward, and new villages were built on

Mimbres bowl with black-on-white horned toad design, c. AD 1050–1150; in the Museum of New Mexico, Santa Fe. Courtesy of the Museum of New Mexico, Santa Fe; photograph, Arthur Taylor (Neg. No. 99666)

the Little Colorado, Puerco, Verde, San Francisco, Rio Grande, Pecos, upper Gila, and Salt rivers.

In their early phases, from about 200 to 650, Mogollon settlements consisted of relatively small villages of pit houses grouped near a large ceremonial structure. Villages of this period were laid out rather randomly, and trash disposal was also haphazard. Houses became more substantial and several innovations in pottery design occurred between about 650 and 850. From about 850 to 1000, Mogollon villages exhibit Ancestral Pueblo influence in such things as construction techniques (shifting from pit houses to pueblos) and pottery design. The Mogollon reached their artistic pinnacle during the Classic Mimbres Period (c. 1000–1150). During the climatic deterioration after 1200, the Mogollon abandoned their territory in southwestern New Mexico.

The Hohokam people of central and southern Arizona built most of their settlements in major river valleys and lived in villages of pit houses that were arrayed along streams and canals. Agriculture was expanded through the use of extensive irrigation canals that may have been built by cooperating villages. Between approximately 775 and 1150, the Hohokam built their largest settlements and experienced a period of cultural innovation. Following this period, and until sometime between 1350 and 1450, Hohokam culture exhibits Ancestral Pueblo and Mexican influences. During this period,

PUEBLO ARCHITECTURE

Taos Pueblo, N.M., with domed oven in the foreground. Ray Manley—Shostal/EB Inc.

The traditional architecture of the Pueblo Indians of the southwestern United States is called pueblo architecture. The multistoried, permanent, attached homes typical of this tradition are modeled after the cliff dwellings built by the Ancestral Pueblo (Anasazi) culture beginning in approximately AD 1150. This architectural form continued to be used by many Pueblo peoples in the early 21st century.

Traditional pueblo construction used limestone blocks or large adobe bricks; the latter were made from clay and water and generally measured approximately 8 by 16 inches (20 by 40 cm), with a thickness of 4 to 6 inches (10 to 15 cm). In the early 21st century, modern construction materials were sometimes used in tandem with adobe, creating stronger and more durable structures.

In a typical pueblo building, adobe blocks form the walls of each room as well as a central courtyard; buildings can be up to five stories tall. Usually each floor is set back from the floor below, so that a given building resembles a stepped pyramid. This architectural form enables the roof of each level to serve as a terrace for the level above. Movement between levels was traditionally accomplished by means of wooden ladders, although staircases are now used as

A Corner of Zuni, photograph by Edward S. Curtis, c. 1903. Courtesy of the Newberry Library, Chicago, Ayer Collection

well. Ground floor rooms had (and in some cases, continue to have) no ground-level doors; used almost exclusively for storage, primarily of grain, they were traditionally entered through rooftop openings. Most rooms above the ground floor can be entered by doorways from adjoining rooms.

Most pueblo residential groups comprise nuclear or extended families; numerous families may live in a given building. Families typically have several connecting rooms, which are often arranged in a line radiating out from the central plaza of the pueblo. Additions to a family's section of the pueblo are generally added above or behind the original rooms. Traditionally each pueblo also had two or more kivas, or ceremonial rooms.

people built more compact settlements, often with a few massive multiroom and two-story buildings that were surrounded by compound walls.

The Ancestral Pueblo were the ancestors of contemporary Pueblo Indians such as the Hopi, Zuni, Acoma, and others. The Hohokam are the ancestors of the Pima and Tohono O'odham. After abandoning their villages, the Mogollon dispersed, probably joining other groups.

EASTERN WOODLAND CULTURES

Outside of the Southwest, Northern America's early agriculturists are typically referred to as Woodland cultures. This archaeological designation is often mistakenly conflated with the eco-cultural delineation of the continent's eastern culture areas: the term *Eastern Woodland cultures* refers to the early agriculturists east of the Mississippi valley, but the term *Eastern Woodlands* refers to the Northeast and Southeast culture areas together.

As in the Southwest, the introduction of corn in the East (*c.* 100 BC) did not cause immediate changes in local cultures; Eastern Archaic groups had been growing locally domesticated plants for some centuries, and corn was a minor addition to the agricultural repertoire. One of the most spectacular Eastern Woodland cultures preceding the introduction of maize was the Adena culture (*c.* 500 BC–AD 100, although perhaps as early as 1000 BC in some areas), which occupied the middle Ohio River valley.

Adena people were hunters, gatherers, and farmers who buried their dead in large earthen mounds, some of which are hundreds of feet long. They also built effigy mounds, elaborate earthen structures in the shape of animals.

This tradition of reshaping the landscape was continued by the Hopewell culture (*c.* 200 BC–AD 500) of the Illinois and Ohio river valleys. Hopewell society was hierarchical and village-based; surplus food was controlled by elites who used their wealth to support highly skilled artisans and the construction of elaborate earthworks. An outstanding feature of Hopewell culture was a tradition of placing elaborate burial goods in the tombs of individuals or groups. The interment process involved the construction of a large boxlike log tomb, the placement of the body or bodies and grave offerings inside, the immolation of the tomb and its contents, and the construction of an earthen mound over the burned materials.

Artifacts found within these burial mounds indicate that the Hopewell obtained large quantities of goods from widespread localities in North America, including obsidian and grizzly bear teeth from as far away as the Rocky Mountains, copper from the northern Great Lakes, and conch shells and other materials from the southeast and along the coast of the Gulf of Mexico. Sites in Ohio were particularly important distribution centres, controlling ceremonial goods and special products over a wide area. Evidence for this so-called Hopewell

Interaction Sphere rapidly faded after about AD 400, although Hopewell traditions continued for another century and Eastern Woodland cultures as a whole persisted for another 300 years.

MISSISSIPPIAN CULTURES

About AD 700 a new cultural complex arose in the Mississippi valley between the present-day cities of St. Louis and Vicksburg. Known as the Mississippian culture, it spread rapidly throughout the Southeast culture area and into some parts of the Northeast. Its initial growth and expansion took place during approximately the same period (700–1200) as the cultural zenith of the Southwest farmers. Some scholars believe that Mississippian culture was stimulated by the introduction of new concepts, religious practices, and improved agricultural techniques from northern Mexico, while others believe it developed in place as a result of climactic change and internal innovation.

Whatever the origin of particular aspects of Mississippian life, the culture as such clearly developed from local traditions; between 700 and 1000, many small Eastern Woodland villages grew into large towns with subsidiary villages and farming communities nearby. Regionally delimited styles of pottery, projectile points, house types, and other utilitarian products reflected diverse ethnic identities. Notably, however, Mississippian peoples were also united by two factors that crosscut ethnicity: a common economy that emphasized corn production and a common religion focusing on the veneration of the sun and a variety of ancestral figures.

One of the most outstanding features of Mississippian culture was the earthen temple mound. These mounds often rose to a height of several stories and were capped by a flat area, or platform, on which were placed the most important community buildings—council houses and temples. Platform mounds were generally arrayed around a plaza that served as the community's ceremonial and social centre; the plazas were quite large, ranging from 10 to 100 acres (4 to 40 hectares). The most striking array of mounds occurred at the Mississippian capital city, Cahokia, located near present-day St. Louis; some 120 mounds were built during the city's occupation. Monk's Mound, the largest platform mound at Cahokia, rises to approximately 100 feet (30 metres) above the surrounding plain and covers some 14 acres (6 hectares).

In some areas, large, circular charnel houses received the remains of the dead, but burial was normally made in large cemeteries or in the floors of dwellings. Important household industries included the production of mats, baskets, clothing, and a variety of vessels for specialized uses, as well as the creation of regalia, ornaments, and surplus food for use in religious ceremonies. In some cases, particular communities seem to have specialized in a certain kind of craft activity, such as the creation of a specific kind of pottery or grave offering. Ritual and religious events were conducted by an organized priesthood that probably also controlled the distribution of surplus food and other goods. Core religious symbols such as the weeping eye, feathered serpent, owl, and spider were found throughout the Mississippian world.

As the Mississippian culture developed, people increased the number and complexity of village fortifications and often surrounded their settlements with timber palisades. This was presumably a response to increasing intergroup aggression, the impetus for which seems to have included control of land, labour, food, and prestige goods. The Mississippian peoples had come to dominate the Southeast culture area by about 1200 and were the predominant groups met and described by Spanish and French explorers in that region. Some Mississippian groups, most notably the Natchez, survived colonization and maintained their ethnic identities into the early 21st century.

Plains Woodland and Plains Village Cultures

Archaic peoples dominated the Plains until about the beginning of the Common Era, when ideas and perhaps people from the Eastern Woodland cultures reached the region; some Plains Woodland sites, particularly in eastern Kansas, were clearly part of the Hopewell Interaction Sphere. Beginning between about AD 1

and 250 and persisting until perhaps 1000, Plains Woodland peoples settled in hamlets along rivers and streams, built earth-berm or wattle-and-daub structures, made pottery and other complex items, and raised corn, beans, and eventually sunflowers, gourds, squash, and tobacco.

On the Plains a regional variation of the favourable agricultural conditions that elsewhere supported the most elaborate forms of culture also fostered a marked increase in settlement size and population density; during this period (locally c. 1000–1250) the hospitable areas along most major streams became heavily occupied. These and subsequent village-dwelling groups are known as Plains Village cultures. These cultures were characterized by the building of substantial lodges, the coalescence of hamlets into concentrated villages, and the development of elaborate rituals and religious practices. Having expanded their populations and territories when conditions were favourable, a period of increasing aridity that began about 1275 caused hardship and in some cases armed conflict among these peoples; at the early 14th-century Crow Creek site (South Dakota), for instance, nearly 500 people were killed violently and buried in a mass grave.

Some village-dwelling peoples sustained their communities through this difficult period, while others retreated eastward and returned when the climate had improved. The descendants of the early Plains Village cultures, such as

Comanche Village, Women Dressing Robes and Drying Meat, *oil on canvas, detail of a painting by George Catlin, 1834–35; in the Smithsonian American Art Museum, Washington, D.C.* National Museum of American Art/Art Resource, New York

the Arikara, Mandan, Hidatsa, Crow, Wichita, Pawnee, and Ponca, greeted European explorers from the 16th century onward and continued to live on the Plains in the early 21st century.

Between 1500 and 1700, the farming peoples of the western and southern Plains, such as the Apache and Comanche, took up a predominantly nomadic, equestrian way of life; most continued to engage in some agriculture, but they did not rely on crops to the same extent as settled village groups. From the early 18th century onward, a number of agricultural groups from the Northeast culture area left their forest homes for the Plains and completely substituted equestrian nomadism for agriculture; perhaps the best known of these were the Sioux and Cheyenne, whose traditional territory had been in present-day Minnesota.

CHAPTER 10

FROM 1492 THROUGH THE 18TH CENTURY

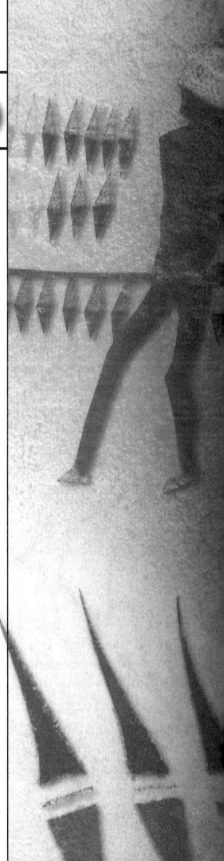

The thoughts and perspectives of indigenous individuals, especially those who lived during the 15th through the 18th and 19th centuries, have survived in written form less often than is optimal for the historian. Because such documents are extremely rare, those interested in the Native American past also draw information from traditional arts, folk literature, folklore, archaeology, and other sources.

Native American history is made additionally complex by the diverse geographic and cultural backgrounds of the peoples involved. As one would expect, indigenous American farmers living in stratified societies, such as the Natchez, engaged with Europeans differently than did those who relied on hunting and gathering, such as the Apache. Likewise, Spanish conquistadors were engaged in a fundamentally different kind of colonial enterprise than were their counterparts from France or England.

NORTH AMERICA AND EUROPE CIRCA 1492

Scholarly estimates of the pre-Columbian population of Northern America have differed by millions of individuals: the lowest credible approximations propose that some 900,000 people lived north of the Rio Grande in 1492, and the highest posit some 18,000,000. In 1910 anthropologist James Mooney undertook the first thorough investigation of the problem. He estimated the precontact population density

CULTURE AREA

In anthropology, geography, and other social sciences a culture area is a contiguous geographic area within which most societies share many traits in common. Delineated at the turn of the 20th century, it remains one of the most widely used frameworks for the description and analysis of cultures. Well-known examples of culture areas and their traditional residents are found on every continent except Antarctica and include Scandinavia, homeland of the Vikings; the North American Plains, home of the Plains Indians; and Africa's Al-Sudd, the seasonal wetland that is home to the Nuer, Dinka, and other cattle pastoralists. Australia, home of the Australian Aborigines, is often treated as a single culture area despite its considerable cultural and geographic diversity.

of each culture area based on historical accounts and carrying capacity, an estimate of the number of people who could be supported by a given form of subsistence. Mooney concluded that approximately 1,115,000 individuals lived in Northern America at the time of Columbian landfall. In 1934 A.L. Kroeber reanalyzed Mooney's work and estimated 900,000 individuals for the same region and period. In 1966 ethnohistorian Henry Dobyns estimated that there were between 9.8 million and 12.2 million people north of the Rio Grande before contact; in 1983 he revised that number upward to 18 million people.

Dobyns was among the first scholars to seriously consider the effects of epidemic diseases on indigenous demographic change. He noted that during the reliably recorded epidemics of the 19th century introduced diseases such as smallpox had combined with various secondary effects (i.e., pneumonia and famine) to create mortality rates as high

as 95 percent, and he suggested that earlier epidemics were similarly devastating. He then used this and other information to calculate from early census data backward to probable founding populations.

Dobyns's figures are among the highest proposed in the scholarly literature. Some of his critics fault Dobyns for the disjunctions between physical evidence and his results, as when the number of houses archaeologists find at a site suggests a smaller population than do his models of demographic recovery. Others, including the historian David Henige, criticize some of the assumptions Dobyns made in his analyses. For instance, many early fur traders noted the approximate number of warriors fielded by a tribe but neglected to mention the size of the general population. In such cases small changes in one's initial presumptions—in this example, the number of women, children, and elders represented by each warrior—can, when multiplied over several generations or centuries, create enormous differences in estimates of population.

A third group suggests that Dobyns's estimates may be too low because they do not account for pre-Columbian contact between Native Americans and Europeans. This group notes that severe epidemics of European diseases may have begun in North America in the late 10th or early 11th century, when the Norse briefly settled a region they called Vinland. The L'Anse aux Meadows site (on the island of Newfoundland), the archaeological remains of a small settlement, confirms the Norse presence in North America about AD 1000. Given that sagas attest to an epidemic that struck Erik the Red's colony in Greenland at about the same time, the possibility that native peoples suffered from introduced diseases well before Columbian landfall must be considered.

Yet another group of demographers protest that an emphasis on population loss obscures the resilience shown by indigenous peoples in the face of conquest. Most common, however, is a middle position that acknowledges that demographic models of 15th-century Native America must be treated with caution, while also accepting that the direct and indirect effects of the European conquest included extraordinary levels of indigenous mortality not only from introduced diseases but also from battles, slave raids, and—for those displaced by these events—starvation and exposure. This perspective acknowledges both the resiliency of Native American peoples and cultures and the suffering they bore.

NATIVE AMERICAN ETHNIC AND POLITICAL DIVERSITY

Determining the number of ethnic and political groups in pre-Columbian Northern America is also problematic, not least because definitions of what constitutes an ethnic group or a polity vary with the questions one seeks to answer. Ethnicity is most frequently equated with some aspect of language, while social or political organization can occur on a number of scales simultaneously. Thus, a given set of people might be defined as an ethnic group through their use of a common dialect or language even as they are recognized as members of nested polities such as a clan, a village, and a confederation. Other factors, including geographic boundaries, a subsistence base that emphasized either foraging or farming, the presence or absence of a social or religious hierarchy, and the inclinations of colonial bureaucrats, among others, also affected ethnic and political classification.

The crosscutting relationships between ethnicity and political organization are complex today and were equally so in the past. Just as a contemporary speaker of a Germanic language—perhaps German or English—might self-identify as German, Austrian, English, Scottish, Irish, Australian, Canadian, American, South African, Jamaican, Indian, or any of a number of other nationalities, so might a pre-Columbian Iroquoian speaker have been a member of the Cayuga, Cherokee, Huron, Mohawk, Oneida, Onondaga, Seneca, or Tuscarora nation. And both the hypothetical Germanic speaker and the hypothetical Iroquoian speaker live or lived in nested polities or quasi-polities: families, neighbourhoods, towns, regions, and so forth, each of which has or had some level of autonomy in its dealings with the outside world. Recognizing that it is difficult to determine precisely how many ethnic or political groups or polities were present in 15th-century Northern America, most researchers favour relative rather than specific quantification of these entities.

The outstanding characteristic of North American Indian languages is their diversity—at contact Northern America was home to more than 50 language families comprising between 300 and 500 languages. At the same moment in history, western Europe had only 2 language families (Indo-European and Uralic) and between 40 and 70 languages. In other words, if one follows scholarly conventions and defines ethnicity through language, Native America was vastly more diverse than Europe.

Politically, most indigenous American groups used consensus-based forms of organization. In such systems, leaders rose in response to a particular need rather than gaining some fixed degree of power. The Southeast Indians and the Northwest Coast Indians were exceptions to this general rule, as they most frequently lived in hierarchical societies with a clear chiefly class. Regardless of the form of organization, however, indigenous American polities were quite independent when compared with European communities of similar size.

EUROPEAN POPULATIONS AND POLITIES

Just as Native American experiences during the early colonial period must be framed by an understanding of indigenous demography, ethnic diversity, and political organization, so must they be contextualized by the social, economic, political, and religious changes that were taking place in Europe at the time. These changes drove European expansionism and are often discussed as part of the centuries-long transition from feudalism to industrial capitalism.

Many scholars hold that the events of the early colonial period are inextricably linked to the epidemics of the Black Death, or bubonic plague, that struck Europe between 1347 and 1400. Perhaps 25 million people, about one-third of the population, died during this epidemic. The population did not return to pre-plague levels until the early 1500s. The intervening period was a time of severe labour shortages that enabled commoners to demand wages for their work. Standards of living increased dramatically for a few generations, and some peasants were even able to buy small farms. These were radical changes from the previous era, during which most people had been tied to the land and a lord through serfdom.

Even as the general standard of living was improving, a series of military conflicts raged, including the Hundred Years' War, between France and England (1337–1453); the Wars of the Roses, between two English dynasties (1455–85); and the Reconquista, in which Roman Catholics fought to remove Muslims from the Iberian Peninsula (c. 718–1492). These conflicts created intense local and regional hardship, as the roving brigands that constituted the military typically commandeered whatever they wanted from the civilian population. In the theatres of war, troops were more or less free to take over private homes and to impress people into labour; famine, rape, and murder were all too prevalent in these areas. Further, tax revenues could not easily be levied on devastated regions, even though continued military expenditures had begun to drain the treasuries of western Europe.

As treasuries were depleted, overseas trade beckoned. The Ottoman Empire controlled the overland routes from Europe to South Asia, with its markets of spices and other commercially lucrative goods. Seeking to establish a sea route to the region, the Portuguese prince Henry the Navigator sponsored expeditions down the Atlantic coast of Africa. Later expeditions attempted to reach the Indian Ocean, but they were severely tested by the rough seas at

the Cape of Good Hope. Christopher Columbus had been a member of several such voyages and proposed an alternative, transatlantic route; in 1484 he requested the sponsorship of John II, the king of Portugal, who refused to support an exploratory journey.

Iberia was a hotbed of activity at the time. Ferdinand II of Aragon and Isabella I of Castille had begun to unify their kingdoms through their 1469 marriage, but they were soon forced to resolve bitter challenges to their individual ascensions. Eventually quelling civil war, the devout Roman Catholic sovereigns initiated the final phase of the Reconquista, pitting their forces against the last Moorish stronghold, Grenada. The city fell in January 1492, an event Columbus reportedly witnessed.

The seemingly endless military and police actions to which Ferdinand and Isabella had been party had severely depleted their financial reserves. This situation was exacerbated by the chief inquisitor of the Spanish Inquisition, Tomás de Torquemada, who persuaded the monarchs to expel any Jews who refused to be baptized. Under his authority some 160,000—and by some accounts as many as 200,000—Jews were ultimately expelled or executed for heresy, including many of Spain's leading entrepreneurs, businessmen, and scientists. Having lost so many of its best minds, Spain faced a very slow economic recovery, if it was to recover at all. Seeking new sources of income, the royal treasurer, Luis de Santángel, urged the monarchs to accept Columbus's proposal to explore a western route to the East. Although Columbus did not find a route with which to sidestep Ottoman trade hegemony, his journey nonetheless opened the way to overseas wealth. Spain used American resources to restore its imperiled economy, a strategy that was soon adopted by the other maritime nations of Europe as well.

COLONIAL GOALS AND GEOGRAPHIC CLAIMS: THE 16TH AND 17TH CENTURIES

Although the situation in 15th-century Iberia framed Columbus's expedition to the Americas, the problems of warfare, financial naïveté, and religious intolerance were endemic throughout Europe. This situation continued into the 16th century, when at least four factors contributed to levels of inflation so high as to be unprecedented: the rise of Protestantism inflamed religious differences and fostered new military conflicts, which in turn hindered free trade; the plague-depleted population recovered, creating an excess of labour and depressing wages; mass expulsions of Jews and Protestants undermined local and regional economies; and an influx of American gold and silver, with additional silver from new mines in Germany, devalued most currencies.

European colonialism was thus begotten in a social climate fraught with war, religious intolerance, a dispossessed peasantry, and inflation. Despite these commonalities, however, each of the countries that attempted to colonize North America in the 16th and 17th centuries—Spain, France, England, the Netherlands, and Sweden—had particular goals, methods, and geographic interests that played an important role in shaping Native American history.

SPAIN

Spain's overseas agenda emphasized the extraction of wealth, with secondary goals that included the relocation of armies, the conversion of indigenous peoples to Roman Catholicism, and the re-creation of the feudal social order to which the Spanish were accustomed. The first country to send large expeditions to the Americas, Spain focused its initial efforts on the conquest of the wealthy Aztec and Inca empires, which fell in 1521 and 1532, respectively. Immense quantities of precious metals were seized from these peoples and shipped to Spain. The initial influx of hard currency provided a period of fiscal relief, but the country suffered bankruptcy in the later 16th century and never fully recovered.

The conquest of the Americas also provided overseas work for the men who had fought in the Reconquista, thus limiting the damage they might have inflicted if left unemployed in Iberia. In lieu of pay or a pension, many conquistadors were provided with *encomiendas*, a form of vassal slavery in which a particular Indian population was granted to a Spaniard. The system alleviated demands on the treasury and also transplanted the Spanish social hierarchy to the colonies. *Encomiendas* were gradually supplanted by haciendas—landed estates or plantations. However, this legal nicety did little to change conditions for the Indians living under Spanish rule.

Having vanquished the indigenous nations of Mexico and Peru, the conquistadors turned their attention to Northern America. In 1540 Francisco Vázquez de Coronado, the governor of Nueva Galicia (northwestern Mexico and the southwestern United States), began the exploration and conquest of the Southwest Indians, taking with him 300 troops. In the same year, Hernando de Soto was authorized to establish Spanish control of La Florida (the southeastern United States) and its residents; he rode out with more than 600 conquistadors. Both expeditions relied upon large complements of native labourers, who were forcibly impressed into service. Coronado, de Soto, and their troops destroyed communities that resisted their demands for tribute, women, supplies, and obeisance. Concerted efforts at settlement north of Mexico began in 1565 in La Florida, with the founding of St. Augustine; similar efforts in the Southwest did not begin until 1598, when Juan de Oñate led 400 settlers to a location near what is now El Paso, Texas. Although its explorers sighted the coast of California in 1542,

Spain did not colonize that area until the second part of the 18th century.

Marriage between Spanish men and native women was acceptable, although concubinage was more common; intermarriage was effectively forbidden to the few Spanish women who lived in the colonies. After a few generations, a complex social order based on ancestry, land ownership, wealth, and noble titles had become entrenched in the Spanish colonies.

The Roman Catholic missionaries that accompanied Coronado and de Soto worked assiduously to Christianize the native population. Many of the priests were hearty supporters of the Inquisition, and their pastoral forays were often violent; beatings, dismemberment, and execution were all common punishments for the supposed heresies committed by Native Americans.

France

France was almost constantly at war during the 15th and 16th centuries, a situation that spurred an overseas agenda focused on income generation, although territorial expansion and religious conversion were important secondary goals. France expressed an interest in the Americas as early as 1524, when the Italian explorer Giovanni da Verrazzano was commissioned to explore the Atlantic coast; in 1534 the French seaman Jacques Cartier entered the Gulf of St. Lawrence and claimed for King Francis I the region that became known as New France. The

French eventually claimed dominion over most of the Northeast, Southeast, and American subarctic peoples. France's North American empire was, however, contested: its warm southern reaches were claimed by both France and Spain, while parts of the northern territory were claimed by both France and England. Native nations, of course, had their own claims to these territories.

Concerned about Spanish claims to the Americas, the French made a number of unsuccessful attempts at settlement in the 16th century. They built (and subsequently abandoned) a fort near present-day Quebec in 1541; they also built a fort near present-day St. Augustine, Fla., in 1564, but the Spanish soon forced them to abandon that facility as well. In 1604 the French successfully established a more permanent presence on the continent, founding Acadia in present-day Nova Scotia. They did not succeed in establishing a major settlement in the south until 1718, when they founded New Orleans.

French colonial settlements were built on major waterways in order to expedite trade and shipping; the city of Quebec was founded in 1608 at the confluence of the St. Lawrence and St. Charles rivers, and Montreal was founded in 1642 at the conjunction of the St. Lawrence and the Ottawa rivers. Although these trading centres were lively, the settlement of northern New France was slowed by several factors. Among these were the lucrative nature of the fur trade, which required a highly mobile and enterprising workforce—quite a different set of habits and skills than those required of farmers—and a cool climate, which produced thick furs but unpredictable harvests. In 1627 a group of investors formed the Company of New France, but governance of the colony reverted to the king in 1663, after the company repeatedly failed to meet the obligations of its charter.

Most of the northern locales where the French founded settlements were already occupied by various Algonquin groups or members of the Iroquoian-speaking Huron (Wendat) confederacy, all of whom had long used the inland waterways of the heavily forested region as trade and transportation routes. These peoples quickly partnered with the French—first as fur trappers, later as middlemen in the trade, and always as a source of staples such as corn. Because the Algonquin, Huron, and French were all accustomed to using marriage as a means of joining extended families, because indigenous warfare caused a demographic imbalance that favoured women, and because few women were eager to leave France for the rough life of the colonies, unions between native women and French men quickly became common. The attitudes of missionaries in New France varied: some simply promoted the adoption of Roman Catholic beliefs and practices, while others actively discouraged and even used force in order to end the practice of indigenous religions.

England

England focused its conquest of North America primarily on territorial expansion, particularly along the Atlantic coast from New England to Virginia. The first explorer to reach the continent under the English flag was John Cabot, an Italian who explored the North Atlantic coast in 1497. However, England did little to follow up on Cabot's exploits until the early 17th century. By that time, the wool trade had become the driving force in the English economy; as a source of foreign exchange, wool sales softened inflation somewhat but did not render the English immune to its effects.

England responded to the pressure of inflation in several ways that influenced Native American history. One response, the intensification of wool production, ensured that the wealthy would remain secure but greatly disrupted the domestic economy. To effect the production of more wool, the landed nobility began to practice enclosure, merging the many small fields that dotted the English countryside into larger pastures. This allowed more sheep to be raised but came at a harsh cost to the burgeoning population of commoners. The landless majority were evicted from their farms, and many had to choose between starvation and illicit activities such as theft, poaching, and prostitution. By the mid-1600s a new option arose for the dispossessed: indentured servitude, a form of contract labour in which transport to a colony and several years' room and board were exchanged for work; petty criminals were soon disposed of through this method as well.

The English elite chartered a variety of commercial entities, such as the Virginia Company, to which King James I granted the control of large swaths of American territory. These business ventures focused especially on the extraction of resources such as tobacco, a new commodity that had proved extremely popular throughout Europe. The monarch also made land grants to religious dissidents, most notably to the Puritan shareholders of the Massachusetts Bay Company, to the Roman Catholic leader Cecilius Calvert, who established the colony of Maryland, and to the Quaker leader William Penn, who established the Pennsylvania colony. English settlements eventually stretched from the Chesapeake Bay north to present-day Massachusetts and included Jamestown (founded in 1607), Plymouth (1620), Boston (1630), St. Mary's City (1634), New York City (formerly New Amsterdam, which England had seized from the Dutch in 1664), and Philadelphia (1681).

England was the only imperial nation in which colonial companies were successful over the long term, in large part because ordinary citizens were eventually granted clear (and thus heritable) title to land. In contrast, other countries generally reserved legal title to overseas real estate for the monarch, a situation that encouraged entrepreneurs to limit their capital investments in the colonies.

In such cases it made much more financial sense to build ships than to improve settler housing or colonial infrastructure; a company could own a ship outright but was at constant risk of losing new construction to the sovereign. Because English real estate practices more or less assured entrepreneurs and colonizers that they would retain any infrastructure they built, they set about the construction of substantial settlements, farms, and transportation systems.

A tradition of enduring title also caused the English to conclude formal compacts with Native Americans, as some of the former believed (and the English courts could potentially have ruled) that indigenous groups held common-law title to the various Northern American territories. As a result, tribes from Newfoundland (Canada) to Virginia (U.S.) engaged in early agreements with the English. However, a fundamental philosophical difference undermined many such agreements: the English held that it was possible to own land outright, while the indigenous American peoples believed that only usufruct, or use rights, to land could be granted. The situation was further complicated by the French custom, soon adopted by the English, of providing native communities with gifts on a seasonal or annual basis. What the colonizers intended as a relatively inexpensive method for currying goodwill, the indigenous peoples interpreted as something akin to rent.

Although mortality was high in the malarial lowlands that the English initially settled, a seemingly endless stream of indentured labourers—and, from 1619 onward, enslaved Africans—poured into the new communities throughout the 17th century. Colonial laws meant to discourage intermarriage generally prevented the children of indigenous-English marriages from inheriting their father's wealth. This effectively forestalled the formation of multiethnic households in areas that were under close colonial control. However, such households were considered unremarkable in indigenous towns.

In contrast to their Spanish and French counterparts, who were invariably Roman Catholic, most English colonizers were members of the Church of England or of various Protestant sects. Evangelization was not particularly important to most of the English elite, who traveled to the Americas for commercial, territorial, or political gain, nor for most indentured servants or criminal transportees. Among those who had left in pursuit of religious freedom, however, some proselytized with zeal. Like the clergy from France, their emphases and methods ranged from the fairly benign to the overtly oppressive.

THE NETHERLANDS AND SWEDEN

The colonial efforts of the Netherlands and Sweden were motivated primarily by commerce. Dutch businessmen formed several colonial monopolies soon after their country gained independence from Spain in the late 16th century. The Dutch West India Company took control of the New Netherland colony (comprising parts of the present-day states of Connecticut, New York, New Jersey, and Delaware) in 1623. In 1624 the company founded Fort Orange (present-day Albany, N.Y.) on the Hudson River; New Amsterdam was founded on the island of Manhattan soon after.

In 1637 a group of individuals formed the New Sweden Company. They hired Peter Minuit, a former governor of New Amsterdam, to found a new colony to the south, in what is now Delaware, U.S. In 1655 New Sweden fell to the Dutch.

Despite some local successes, the Dutch ceded their North American holdings to the English after just 40 years, preferring to turn their attention to the lucrative East Indies trade rather than defend the colony. The English renamed the area New York and allowed the Dutch and Swedish colonists to maintain title to the land they had settled.

NATIVE AMERICANS AND COLONIZATION: THE 16TH AND 17TH CENTURIES

From a Native American perspective, the initial intentions of Europeans were not always immediately clear. Some Indian communities were approached with respect and in turn greeted the odd-looking visitors as guests. For many indigenous nations, however, the first impressions of Europeans were characterized by violent acts including raiding, murder, rape, and kidnapping. Perhaps the only broad generalization possible for

the cross-cultural interactions of this time and place is that every group—whether indigenous or colonizer, elite or common, female or male, elder or child—responded based on their past experiences, their cultural expectations, and their immediate circumstances.

THE SOUTHWEST INDIANS

Although Spanish colonial expeditions to the Southwest had begun in 1540, settlement efforts north of the Rio Grande did not begin in earnest until 1598. At that time the agricultural Pueblo Indians lived in some 70 compact towns, while the hinterlands were home to the nomadic Apaches, Navajos, and others whose foraging economies were of little interest to the Spanish.

Although nomadic groups raided the Pueblos from time to time, the indigenous peoples of the Southwest had never before experienced occupation by a conquering army. As an occupying force, the Spanish troops were brutal. They continued to exercise the habits they had acquired during the Reconquista, typically camping outside a town from which they then extracted heavy tribute in the form of food, impressed labour, and women, whom they raped or forced into concubinage.

The missionaries who accompanied the troops in this region were often extremely doctrinaire. They were known to beat, dismember, torture, and execute Indians who attempted to maintain traditional religious practices; these

PUEBLO REBELLION

The Pueblo Rebellion (1680) was a carefully organized revolt of Pueblo Indians (in league with Apaches), who succeeded in overthrowing Spanish rule in New Mexico for 12 years. A traditionally peaceful people, the Pueblos had endured much after New Mexico's colonization in 1598. Catholicism was forced on them by missionaries who burned their ceremonial pits (kivas), masks, and other sacred objects. Indians were tried in Spanish courts and received severe punishments—hanging, whipping, dismemberment (of hands or feet), or condemnation to slavery.

From 1645 on there were several abortive revolts, after each of which medicine men were especially singled out for reprisals. One medicine man, Popé of the San Juan pueblo, embittered by imprisonment, believed himself commanded by the tribal ancestor spirits (kachinas) to restore the old customs; on Aug. 10, 1680, he led a full-scale revolt in which almost all the Pueblos participated. On August 21 the Spaniards were forced to flee, leaving 400 dead, including 21 priests. The Indians celebrated their victory by washing off the stains of Christian baptism, annulling Christian marriages, and destroying churches. They remained free until 1692, when New Mexico was reconquered by Gov. Pedro de Vargas.

punishments were also meted out for civil offenses. Such depredations instigated a number of small rebellions from about 1640 onward and culminated in the Pueblo Rebellion (1680)—a synchronized strike by the united Pueblo peoples against the Spanish missions and garrisons. The Pueblo Rebellion cost the lives of some 400 colonizers, including nearly all the priests, and caused the Spanish to remove to Mexico.

The Spanish retook the region beginning in 1692, killing an estimated 600 native people in the initial battle. During subsequent periods, the Southwest tribes engaged in a variety of nonviolent forms of resistance to Spanish rule. Some Pueblo families fled their homes and joined Apachean foragers, influencing the Navajo and Apache cultures in ways that continue to be visible even in the 21st century. Other Puebloans remained in their towns and maintained their traditional cultural and religious practices by hiding some activities and merging others with Christian rites.

THE SOUTHEAST INDIANS

Most Southeast Indians experienced their first sustained contact with Europeans through the expedition led by Hernando de Soto (1539–42). At that time most residents were farmers who supplemented their agricultural produce with wild game and plant foods. Native communities ranged in size from hamlets to large towns, and most Southeast

Timucua Indians preparing land and sowing seeds, *engraving by Theodor de Bry from a drawing by Jacques Le Moyne, c. 1564; first published in 1591.* Library of Congress, Washington, D.C. (neg. no. LC-USZ62-31869)

societies featured a social hierarchy comprising a priestly elite and commoners.

Warfare was not unknown in the region, but neither was it endemic. The indigenous peoples of present-day Florida treated de Soto and his men warily because the Europeans who had visited the region previously had often, but not consistently, proved violent. As the conquistadors moved inland, tribes at first treated them in the manner accorded to any large group of visitors, providing gifts to the leaders and provisions to the rank and file. However, the Spaniards either misread or ignored the intentions of their hosts and often forced native commoners, who customarily provided temporary labour to visitors as a courtesy gesture, into slavery.

News of such treatment traveled quickly, and the de Soto expedition soon met with military resistance. Indigenous warriors harassed the Spanish almost constantly and engaged the party in many battles. Native leaders made a number of attempts to capture de Soto and the other principals of the party, often by welcoming them into a walled town and closing the gates behind them. Such actions may have been customary among the Southeast Indians at this time—diplomatic customs in many cultures have

Hernando de Soto committing atrocities against Indians in Florida, engraving by Theodor de Bry in Brevis narratio eorum quae in Floridae Americae provincia Gallis acciderunt, *1591.* Library of Congress, Washington, D.C.

included holding nobles hostage as a surety against the depredations of their troops. Such arrangements were common in Europe at the time and were something with which the conquistadors were presumably familiar. However, the Spanish troops responded to these situations with violence, typically storming the town and setting upon the fleeing residents until every inhabitant was either dead or captured.

As losses to capture, slaughter, and European diseases progressively decimated the Native American population, the Spanish began to focus on extracting the region's wealth and converting its inhabitants to Christianity. The Southeast nations had little gold or silver, but they had accumulated a plenitude of pearls to use as decoration and in ritual activities. The slave trade was also extremely lucrative, and many of those who survived the immediate effects of conquest were kidnapped and transported to the Caribbean slave markets. Some indigenous communities relocated to Catholic missions in order to avail themselves of the protection offered by resident priests, while others coalesced into defensible groups or fled to remote areas.

THE NORTHEAST INDIANS

The Northeast Indians began to interact regularly with Europeans in the first part of the 16th century. Most of the visitors were French or English, and they were initially more interested in cartography and trade than in physical conquest. Like their counterparts in the Southeast, most Northeast Indians relied on a combination of agriculture and foraging, and many lived in large walled settlements. However, the Northeast tribes generally eschewed the social hierarchies common in the Southeast. Oral traditions and archaeological materials suggest that they had been experiencing increasingly fierce intertribal rivalries in the century before colonization. It has been surmised that these ongoing conflicts made the Northeast nations much more prepared for offensive and defensive action than the peoples of the Southwest or the Southeast had been.

Discussions of the early colonial period in this region are typically organized around categories that conjoin native political groupings and European colonial administrations. The discussion in this chapter considers two broad divisions: the Algonquian-speaking tribes of the mid-Atlantic region, an area where the English settled, and the Algonquian- and Iroquoian-speaking tribes of New England and New France, where the English and the French competed in establishing colonial outposts.

THE MID-ATLANTIC ALGONQUIANS

The mid-Atlantic groups that spoke Algonquian languages were among the most populous and best-organized indigenous nations in Northern America at the time of European landfall. They were accustomed to negotiating boundaries with neighbouring groups and expected all parties to abide by such understandings. Although they allowed English colonizers to build, farm, and hunt in particular areas, they found that the English colonial agenda inherently promoted the breaking of boundary agreements. The businessmen who sponsored the early colonies promoted expansion because it increased profits; the continuous arrival of new colonizers and slaves caused settlements to grow despite high mortality from malaria and misfortune; and many of the individuals who moved to the Americas from England—especially the religious freethinkers and the petty criminals—were precisely the kinds of people who were likely to ignore the authorities.

The earliest conflict between these Algonquians and the colonizers occurred near the Chesapeake Bay. This region was home to the several hundred villages of the allied Powhatan tribes, a group that comprised many thousands of individuals. In 1607 this populous area was chosen to be the location of the first permanent English settlement in the Americas, the Jamestown Colony. Acting from a position of strength, the Powhatan were initially friendly to the people of

Jamestown, providing the fledgling group with food and the use of certain lands.

By 1609 friendly interethnic relations had ceased. Powhatan, the leader for whom the indigenous alliance was named, observed that the region was experiencing a third year of severe drought; dendrochronology (the study of tree rings) indicates that this drought ultimately spanned seven years and was the worst in eight centuries. In response to English thievery (mostly of food), Powhatan prohibited the trading of comestibles to the colonists. He also began to enforce bans against poaching. These actions contributed to a period of starvation for the colony (1609–11) that nearly caused its abandonment.

It is not entirely clear why Powhatan did not press his advantage, but after his death in 1618 his brother and successor, Opechancanough, attempted to force the colonists out of the region. His men initiated synchronized attacks against Jamestown and its outlying plantations on the morning of March 22, 1622. The colonists were caught unawares, and, having killed some 350 of the 1,200 English, Opechancanough's well-organized operation created so much terror that it nearly succeeded in destroying the colony.

The so-called Powhatan War continued sporadically until 1644, eventually resulting in a new boundary agreement between the parties; the fighting ended only after a series of epidemics had decimated the region's native population, which shrank even as the English population grew. Within five years, colonists

were flouting the new boundary and were once again poaching in Powhatan territory. Given the persistence of the mid-Atlantic Algonquians, their knowledge of local terrain, and their initially large numbers, many scholars argue that the Algonquian alliance might have succeeded in eliminating the English colony had Powhatan pressed his advantage in 1611 or had its population not been subsequently decimated by epidemic disease.

THE IROQUOIANS OF HURONIA

During the 15th and early 16th centuries, warfare in the Northeast culture area fostered the creation of extensive political and military alliances. It is generally believed that this period of increasing conflict was instigated by internal events rather than by contact with Europeans; some scholars suggest that the region was nearing its carrying capacity. Two of the major alliances in the area were the Huron confederacy (which included the Wendat alliance) and the Five Tribes (later Six Tribes), or Iroquois Confederacy. The constituent tribes of both blocs spoke Iroquoian languages; the term Iroquoian is used to refer generally to the groups speaking such languages, while references to the Iroquois generally imply the tribes of the Iroquois Confederacy alone.

The Huron were a relatively tight alliance of perhaps 20,000–30,000 people who lived in rather dense settlements between Hudson Bay and the St. Lawrence River, an area thus known as

Huronia. This was the northern limit at which agriculture was possible, and the Huron grew corn to eat and to trade to their subarctic Indian neighbours—the Innu to the north and east and the Cree to the west—who provided meat and fish in return. The Huron confederacy is believed to have coalesced in response to raids from other Iroquoians and to have migrated northward to escape pressure from the Five Tribes to their south and southeast. Although the Huron coalition's major goal was defense, the strength of the alliance also helped them to maintain trading, rather than raiding, relationships with the Innu, the Cree, and later the French.

The Five Tribes of the Iroquois Confederacy lived south of the St. Lawrence River and Lake Erie, for the most part in the present-day state of New York. The alliance comprised the Mohawk, Oneida, Onondaga, Cayuga, and Seneca peoples; the Tuscarora joined the confederacy later. Evenly matched with the Huron alliance in terms of aggregate

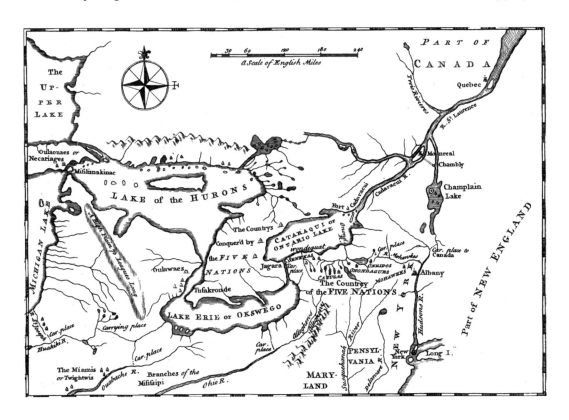

Map of the initial nations of the Iroquois Confederacy, from History of the Five Indian Nations Depending on the Province of New-York, *by Cadwallader Colden, 1755.* Library of Congress, Rare Book Division, Washington, D.C.

size, the Iroquois were more loosely united and somewhat less densely settled across the landscape. While the Huron nations traded extensively for food, this was less the case for the Five Tribes, who relied more thoroughly upon agriculture. Before colonization they seem to have removed southward, perhaps in response to raids from the Huron to their north. The alliances among the Five Tribes were initiated not only for defense but also to regulate the blood feuds that were common in the region. By replacing retributory raids among themselves with a blood money payment system, each of the constituent nations was better able to engage in offensive and defensive action against outside enemies.

The Northeast was crisscrossed by an extensive series of trade routes that consisted of rivers and short portages. The Huron used these routes to travel to the Cree and Innu peoples, while the Iroquois used them to travel to the Iroquoians on the Atlantic coast. The French claimed the more northerly area and built a series of trade entrepôts at and near Huron communities, whose residents recognized the material advantages of French goods as well as the fortifications' defensive capabilities. The Huron alliance quickly became the gatekeeper of trade with the subarctic, profiting handsomely in this role. Its people rapidly adopted new kinds of material culture, particularly iron axes, as these were immensely more effective in shattering indigenous wooden armour than were traditional stone tomahawks.

For a period of time the new weapons enabled the Huron confederacy to gain the upper hand against the Iroquois, who did not gain access to European goods as quickly as their foes. By about 1615 the long traditions of interethnic conflict between the two alliances had become inflamed, and each bloc formally joined with a member of another traditional rivalry—the French or the English. Initially the Huron-French alliance held the upper hand, in no small part because the French trading system was in place several years before those of the Dutch and English. The indigenous coalitions became more evenly matched after 1620, however, as the Dutch and English trading system expanded. These Europeans began to make guns available for trade, something the French had preferred not to do. The Huron found that the technological advantage provided by iron axes was emphatically surpassed by that of the new firearms.

French records indicate that a smallpox epidemic killed as many as two-thirds of the Huron alliance in 1634–38; the epidemic affected the Iroquois as well, but perhaps to a lesser extent. At about the same time, it became increasingly clear that beavers, the region's most valuable fur-bearing animals, had been overhunted to the point of extinction in the home territories of both groups. The Iroquois blockaded several major rivers in 1642–49, essentially halting canoe traffic between Huronia and the subarctic. The combination of smallpox, the collapse of the beaver population, and the

BLOOD FEUD

A blood feud is a continuing state of conflict between two groups within a society (typically kinship groups) characterized by violence, usually killings and counterkillings. It exists in many nonliterate communities in which there is an absence of law or a breakdown of legal procedures and in which attempts to redress a grievance in a way that is acceptable to both parties have failed.

The feud is usually initiated to secure revenge, reprisal, or honour for a member of the injured group. The hostile groups are related in some way, such as being members of the same political or cultural unit. Within each group there is a strong sense of collective solidarity that protects individual members against injury by outsiders. Members of any other such group are held collectively responsible for any injury suffered at the hands of the members of that group. If, however, both parties accept as "due process" a counterkilling in response to an original homicide, a feud will not result.

Most nonliterate societies have institutions that forestall blood feud or bring it to a close. Even though many peoples profess that honour demands revenge, payment of compensation is more common than reciprocal killing. Regulated combat may also serve as a substitute for blood feud. The establishment of a strong centralized political authority generally results in the suppression of blood feud.

stoppage of trade precipitated an economic crisis for the Huron, who had shifted so far from a subsistence economy to one focused on exchange that they faced starvation. Decades of intermittent warfare culminated in fierce battles in 1648–49, during which the Iroquois gained a decisive victory against the Huron and burned many of their settlements. In 1649 the Huron chose to burn their remaining villages themselves, some 15 in all, before retreating to the interior.

Having defeated the Huron confederacy to their north and west, the Iroquois took the Beaver Wars to the large Algonquin population to their north and east, to the Algonquian territory to their west and south, and to the French settlements of Huronia. They fought the alliances of these parties for the remainder of the 17th century, finally accepting a peace agreement in 1701. With both the Huron and the Iroquois confederacies having left Huronia, mobile French fur traders took over much of the trade with the Innu and Cree, and various bands of Ojibwa began to enter the depopulated region from their original homelands to the south of the Great Lakes.

THE SUBARCTIC INDIANS AND THE ARCTIC PEOPLES

The European exploration of the subarctic was for many decades limited to the coasts of the Atlantic and Hudson Bay, an inland sea connected to the Atlantic and the Arctic oceans. The initial European exploration of the bay occurred in 1610. It was led by the English navigator Henry Hudson, who had conducted a number of voyages in search of a northwest passage from the Atlantic to the Pacific.

The subarctic climate and ecosystem were eminently suited to the production of fur-bearing animals. This circumstance was well understood by the Huron alliance, which maintained a virtual lock on trade between this region and the French posts to the south until about 1650. Although the French colonial administration purported to encourage entrepreneurial individuals, its bureaucracy could be difficult to work with. In the 1660s, brothers-in-law Pierre Esprit Radisson and Médard Chouart des Groseilliers, their pelts seized by authorities for the lack of a proper license, offered the English their services as guides to the region around Hudson Bay. The English hired the men and sponsored an exploratory voyage in 1668. The expedition was well received by the resident Cree, who had relied upon the Hurons for trade goods and found their supply greatly diminished in the wake of the Beaver Wars.

The initial voyage was successful enough to instigate the creation of the Hudson's Bay Company, which was chartered in 1670. Its first governor was Prince Rupert, an experienced military commander and the cousin of King Charles II. The company was granted proprietary control of the vast territory from Labrador to the Rocky Mountains, a region that soon became known as Rupert's Land. Company traders spent the remainder of the 17th century building relationships with the local Cree, Innu, and Inuit peoples. The Hudson's Bay Company eventually became one of the most dominant forces of colonialism in Northern America, maintaining political control over Rupert's Land until 1870 and economic control of the north for decades more.

By about 1685 the company had built a series of trading posts around the bay. These posts were staffed by company employees who were instructed not to travel far afield. As a result, indigenous peoples came to the posts to trade, and particular bands became associated with particular posts. Known as Home Guard Indians, the relatively close proximity of these bands and Hudson's Bay Company employees often led to intermarriage, adoption, and other forms of kinship. Band members with limited mobility might spend most of the year at a post community, and all of the population would usually reside there for some part of the year.

The French built a few trading posts in the subarctic but found that having independent contractors transport goods to native communities was more profitable—as was the practice of taking over Hudson's Bay Company posts after running off the staff. Accustomed to the difficult conditions of the boreal forest and the tundra, the Innu, Cree, and Inuit could easily defend themselves against potential depredations by Europeans. Many bands chose not to form an exclusive alliance with either colonial power. Instead, they played the French and the English against one another in order to gain advantageous terms of exchange, profiting as the two colonial powers squabbled for control over the northern trade.

THE CHESSBOARD OF EMPIRE: THE LATE 17TH TO THE EARLY 19TH CENTURY

In general, this period was characterized by indigenous resistance to colonial efforts at establishing anything more than toeholds in Northern America. Had victory been based on military skill and tenacity alone, Native Americans might well have avoided or significantly delayed colonization. However, epidemic diseases, the slave trade, and a continuous stream of incoming Europeans proved to be more decisive elements in the American narrative.

EASTERN NORTH AMERICA AND THE SUBARCTIC

During the 17th century the Iroquois Confederacy and the English had created a strong alliance against the competing coalitions formed by the Huron, Algonquin, Algonquian, and French. The tradition of forming such alliances continued in the 18th century. Some of these coalitions were very strong, while loyalties shifted readily in others. Indigenous leaders often realized that they could reap the most benefit by provoking colonial rivalries and actively did so. Many also recognized that the Europeans were no more consistent in maintaining alliances than they were in observing territorial boundaries, and so they became wary of colonial opportunism. Such was the case for the Iroquois: about 1700 they adopted a policy of neutrality between the English and French that held for some 50 years.

Colonial administrative decisions of the 18th century were thoroughly coloured by issues in Europe, where the diplomatic and military milieus were characterized by constant tension. England, France, Spain, Austria, Prussia, and other countries engaged in several conflicts that either spread to or greatly influenced events in eastern North America during this period. The most important of these conflicts are discussed below.

QUEEN ANNE'S WAR (1702–13) AND THE YAMASEE WAR (1715–16)

The War of the Spanish Succession (1702–13) pitted France and Spain against England, the Dutch Republic, and Austria in a fight to determine the European balance of power. One theatre of this war was Northern America, where the conflict became known as Queen Anne's War. It set an alliance of the English and some Southeast Indian nations, notably the Creek and the eastern Choctaw, against one comprising the French, the Spanish, and other Southeast Indians, notably the western Choctaw.

The latter alliance lost, and treaties negotiated in Europe caused France to relinquish claim to a vast area including Newfoundland, French Acadia (renamed Nova Scotia), and Rupert's Land. The French presence in the north was thin and had always been contested by the English; as a result, the war had few immediate effects on First Nations peoples (the Native Americans of Canada) other than to cement the position of the Hudson's Bay Company. The company remained paramount in the north until 1783, when its hegemony was challenged by the rival North West Company.

In the Southeast the war caused widespread havoc. Many communities, both native and colonial, were forced to move or risk destruction. With territorial boundaries in disarray, the war's aftermath included a series of smaller engagements through which Native Americans tried to avoid being squeezed between the westward expansion of the English, who held the Atlantic coast, and the French expansion eastward from their Mississippi River entrepôts.

One of the better-known of these conflicts was the Yamasee War (1715–16), in which an alliance of Yamasee, Creek, and other tribes fought against English expansion. Their resistance was ultimately unsuccessful, and some of the refugees fled south to Florida, where their descendants later joined with others to found the Seminole nation. The Yamasee War inspired the Creek to take a neutral stance between the colonizers; they subsequently became one of the most successful groups in profiting from colonial rivalries. However, the Creek and their traditional rivals, the Cherokee, continued intermittent raids against one another until the late 1720s. At the same time, the neighbouring Chickasaw were shifting their trade from the French to the English because the goods provided by the latter were generally less expensive and of better quality than those of the former. The Chickasaw defended themselves from repeated Choctaw-French attacks and successfully avoided French trade hegemony. The Natchez were less fortunate: their resistance was quashed by the Choctaw-French alliance, which captured hundreds of Natchez people and sold them into the Caribbean slave trade.

THE FRENCH AND INDIAN WAR (1754–63) AND PONTIAC'S WAR (1763–64)

During the years from 1754 to 1763, disputes between the European empires ignited conflicts in Europe, Asia, and North America. The fighting that took place in Europe became known as the Seven Years' War (1756–63) and pitted the joint forces of Prussia, Hanover, and England against an alliance comprising Austria, France, Russia, Saxony, and Sweden.

Although they participated in the European theatre of war, for France and England the most important battlegrounds were their colonies in Asia and America. The last of the Carnatic Wars (1756–63) saw these two colonial powers battle for control over eastern India—a contest in which England's victory was decisive.

The international conflict was most prolonged in North America, where it became known as the French and Indian War (1754–63). There it pitted the English, allied with the Iroquois Confederacy once again, against a much larger coalition comprising many Algonquian-speaking tribes, the French, and the Spanish. Most of the fighting occurred in the Ohio River watershed and the Great Lakes region. Surprisingly, given their smaller numbers, the Iroquois-English alliance prevailed. Under the terms of the Treaty of Paris (1763), France ceded to England its colonies east of the Mississippi River. England now ruled a vast landmass reaching from Hudson Bay to the Gulf of Mexico and from the Atlantic coast to the Mississippi River.

Treaties at this time generally transferred sovereignty over a territory from one monarch to another but did not dispossess locals of their property nor abrogate prior agreements between monarch and subject. Categories of people were seen as rather interchangeable—if the sovereign (in this case, of France) had made a promise to subjects in a territory that was to become the domain of another monarch (in this case, of England), the latter was expected to honour the arrangement. The subjects living in the region, here the native and colonial peoples of New France, were likewise expected to transfer their loyalty from the first monarch to the second. Although European and Euro-American colonists were accustomed to having no voice in such matters, the region's indigenous residents objected to being treated as subjects rather than nations; not having been party to the treaty, they felt little need to honour it.

With English rule came the usual flood of settlers. Like their compatriots in New England and the mid-Atlantic, the First Nations in the former French territory observed that the English were unwilling or unable to prevent trespass by squatters. Indigenous groups throughout the Great Lakes region were further piqued because the annual giveaway of trade goods had been suspended. The English had come to view the giveaway as an unnecessary expense and were glad to be rid of it. In contrast, the First Nations felt that they were being deprived of income they were owed for allowing foreign access to the North American interior.

These and other issues caused the indigenous nations to press their advantage during the disorderly period marking the end of the French and Indian War. Recognizing that strength of unified action, the Ottawa leader Pontiac organized a regional coalition of nations. Among other actions in the conflict that became known as Pontiac's War (1763–64), the native coalition captured several English forts near the Great Lakes. These and other demonstrations of military skill and numerical strength prompted King George III's ministers to issue the Proclamation of 1763, one of the most important documents in Native American legal history. It reserved for the use of the tribes "all the Lands and Territories lying to the Westward of the sources of the Rivers which fall into the Sea from the West and Northwest." That is, the land between the Appalachian Mountains and the Mississippi River, and from the Great Lakes almost to the Gulf of Mexico, was declared reserved for Indian use exclusively. The proclamation also reserved to the English monarch the exclusive right to purchase or otherwise control these tribal lands.

The proclamation also required all settlers to vacate the region. Despite this mandate, thousands of English settlers followed their forebears' tradition of ignoring the colonial authorities and moved into the reserved territory during the relatively quiescent period following Pontiac's War. French Canadians were also on the move, not least because British law prohibited Roman Catholics from a number of activities, such as holding public office. The British attempted to address French Canadian discontent by passing the Quebec Act (1774). It included a number of provisions ensuring the free practice of religion and the continuation of French civil law.

More important from an indigenous view, it extended Quebec's boundaries northward to Hudson Bay and southward to the confluence of the Ohio and Mississippi rivers, the site of present-day Cairo, Ill. Although England saw this as an expedient way to establish the governor of Quebec's political authority over

remote French Canadian settlements, Native Americans saw the act as an abrogation of the Proclamation of 1763. In addition, Euro-American settlers who had entered the region after pacification saw it as an attempt to curtail what they believed was their God-given right to expand into the west. The feelings among these parties soon became so inflamed that they led to the brink of yet another war.

THE AMERICAN REVOLUTION (1775–83)

The discontentment caused by the Quebec Act contributed directly to a third 18th-century war of empire, the American Revolution (1775–83), in which 13 of the English colonies in North America eventually gained political independence. This war was especially important to the Iroquois Confederacy, which by then included the Tuscarora. The confederacy had long been allied with the English against the Huron, the northern Algonquians, and the French. Now the Iroquois were faced with a conundrum: a number of the English individuals with whom they had once worked were now revolutionaries and so at least nominally allied with France. All the foreigners, whether English loyalists, revolutionaries, or French, promised to uphold the sovereignty of Iroquois lands, but by this time most Indians recognized that such promises were as likely to be expediencies as they were to be true pledges. This left the council of the

Iroquois Confederacy with the problem of balancing its knowledge of individual colonizers, some of whom were trustworthy allies, against its experiences with the colonial administrations, which were known to be inconstant. Despite much deliberation, the council was unable to reach consensus. As its decisions could only be enacted after full agreement, some individuals, families, and nations allied themselves with the English loyalists and others with the colonial upstarts and their French allies.

For the colonizers, the war ended with the Peace of Paris (1783). The treaties between England and the new United States included the English cession of the lands south of the St. Lawrence River and the Great Lakes and as far west as the Mississippi River. The indigenous nations were not consulted regarding this cession, which placed those Iroquois who had been allied with the English loyalists in what was now U.S. territory. Realizing that remaining in the territory would expose them to retribution, several thousand members of the Iroquois-English alliance left their homes and resettled in Canada.

The nascent United States was deeply in debt after the war and had a military too small to effectively patrol its extensive borders. Hoping to overextend and reconquer the upstarts, their rivals—formidable alliances comprising the displaced Iroquois, the Algonquians, and the English in the north and the Spanish with some of the Chickasaw, Creek,

Cherokee, and Choctaw in the south—engaged in munitions trading and border raids. The United States committed to a number of treaties in order to clarify matters with indigenous nations, but in eastern North America the end of the 18th century was nonetheless characterized by confusion over, and lack of enforcement of, many territorial boundaries.

THE WAR OF 1812 (1812–14)

American Indian experiences of the transition from the 18th to the 19th century were rather thoroughly, if indirectly, affected by the French revolutionary and Napoleonic wars (1789–1815). The fall of the French monarchy worried Europe's elite, who began to decrease the level of conspicuous consumption to which they had previously been accustomed. The subsequent suppression of Napoleon's armies required a concentrated international military effort that was enormously expensive in both cash and lives and which further encouraged relative frugality. This social and economic climate caused a serious decline in the fur trade and much hardship for those who depended upon it, including indigenous North Americans.

By 1808–10, despite assurances from the U.S. government that the Proclamation of 1763 would be honoured, settlers had overrun the valleys of the Ohio and Illinois rivers. Game and other wild food was increasingly scarce, and settlers were actively attempting to dislocate native peoples. Tensions that had been building since the American Revolution were worsened by the decline in the fur trade and a multiyear drought during which native and settler crops alike failed.

Realizing that the fates of indigenous peoples throughout the Great Lakes region were intertwined, Tecumseh, a Shawnee leader who had served with the British during the American Revolution, began to advocate for a pan-Indian alliance. He recommended a renewed association with the English, who seemed less voracious for land than the Americans. By all accounts, however, Tecumseh was simply choosing the less odious of two fickle partners. He had fought in the Battle of Fallen Timbers (1794), one of several postrevolutionary engagements in which Indian-English coalitions attempted to prevent the United States' settlement of the Ohio valley. Tecumseh's brother and hundreds of other native combatants were killed at Fallen Timbers because the British would neither send reinforcements nor open the gates of their fort to the fleeing warriors. British inconstancy in events with such severe and personal consequences was not soon forgotten.

For the Native American coalition that participated in the War of 1812, the conflict centred on territorial rights; for the English and the Euro-Americans, it was a conflict over transatlantic shipping rights. Eventually, the actions of future U.S. president William Henry Harrison, who attempted to break the nascent native alliance by burning its settlement at Prophetstown during the Battle of Tippecanoe (1811), sealed the indigenous leaders' decision to support England.

Tecumseh's coalition won a number of early victories. One of the most notable was the 1813 capture of Fort Detroit—through canny tactics that made his troops seem much greater in number than they were, Tecumseh caused the fort's commander, Gen. William Hull, to panic. Hull surrendered without mounting a defense and was later court-martialed.

Despite these and other victories won by the alliance of Indians and English, the War of 1812 was ultimately a draw between England and the United States. They agreed to terms in the Treaty of Ghent (1814); England did not consult with its native allies regarding the terms of the agreement, which for the most part returned Northern America to its prewar status. That status did not hold in southern Quebec, however, which at the time extended well south of the Great Lakes. Instead, the English relinquished their claims to the Ohio River basin area and left the members of Tecumseh's coalition to fend for themselves. This was a tremendous blow, as the resident nations were immediately subject to displacement by Euro-American settlers. With the fur trade in the doldrums and peaceful relations between England and the United States, the pelts and military assistance that had been the economic mainstays of the Northeast tribes had lost their value. Indigenous prosperity and power in the region entered a period of rapid decline.

THE SOUTHWEST AND THE SOUTHERN PACIFIC COAST

While the 18th-century wars of empire raged in Europe and eastern North America, colonization continued apace in the western part of the continent. There the principal imperial powers were Spain and Russia. In the Southwest the Spanish continued to dominate the indigenous nations. The tribes there, particularly the Puebloans, continued to face severe punishment for "heretical" practices and other forms of direct resistance to colonization. They maintained their cultural heritage through a combination of overt acceptance of European conventions and private practice of their own traditions. Most hunting and gathering groups in the region continued to live in areas that were not amenable to farming or ranching and so encountered the colonizers less often.

European explorers had sighted California in 1542 but did not attempt to occupy it until 1769. Following the Pacific coast northward from Mexico, the Franciscan friar Junípero Serra and his successors established 21 missions, while their military and civilian counterparts chose nearby sites for presidios (forts) and haciendas (estates).

The arrival of the Spanish proved disastrous for the California Indians. The resident nations of California were unusually prosperous hunters and gatherers, making a living from a landscape that was extremely rich with wild foods. These peoples used a form of political organization known as the tribelet: moderately sized sedentary groups characterized by hierarchical but highly independent relationships both within and between polities.

The California nations were accustomed to negotiating agreements among themselves but, like their Southwestern counterparts, had no experience of occupation. As elsewhere, the Spanish occupation was brutal. Having selected a building site, Spanish leaders dispatched troops to indigenous villages, where they captured the residents. Having been marched to the chosen location, the people were forced to labour as builders and farmers and were forbidden to leave. In both hacienda and mission contexts, but more so in the missions, rules often mandated that native individuals be separated by gender, a practice that left women and children especially vulnerable to physical and sexual abuse at the hands of clergy and soldiers. As in the Southwest, resistance to any aspect of the missionizing experience was often harshly punished; nonetheless, many native Californians sought to escape the conquest by fleeing to distant areas and rebuilding their lives.

THE NORTHERN PACIFIC COAST

North America's northern Pacific coast was home to Arctic peoples and Northwest Coast Indians. These groups made their living primarily from the sea. Like their counterparts in the Northeast culture area, they were accustomed to

TECUMSEH

Born in 1768 in Old Piqua (modern Clark county, Ohio, U.S.), Tecumseh was a Shawnee Indian chief, orator, military leader, and advocate of intertribal Indian alliance who directed Indian resistance to white rule in the Ohio River valley.

After settling in the area of present-day Indiana, Tecumseh, with inexhaustible energy, began to form an Indian confederation to resist white pressure after about 1808. He made long journeys in a vast territory, from the Ozarks to New York and from Iowa to Florida, gaining recruits (particularly among the tribes of the Creek Confederacy, to which his mother's tribe belonged). The tide of settlers had pushed game from the Indians' hunting grounds, and, as a result, the Indian economy had broken down.

Seeing the approach of war (the War of 1812) between the Americans and British, Tecumseh assembled his followers and joined the British forces at Fort Malden on the Canadian side of the Detroit River. There he brought together perhaps the most formidable force ever commanded by a North American Indian, an accomplishment that was a decisive factor in the capture of Detroit and of 2,500 U.S. soldiers (1812).

Fired with the promise of triumph after the fall of Detroit, Tecumseh departed on another long journey to arouse the tribes, which resulted in the uprising of the Alabama Creeks in response to his oratory, though the Chickasaws, Choctaws, and Cherokees rebuffed him. He returned north and joined the British general Henry A. Procter in his invasion of Ohio. Together they besieged Fort Meigs, held by William Henry Harrison, on the Maumee River above Toledo, where by a stratagem Tecumseh intercepted and destroyed a brigade of Kentuckians under Colonel William Dudley that had been coming to Harrison's relief. He and Procter failed to capture the fort, however, and were put on the defensive by Oliver Hazard Perry's decisive victory over the British fleet on Lake Erie (Sept. 10, 1813).

Harrison thereupon invaded Canada. Tecumseh with his Indians reluctantly accompanied the retiring British, whom Harrison pursued to the Thames River, in present-day southern Ontario. There, on Oct. 5, 1813, the British and Indians were routed, and Harrison won control of the Northwest. Tecumseh, directing most of the fighting, was killed. His body was carried from the field and buried secretly in a grave that has never been discovered. Nor has it ever been determined who killed Tecumseh.

Tecumseh's death marked the end of Indian resistance in the Ohio River valley and in most of the lower Midwest and South, and soon thereafter the depleted tribes were transported beyond the Mississippi River.

offensive and defensive military action. They also participated in an indigenous trade network so extensive that it necessitated its own pidgin, or trade language, known as Chinook Jargon.

By the early 18th century, European elites had begun to recognize the potential profitability of trade relations with the peoples of North America's Pacific coast. From the mid-18th century on, the northern Pacific trade was dominated by Russia, although explorers and traders from other countries also visited the region.

Russian elites initially saw North America as rich but so distant that attempts at occupation might prove ill-advised. This perception was soon reversed, however. The Russian tsar Peter I sent Vitus Bering to explore the northern seas in 1728, and Russian traders reached the Aleutian Islands and the coasts of present-day Alaska (U.S.) and British Columbia (Can.) in the 1740s.

Russian trade was conducted by a rugged group of Siberian sailors and trappers, the *promyshlenniki*. Like their French counterparts, they wished to establish themselves in the lucrative fur trade, but, whereas the French sought beaver pelts for the European markets, the Russians sought the rich pelts of sea otters for trade with China. The differences between the French and Russian traders were more substantial than their pelt preferences, however. Where the 17th-century French traders had generally built settlements near native towns and partnered with local peoples, the 18th-century Russians imposed a devastating occupation that replicated the brutal social order to which they were accustomed—one in which they assumed the status of elites and exercised the power of life and death over their indigenous "serfs."

The initial encounters between the native peoples of the northern Pacific coast and Russian traders presaged terrible hardships to come. In 1745 a group of *promyshlenniki* overwintered in the Aleutian Islands; their behaviour was so extreme that the Russian courts eventually convicted several members of the party of atrocities. The Aleuts and the neighbouring Koniag mounted a spirited resistance against Russian incursions over the next 20 years but were outgunned. The Native Alaskan men who survived these early battles were immediately impressed into service hunting sea otters from light boats; their absences could range in length from days to months. During these periods the colonizers held entire villages hostage as surety and demanded food, labour, and sex from the remaining residents. This caused extraordinary human suffering; many communities endured cruel exploitation and prolonged periods of near-starvation.

During the last decade of the 18th century, Russian attempts to expand operations southward met with fierce military resistance from the Northwest Coast Indians, especially the Tlingit. With larger numbers than the Aleuts and Koniag, access to firearms, and the ability to retreat to the interior, the Tlingit nation successfully repelled the Russian colonizers. Having gained control of the region's harbours and waterways, the Tlingit and other Northwest Coast peoples profited by charging European (and later Euro-American) traders tolls for passage therein and by selling them immense quantities of fish, game, and potatoes.

In 1799 Russia's many independent trading outfits coalesced into a single monopoly, the Russian-American Company. Over the next decade it became clear that the practice of hunting mature female otters, which had more-luxurious pelts than males, was seriously depleting the sea otter population. Desiring a permanent southern outpost from which to stage hunts as well as a source for cheaper comestibles, in 1812 the company founded the northern California trading post of Fort Ross (about 90 miles [140 km] north of what is now San Francisco). The *promyshlenniki* continued to force Aleut and Koniag men on extended hunting trips. In many cases, local Pomo women married these Native Alaskan men, and together they built a unique multiethnic community.

In the early decades of the 19th century, voluntary cohabitation and intermarriage between native women and Russian men began to soften colonial relations in Alaska. Equally important, the multiethnic progeny of these matches and of the Native Alaskan-Pomo couples at Fort Ross began to ascend into the administrative ranks of the fur trade. By the 1850s, common customs in the northern Pacific colonies included wage rather than impressed labour; ritual godparenting, a Russian custom in which an adult makes a serious and public commitment to ensuring the physical, economic, and spiritual well-being of another person's child; and name exchanges, a Native Alaskan custom in which one receiving a name (usually of a deceased person) assumes some of the rights of its previous owner.

THE PLAINS AND PLATEAU CULTURE AREAS

The European conquest of North America proceeded in fits and starts from the coasts to the interior. During the early colonial period, the Plains and the Plateau peoples were affected by epidemics of foreign diseases and a slow influx of European trade goods. However, sustained direct interaction between these nations and colonizers did not occur until the 18th century.

In 1738 the Mandan villages on the upper Missouri River hosted a party led by the French trader Pierre Gaultier de Varennes et de la Vérendrye; this is often characterized as the event that initiated lasting contact between the peoples of the northern Plains and the colonial powers. Certainly a significant number of traders, such as David Thompson, were living with the Mandans and other Plains peoples by the late 18th century. Accounts of daily life in the region, gleaned from the diaries and letters of these traders, indicate that the interior nations were adept negotiators who enjoyed a relatively prosperous lifestyle; indeed, many visitors commented on the snug nature of the earth lodges in which Plains families lived and on the productivity they witnessed in the region. Although somewhat less historical data exists for the Plateau peoples of this era, it is clear that the 18th century was a time of great change for both groups. Three key factors influenced the trajectory of change: the arrival of horses, the arrival of guns, and the arrival of native peoples from adjacent culture areas.

Horses were introduced to the Americas by the Spanish conquistadors. The advantages of using horses, whether as pack animals or as mounts, were obvious to the Plains and Plateau peoples, who had until then been obligated to travel overland by foot or in small boats on the regions' few navigable rivers. Horses might be acquired in one of several ways: through purchase or trade, by capture from a rival group, or by taming animals from the wild herds that soon arose.

The dense forests of the Northeast, Southeast, and subarctic had discouraged the widespread use of horses; in those

Plains bullboats, in Mih-tutta-Hangkusch, a Mandan Village, *one of a series of aquatint engravings by Karl Bodmer, 1843–44.* Library of Congress, Washington, D.C.

regions, abundant waterways provided a more readily negotiated system of transportation. Thus, horses spread from the Southwest culture area to the Plains and the Plateau following a northerly and easterly trajectory. As horses spread, the pedestrian foragers of the southwestern Plains quickly incorporated them into bison hunts. Previously these had been dangerous affairs: the range of the bow and arrow was not great and so required hunters to approach animals rather closely, while the alternative method of hunting was to stampede a herd of bison toward a cliff, from which they would fall to their deaths. The speed and mobility provided by horses were great improvements over these earlier conditions.

Spanish law expressly forbade the distribution of firearms to indigenous individuals, but the English and Dutch traded them freely. Initially used in battle and to hunt the large game of the eastern and boreal forests, firearms were readily incorporated into the bison hunt by the pedestrian forager-farmers of the northeastern Plains. The horse's speed and agility had inspired a more effective form of hunting in the southern Plains; in the north a similar increase in productivity occurred as guns replaced bows and arrows. A rifle's greater firepower allowed more distance between hunter and hunted, lessening the danger of attack from a charging animal.

Horses and guns spread to the interior over the course of about 100 years, from roughly 1600 to 1700. By approximately 1700 many tribes were moving to the interior as well. Those from the Northeast were agriculturists pushed west by the intertribal hostilities of the Huron-Algonquian-French and Iroquois-English alliances. Those from the Southwest were Apachean and other hunters and gatherers who, having acquired horses, were able for the first time to match the movement of the bison herds.

By the 1750s the horse culture of the southern interior had met with the gun culture of the northern interior. The combination of guns and horses was invaluable: nations could follow herds of bison across the landscape and also take advantage of the greater distance and power allowed by firearms. From the mid-18th century to the first part of the 19th century, horses and guns enabled the indigenous nations of the North American interior to enjoy an unprecedented level of prosperity.

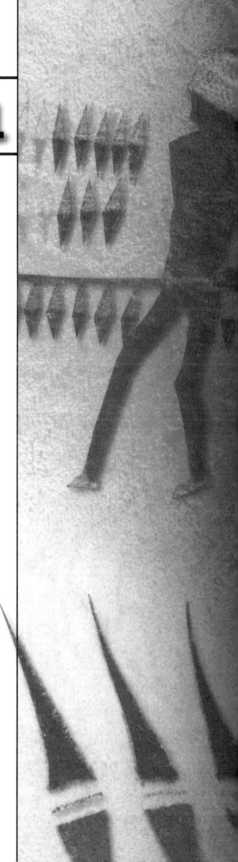

CHAPTER 11

FROM THE 19TH TO THE 21ST CENTURY

While Native American experiences of the 18th century were influenced by internecine warfare between the European powers, their experiences of the 19th century reflected an increasing political shift from overseas colonialism to domestic expansionism. Events of the 19th century made two things clear to indigenous nations: There were no longer any territories so remote as to escape colonization, and, for the most part, colonizers continued to prove inconstant and unable—or unwilling—to fulfill the commitments to which they agreed.

REMOVAL OF THE EASTERN NATIONS

The first full declaration of U.S. policy toward the country's indigenous peoples was embodied in the third of the Northwest Ordinances (1787):

> The utmost good faith shall always be observed toward the Indians, their lands and property shall never be taken from them without their consent; and in their property, rights, and liberty, they shall never be invaded or disturbed, unless in just and lawful wars authorized by Congress; but laws founded in justice and humanity shall from time to time be made, for preventing wrongs being done to them, and for preserving peace and friendship with them.

Within a few decades this guarantee of legal, political, and property rights was undermined by a series of Supreme

Court decisions and the passage of a new federal law.

The rulings in question were written by Chief Justice John Marshall. In *Johnson* v. *M'Intosh* (1823), the court ruled that European doctrine gave a "discovering" (e.g., colonial) power and its successors the exclusive right to purchase land from aboriginal nations. This ruling removed control of land transactions from the tribes, which had previously been able to sell to whomever they wished. In *Cherokee Nation* v. *Georgia* (1831), the court further opined that the political autonomy of indigenous polities was inherently reliant on the federal government, defining them as domestic (dependent) nations rather than foreign (independent) nations. This status prevented tribes from invoking a number of privileges reserved to foreign powers, such as suing the United States in the Supreme Court. In a third case, *Worcester* v. *Georgia* (1832), the court ruled that only the federal government, not the states, had the right to impose their regulations on Indian land. This created an important precedent through which tribes could, like states, reserve some areas of political autonomy. Together these three decisions suggested that Indian nations were simultaneously dependent upon and independent from federal control; subsequent case law has often focused on defining exactly which form of relationship obtains in a particular situation.

Even as these cases made their way through the U.S. courts, Congress was passing the Indian Removal Act (1830). The act was initiated after the 1828 discovery of gold on Cherokee land in Georgia. Speculators hoping to profit from the discovery, including President Andrew Jackson, subsequently pressured Congress to find a way to legally divest the tribe of its land. Jackson's speech *On Indian Removal*, presented to Congress in December 1830, provides a sample, although certainly not a full account, of his rationalizations for such action.

The Indian Removal Act enabled the president to designate tracts of land west of the Mississippi as new Indian Territories, to negotiate with tribes to effect their removal from east of the Mississippi, and to fund these transactions and associated transportation costs. The Native American population had not been consulted in these matters and responded in a variety of ways: Black Hawk led the Sauk and Fox in defending their territory, the Cherokee pursued resolution through the courts, the Choctaw agreed to arrange a departure plan with the designated federal authorities, and the Chickasaw gained permission to sell their property and arrange their own transportation to points west. Perhaps the most determined to remain in place were the Seminoles, who fiercely defended their homes; the Seminole Wars (1817–18, 1835–42, and 1855–58) came to be the most expensive military actions undertaken by the U.S. government up to that point.

Ultimately, all the eastern tribes found that overt resistance to removal was met with military force. In the decade after 1830, almost the entire U.S. population of perhaps 100,000 eastern Indians—including nearly every nation from the Northeast and Southeast culture areas—moved westward, whether voluntarily or by force. Encountering great difficulties and losing many people to exposure, starvation, and illness, those who survived this migration named it the Trail of Tears.

THE CONQUEST OF THE WESTERN UNITED STATES

In 1848 the Treaty of Guadalupe Hidalgo granted the United States all of Mexico's territories north of the Rio Grande; in the same year, gold was discovered in California. Thousands of miners and settlers streamed westward on the Oregon Trail and other routes, crossing over and hunting on indigenous land without asking leave or paying tribute. From the resident nations' perspective, these people were trespassers and poachers, although their presence was somewhat ameliorated by the goods and services they purchased from the tribes.

Contrary to their frequent portrayal in 20th-century popular culture, few armed conflicts between travelers and Indians took place, although tense situations certainly occurred. These circumstances moved the U.S. government to initiate a series of treaties through which to pacify the trans-Mississippi west. Perhaps the most important of these was the first Treaty of Fort Laramie

(1851), which was negotiated with the Arapaho, Arikara, Assiniboin, Blackfoot, Cheyenne, Crow, Dakota Sioux, Hidatsa, and Mandan nations. Among other issues, it explicitly defined the home territories of each of these peoples, disputes over which had fostered intertribal conflict. It also required the signatory nations to forego battle among themselves and against Euro-Americans and gave the United States the right to build and protect roads through the Plains. In return, the United States agreed to provide a variety of goods and services to the tribes.

Notably, while the impetus for the first Treaty of Fort Laramie was federal concern about the safety of travelers, indigenous actions against these people paled before the depredations of Euro-Americans, which have been described as genocidal. In the first three decades following the 1848 gold strike, for example, California's Native American population declined from between 100,000 and 150,000—a figure already depleted by the decades of poor conditions the "novitiates" had experienced at the hands of Spanish missionaries and businessmen—to perhaps 15,000 individuals. In 1850 the California legislature legalized the de facto slavery of indigenous individuals by allowing Euro-American men to declare them "vagrant" and to bind such "vagrants" by indenture. Thousands of people were enslaved under this statute, and many died of maltreatment. Between 1851 and 1857 the state legislature also authorized some $1.5 million for reimbursement to

ON INDIAN REMOVAL

Westward expansion brought the United States into contact with numerous Indian tribes, and the admission of new states brought certain Indian lands within the national boundaries. In a message to Congress on December 6, 1830, Pres. Andrew Jackson inaugurated the policy of extinguishing all Indian title to such lands and removing Native Americans to an area beyond the Mississippi River. The policy was upheld by the Supreme Court in the case of Cherokee Nation v. State of Georgia, but when Chief Justice John Marshall ruled in Worcester v. Georgia that the Indians retained certain rights in their own lands, Jackson is said to have retorted, "John Marshall has made his decision, now let him enforce it."

The following excerpt from Jackson's message to Congress is taken from A Compilation of the Messages and Papers of the Presidents 1789–1897, *James D. Richardson, ed., Washington, 1896–1899, Vol. II, pp. 500–529.*

It gives me pleasure to announce to Congress that the benevolent policy of the government, steadily pursued for nearly thirty years, in relation to the removal of the Indians beyond the white settlements is approaching to a happy consummation. Two important tribes have accepted the provision made for their removal at the last session of Congress, and it is believed that their example will induce the remaining tribes also to seek the same obvious advantages.

The consequences of a speedy removal will be important to the United States, to individual states, and to the Indians themselves. The pecuniary advantages which it promises to the government are the least of its recommendations. It puts an end to all possible danger of collision between the authorities of the general and state governments on account of the Indians. It will place a dense and civilized population in large tracts of country now occupied by a few savage hunters. [...]

It will separate the Indians from immediate contact with settlements of whites; free them from the power of the states; enable them to pursue happiness in their own way and under their own rude institutions; will retard the progress of decay, which is lessening their numbers, and perhaps cause them gradually, under the protection of the government and through the influence of good counsels, to cast off their savage habits and become an interesting, civilized, and Christian community. These consequences, some of them so certain and the rest so probable, make the complete execution of the plan sanctioned by Congress at their last session an object of much solicitude.

Toward the aborigines of the country no one can indulge a more friendly feeling than myself, or would go further in attempting to reclaim them from their wandering habits and make them a happy, prosperous people. [...]

Humanity has often wept over the fate of the aborigines of this country, and philanthropy has been long busily employed in devising means to avert it, but its progress has never for a moment been arrested, and one by one have many powerful tribes disappeared from the earth.

To follow to the tomb the last of his race and to tread on the graves of extinct nations excite melancholy reflections. But true philanthropy reconciles the mind to these vicissitudes as it does to the extinction of one generation to make room for another. [...] Philanthropy could not wish to see this continent restored to the condition in which it was found by our forefathers. What good man would prefer a country covered with forests and ranged by a few thousand savages to our extensive republic, studded with cities, towns, and prosperous farms, embellished with all the improvements which art can devise or industry execute, occupied by more than 12 million happy people, and filled with all the blessings of liberty, civilization, and religion?

The present policy of the government is but a continuation of the same progressive change by a milder process. The tribes which occupied the countries now constituting the Eastern states were annihilated or have melted away to make room for the whites. The waves of population and civilization are rolling to the westward, and we now propose to acquire the countries occupied by the red men of the South and West by a fair exchange, and, at the expense of the United States, to send them to a land where their existence may be prolonged and perhaps made perpetual. [...]

private individuals who quelled native "hostilities." Most of these private expeditions were little more than shooting sprees and slave raids against peaceful indigenous settlements.

For a time, the conquest of the West was overshadowed by the American Civil War (1861–65). Conflicts in the Plains increased during this period and included two of the worst interethnic atrocities of 19th-century America: the Sioux Uprising (1862), in which Santee warriors killed some 400 settlers in Minnesota, many of whom were women and children, and the Sand Creek Massacre (1864), in which members of the Colorado militia killed at least 150 and perhaps as many as 500 people, mostly women and children, at a Cheyenne village known to be peaceable.

As the Civil War ended, increasing numbers of U.S. troops were sent to pacify the North American interior. The federal government also began to develop the policies that eventually confined the nations of the West to reservations, and to pursue treaties with Native American polities in order to effect that goal. These agreements generally committed tribes to land cessions, in exchange for which the United States promised to designate specific areas for exclusive indigenous use and to provide tribes with annual payments (annuities) comprising cash, livestock, supplies, and services. A second major treaty convention occurred at Fort Laramie in 1868, but treaty making ceased with the passage of the Indian Appropriation Act (1871), which declared that "hereafter no Indian nation or tribe" would be recognized "as an independent power with whom the United States may contract by treaty." Indian affairs were thus brought under the legislative control of the Congress to a much greater extent than previously.

These actions eventually had an enormous effect on native nations. However, policy changes made from afar are difficult to enforce, and Washington, D.C., was nearly 1,700 miles (2,700 km) away from the communication nexus at Fort Laramie. The tasks of finding, moving, and restricting the nomadic nations to their designated reservations were given to the U.S. military. The best-known event of the conquest of the American West, the Battle of the Little Bighorn (June 25, 1876), arose directly from this delegation of authority. Notably, and despite its notoriety, this engagement caused few or no injuries to noncombatants; only military personnel were directly injured or killed.

During the battle a combined group of Cheyenne and Sioux warriors defended their families from George Armstrong Custer and the U.S. 7th Cavalry. Custer's mission had been to remove these people (several hundred in all) to their reservations, and he had intended to forcibly capture or kill every member of the community, including women, children, the aged, and the infirm, in order to do so. With the exception of a small group of soldiers led by Maj. Marcus Reno, who were trapped under fire on a hill, Custer and his troops were completely annihilated. Unfortunately for the western

nations, this event—and particularly Elizabeth Custer's decades-long promotion of her husband's death as an atrocity, despite his status as a recognized combatant—spawned a prolonged media sensation that reignited the United States' commitment to complete hegemony over Native America.

By the late 1880s an indigenous millenarian movement, the Ghost Dance religion, had arrived on the Plains. Growing from an older tradition known as the Round Dance, the new religion was based on the revelations of a young Paiute man, Wovoka, who prophesied the departure of the Euro-Americans and a reunion of Indians and their departed kin. The songs and ceremonies born of Wovoka's revelation swept the Plains, offering hope to indigenous believers but also shifting over time and space from a pacifist set of practices to one with at least some military aspects. Concerned that the Ghost Dance would disturb the uneasy peace of the northern Plains, U.S. government agents moved to capture its proponents. Among them was the Sioux leader Sitting Bull, who was killed on Dec. 15, 1890, while being taken into custody.

Just 14 days later the U.S. 7th Cavalry—Custer's regiment reconstituted—encircled and shelled a peaceful Sioux encampment at Wounded Knee, S.D., an action many have argued was taken in revenge of the Little Bighorn battle. More than 200 men, women, children, and elders who were waiting to return to their homes were killed. Although this massacre marked the effective end of native military resistance in the western United States, tribes and individuals continued to resist conquest in a variety of other ways.

THE CONQUEST OF WESTERN CANADA

For the indigenous peoples of the Canadian West, the 19th century was a time of rapid transformation. The fur trade and a variety of large prey animals were in decline, and, with the elimination of government tribute payments, this created a period of economic hardship for the tribes. In addition, Canada's northern forests and Plains saw an influx of European and Euro-American settlers and a series of treaties that greatly reduced the landholdings of aboriginal peoples.

Many legal issues of import to aboriginal nations were decided early in the century, before Canadian independence. Among the most important of these policies was the Crown Lands Protection Act (1839), which affirmed that aboriginal lands were the property of the crown unless specifically titled to an individual. By disallowing indigenous control of real estate, a requirement for full citizenship in most of Canada, the act disenfranchised most native peoples. Through the 1850s a series of additional laws codified Indian policy in Canada. Initiated by the assimilationist Bagot Commission (1842–44), these laws defined what constituted native identity, mandated that individuals carry only one legal status (e.g.,

aboriginal or citizen), prohibited the sale of alcohol to native peoples, and shifted the administration of native affairs from the British Colonial Office to Canada.

For native peoples, the most momentous legal changes in the later 19th century included the creation of the Dominion of Canada (1867) and the passage of legislation including the Gradual Civilization Act (1857), the Act Providing for the Organisation of the Department of the Secretary of State of Canada and for the Management of Indian and Ordnance Lands (1868), the Manitoba Act (1870), and the first consolidated Indian Act (1876). Events of the 19th century were also heavily influenced by the intensifying competition between the Hudson's Bay Company and the North West Company, a rivalry with roots a century old.

THE RED RIVER CRISIS AND THE CREATION OF MANITOBA

The Hudson's Bay Company (HBC) and the North West Company (NWC) had initially exploited different territories: the HBC took northern Huronia, Hudson Bay, and the land from the bay's western shore to the Rocky Mountains, while the NWC took the region lying between Lake Superior and the Rockies. In 1810 Thomas Douglas, 5th earl of Selkirk, became the major shareholder of the HBC. Selkirk was a Scottish philanthropist who felt that emigration was the most reasonable response to enclosure, which in Scotland was causing the precipitous eviction and impoverishment of literally thousands of farm families. He arranged to have the HBC provide nearly 120,000 square miles (approximately 310,000 square km) for settlement in and around the Red River valley of present-day Manitoba and North Dakota. The area was referred to as Assiniboia, named after the Assiniboin nation, which resided there.

The scheme was not well received by the established residents of the area. The population of Assiniboia was a heterogeneous mix of aboriginal and Euro-American individuals, essentially all of whom were engaged in the fur trade in one form or another. Members of the Métis nation were among the region's most prominent residents—economically successful, numerous, and well-traveled. Their economy emphasized commercial hunting, trapping, fishing, trading, and cartage; by generally limiting farming to such labour as was required to meet subsistence needs, they preserved the habitat of the animals upon which the fur trade relied. Métis culture arose from the marriages of indigenous women, who were most often Cree, to European traders, who were most often French or Scottish. In the early 19th century, some Métis identified most closely with their indigenous heritage, some with their European heritage, and some with both equally. A fourth group saw themselves as members of a unique culture that drew from, but was independent of, those of their ancestors. Given that the first interethnic marriages had occurred some two centuries earlier and that new individuals were constantly admixing into Métis communities, each of these perspectives could be reasonably held.

A number of Métis were officers in the NWC; the HBC, however, eschewed hiring them (and all indigenous individuals) for anything but the most basic labour. This rankled the Métis, many of whom supposed that Selkirk's settlers and their intensive farming were meant to dispossess the residents of Assiniboia of their lands and livelihoods. The NWC shareholders encouraged these sentiments. The two companies' dispute over control of the territory became quite heated; the NWC had a longer presence there, but both had trading posts in the region, and the crown's grant of Rupert's Land to the HBC seemed—to HBC shareholders, at least—to prove the superiority of the HBC claim.

In 1812 the first of the Selkirk settlers arrived at the Red River Settlement (near present-day Winnipeg, Man.). Additional immigrants arrived in succeeding years; they were often harassed, and in some cases their buildings were burned and their crops destroyed. Tensions between the NWC-Métis contingent and the HBC-settler contingent were compounded in the severe winter of 1815–16, which produced widespread starvation. When a group of NWC men, almost entirely Métis, attacked and captured an HBC supply convoy, the HBC-appointed governor of the colony led a group of some 20–25 troops to retaliate. The NWC men killed 20 of this group in an engagement known as the Seven Oaks Massacre

(1816). Many historians credit this event with fostering the unified Métis identity that later proved to be a key element in shaping the Canadian West and that continues to exist today.

In 1818 the Canadian courts, packed with judges who were NWC shareholders and supporters, ordered Selkirk to pay the NWC a very large settlement. The animosity between the rival companies was not resolved until 1821, when the British government insisted that they merge. The resultant corporation retained the Hudson's Bay Company name and many of its policies, including the use of discriminatory employment practices. Many Métis thus lost their primary employment as trappers, traders, and carters and began to move from the countryside into the Red River Settlement. Over the next several decades they made numerous petitions to the colonial and British governments requesting recognition of their status as an independent people, an end to the HBC monopoly, and colony status for Assiniboia, among other things. Their petitions were denied, although in some cases only after heated debate in the British Parliament.

Parliament granted Canada independence through the British North America Act (1867), legislation that included little acknowledgement of the concerns of the Métis or other aboriginal nations. Instead, Canada's 1868 Act Providing for the Organisation of the Department of the Secretary of State of Canada and for the Management of Indian and Ordnance Lands (sometimes referred to as the first Indian Act, although an act by that name was not passed until 1876) defined the ways that the dominion government would relate to native nations, essentially codifying the colonial legislation that had been passed during the 1850s.

Britain's Parliament also approved the transfer of Rupert's Land from the HBC to Canada, to be effective Dec. 1, 1869. Convinced that this would result in the seizure of their homes and land, the Métis formed a coalition through which they hoped to negotiate with the new dominion government. Led by Louis Riel, a young Métis who had studied law in Montreal, the coalition waded into a political morass that pitted an assortment of competing interests against one another. The parties included not only the Métis but also various First Nations groups, the Canadian Parliament, the HBC, and a variety of entities whose interests were diametrically opposed, such as Irish Catholic Fenians and Irish Protestant Orange Order members, French Canadian Catholics and British Canadian Protestants, and fur traders and farmers. The United States followed the proceedings closely, hoping to connect the lower 48 states with Alaska through the purchase or annexation of Rupert's Land; the state of Minnesota even offered Canada $10 million for the territory.

In an attempt to ensure that their concerns were heard, Riel's men prevented William McDougall, the commissioner of crown lands, from entering Assiniboia to implement the transfer of Rupert's Land from the HBC to the dominion. A frustrated McDougall nevertheless executed the part of the proclamation eliminating HBC rule over the region, unwisely leaving it without an official government. Riel quickly emplaced a provisional government as allowed under law.

Soon after, in one of the communities governed by the Riel coalition, an Orangeman was tried for disturbing the peace; his trial, despite its legality, and subsequent execution created an uproar throughout Canada. Hoping to quell the situation, the Canadian Parliament quickly wrote and passed the Manitoba Act (1870). Among other provisions, it recognized the property claims of the area's occupants and set aside 1,400,000 acres (some 565,000 hectares) for future Métis use. It also mandated legal and educational parity between the English- and French-speaking communities, as that had become the key political issue for most of the Canadian public.

THE NUMBERED TREATIES AND THE SECOND RIEL REBELLION

The Red River crisis laid the groundwork for the Numbered Treaties, 11 in all, that were negotiated between 1871 and 1921. For the most part these involved the cession of indigenous land in exchange for reserve areas and the governmental provision of annuities, including cash, equipment, livestock, health care, and public education, all in perpetuity. Leaders from all the involved parties generally felt it better to negotiate than to fight, as the human and financial costs of the conflicts in the western United States were well publicized at the time.

No aboriginal nation was able to negotiate everything it desired through the Numbered Treaties, although many native leaders were successful in pushing the dominion well beyond its preferred levels of remuneration. In addition to their own negotiating skills, which were considerable, these leaders relied upon individuals who were trained to repeat discussions verbatim—a group whose talents were especially useful when the colonizers "forgot" important clauses of agreements. By the end of 1876, Treaties 1 through 6 had been negotiated by the nations of the southern reaches of present-day Ontario, Manitoba, Alberta, and Saskatchewan. A particularly interesting idea had been advocated by the Plains Cree leader Big Bear, who persuaded the leaders of other nations to join him in requesting adjoining reserves. Their request was denied on the grounds that it would create an indigenous nation within a nation, which had of course been exactly the goal Big Bear wished to achieve.

The Métis fared poorly during the implementation of the Manitoba Act and the Numbered Treaties despite their earlier role in instigating dominion consultation with indigenous peoples in the Canadian West. Government assurances that Métis property claims in Manitoba would be recognized had been negated by the post hoc addition of development requirements—approximately 90 percent of Métis title requests were refused on the basis of insufficient improvements such as too few cultivated acres or housing that was deemed unsuitable. A large number moved to Saskatchewan, where the government insisted they file individual land claims as regular citizens. As an aboriginal nation, the Métis argued against this, noting that new block reserves should replace the land they had lost in Manitoba. From the perspective of the dominion, however, the matter was closed.

Even before the 1876 completion of Treaties 1–6, many members of the northern Plains nations were taking up farming and ranching. Most also continued to rely on bison for meat and for robes or finished hides, which had become very popular trade items. The Métis engaged in the same activities, and, while the resident tribes were not happy with the arrival of competitors, they and the Métis were generally sympathetic to each others' human rights causes.

The bison robe trade peaked in the late 1870s. Consumers preferred the lush robes of young cows, and the hunting of animals in their prime reproductive years contributed heavily to the imminent collapse of the bison population. Even as bison became scarce, harvests failed, and for several years in the early 1880s starvation became a real possibility for many people. For indigenous nations, these hardships were worsened by government agents who refused to fulfill their legal obligations to distribute annuities or who distributed only partial or substandard goods.

In 1884, at the suggestion of Big Bear, more than 2,000 people convened for a pan-tribal gathering. Although tribal leaders had been quietly meeting for years to arrange the scheduling of bison hunts, this was by far the largest indigenous gathering the Canadian Plains had seen. Government agents subsequently prohibited inter-reserve travel and began in earnest to use the withholding of food as a method of control.

Their actions ultimately precipitated a crisis. Late in 1884 Louis Riel arrived in Saskatchewan, having spent several years in exile in the United States. He attempted to engage the dominion government, advocating for colony status, a position supported by Big Bear's pan-tribal alliance, the Métis, and local Euro-Americans alike. In early 1885 a few starving tribal members looted Euro-American storage facilities and convoys, provoking government retaliation. Big Bear and another Plains Cree leader, Poundmaker, were able to intercede before the resultant skirmishes became full-blown engagements, thus preventing the deaths of many settlers and Royal Canadian Mounted Police officers. Government troops and ordnance were quickly transported to the area, and within a few weeks Big Bear, Poundmaker, Riel, and other alliance leaders had surrendered. They were soon convicted of various crimes. Riel was executed for treason, and, although their actions had clearly saved many lives, Big Bear and Poundmaker were sentenced to prison, where their health was quickly broken; both died within two years. Although Treaties 7 through 11 remained to be negotiated, colonial conquest was complete in the most populated portions of western Canada.

ASSIMILATION VERSUS SOVEREIGNTY: THE LATE 19TH TO THE LATE 20TH CENTURY

In many parts of the world, including Northern America, the indigenous peoples who survived military conquest were subsequently subject to political conquest, a situation sometimes referred to colloquially as "death by red tape." Formulated through governmental and quasi-governmental policies and enacted by nonnative bureaucrats, law enforcement officers, clergy, and others, the practices of political conquest typically fostered structural inequalities that disenfranchised indigenous peoples while strengthening the power of colonizing peoples.

Although the removals of the eastern tribes in the 1830s initiated this phase of conquest, the period from approximately 1885 to 1970 was also a time of intense political manipulation of Native American life. The key question of both eras was whether indigenous peoples would be better served by self-governance or by assimilation to the dominant colonial cultures of Canada and the United States.

For obvious reasons, most Indians preferred self-governance, also known as sovereignty. Although many Euro-Americans had notionally agreed with this position during the removal era, by the late 19th century most espoused assimilation. Many ascribed to progressivism, a loosely coherent set of values and beliefs that recognized and tried to ameliorate the growing structural inequalities they observed in Northern America. Generally favouring the small businessman and farmer over the industrial capitalist, most progressives realized that many inequities were tied to race or ethnicity and believed that assimilation was the only reasonable means through which the members of any minority group would survive.

This view held that the desire among American Indians to retain their own cultures was merely a matter of nostalgia and that it would be overcome in a generation or two, after rationalism replaced indigenous sentimentality. In Canada, early assimilationist legislation included the Crown Lands Protection Act (1839) and the many acts flowing from Canada's Bagot Commission, such as the Act to Encourage the Gradual Civilization of the Indian Tribes of the Canadas (1857). In the United States, the most prominent example of such legislation was the Indian Civilization Act (1819).

Although assimilationist perspectives were often patronizing, they were also more liberal than some of those that had preceded them. The reservation system had been formulated through models of cultural evolution (now discredited) that claimed that indigenous cultures were inherently inferior to those originating in Europe. In contrast to those who believed that indigenous peoples were inherently incompetent, assimilationists believed that any human could achieve competence in any culture.

Programs promoting assimilation were framed by the social and economic ideals that had come to dominate the national cultures of Canada and the United States. Although they varied in detail, these ideals generally emphasized Euro-American social structures and habits such as nuclear or, at most, three-generation families; patrilineal kinship; differential inheritance among "legitimate" and "bastard" children; male-led households; a division of labour that defined the efforts of women, children, and elders as "domestic help" and those of men as "productive labour"; sober religiosity; and corporal punishment for children and women. Economically, they emphasized capitalist principles, especially the ownership of private property (particularly of land, livestock, and machinery); self-directed occupations such as shop keeping, farming, and ranching; and the self-sufficiency of the nuclear household.

Most Native American nations were built upon different social and economic ideals. Not surprisingly, they preferred to retain self-governance in these arenas as well as in the political sphere. Their practices, while varying considerably from one group to the next, generally stood in

opposition to those espoused by assimilationists. Socially, most indigenous polities emphasized the importance of extended families and corporate kin groups, matrilineal or bilateral kinship, little or no consideration of legitimacy or illegitimacy, households led by women or by women and men together, a concept of labour that recognized all work as work, highly expressive religious traditions, and cajoling and other nonviolent forms of discipline for children and adults. Economically, native ideals emphasized communitarian principles, especially the sharing of use rights to land (e.g., by definition, land was community, not private, property) and the self-sufficiency of the community or kin group, with wealthier households ensuring that poorer neighbours or kin were supplied with the basic necessities.

Assimilationists initiated four movements designed to ensure their victory in this contest of philosophies and lifeways: allotment, the boarding school system, reorganization, and termination. Native peoples unceasingly fought these movements. The survival of indigenous cultures in the face of such strongly assimilationist programming is a measure of their success.

ALLOTMENT

Within about a decade of creating the western reservations, both Canada and the United States began to abrogate their promises that reservation land would be held inviolable in perpetuity. In Canada the individual assignment, or allotment, of parcels of land within reserves began in 1879. By 1895 the right of allotment had officially devolved from the tribes to the superintendent general. In the United States a similar policy was effected through the Dawes General Allotment Act (1887).

Although some reservations were large, they consistently comprised economically marginal land. Throughout the colonial period, settlers and speculators—aided by government entities such as the military—had pushed tribes to the most distant hinterlands possible. Further, as treaty after treaty drew and redrew the boundaries of reservations, the same parties lobbied to have the best land carved out of the reserves and made available for sale to non-Indians. As a result, confinement to a reservation, even a large one, generally prevented nomadic groups from obtaining adequate wild food; farming groups, who had always supplemented their crops heavily with wild fare, got on only slightly better.

Native leaders had insisted that treaties include various forms of payment to the tribes in exchange for the land they ceded. Although the governments of the

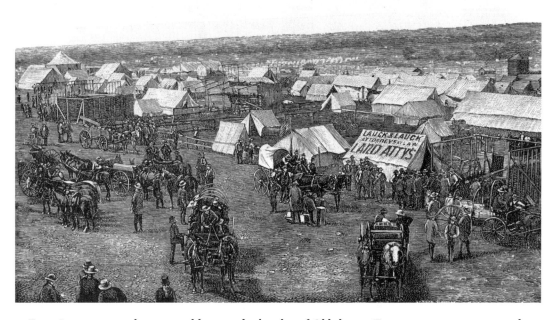

Euro-American settlers assembling at the border of Oklahoma Territory, preparing to stake claims on land made available by the Dawes General Allotment Act (1887). Library of Congress, Washington, D.C.

United States and Canada were obliged to honour their past promises of annuities, many of the bureaucrats entrusted with the distribution of these materials were corrupt. The combination of marginal land and bureaucratic malfeasance created immense poverty in native communities.

Ignorant of the legal and bureaucratic origins of reservation poverty, many Euro-Americans in the United States and Canada developed the opinion that reservation life, particularly its communitarian underpinnings, fostered indolence. They came to believe that the privatization of land was the key to economic rehabilitation and self-sufficiency. The right to allot reserves was held by the government in Canada, which at the time dictated that individual title and full citizenship were restricted to those who relinquished their aboriginal status. In the United States, the Dawes Act authorized the president to divide reservations into parcels and to give every native head of household a particular piece of property. The land would be held in trust for a period of 25 years, after which full title would devolve upon the individual. With title would go all the rights and duties of citizenship. Reservation land remaining after all qualified tribal members had been provided with allotments was declared "surplus" and could be sold by the government, on behalf of the tribe, to non-Indians. In the United States a total of 118 reservations were allotted in this manner. Through the alienation of the surplus lands and the patenting of individual holdings, the nations living on these reservations lost 86 million acres (34.8 million hectares), or 62 percent, of the 138 million acres (55.8 million hectares) that had been designated by treaty as Native American common property.

Although the particulars of allotment were different in the United States and Canada, the outcomes were more or less the same in both places: indigenous groups and individuals resisted the partitioning process. Their efforts took several forms and were aided by allotment's piecemeal implementation, which continued into the early 20th century.

A number of tribes mounted legal and lobbying efforts in attempts to halt the allotment process. In the United States these efforts were greatly hindered when the Supreme Court determined, in *Lone Wolf* v. *Hitchcock* (1903), that allotment was legal because Congress was entitled to abrogate treaties. In Canada the decision in *St. Catherine's Milling & Lumber Company* v. *The Queen* (1888) found that aboriginal land remained in the purview of the crown despite treaties that indicated otherwise and that the dominion, as an agent of the crown, could thus terminate native title at will.

In the United States, some tribes held property through forms of title that rendered their holdings less susceptible to the Dawes Act. For instance, in the 1850s some members of the Fox (Meskwaki) nation purchased land on which to reside. Their original purchase of 80 acres (32

INDIANS AND WHITES

The book A Century of Dishonor *(1881) by Helen Hunt Jackson documented the dealings of the federal government with various Native American peoples. Theodore Roosevelt, for one, refused to accept Jackson's findings and included her among those whom he called "these foolish sentimentalists."*

The following is an excerpt from the concluding chapter of A Century of Dishonor, *Boston, 1887.*

[...] There is not among these 300 bands of Indians one which has not suffered cruelly at the hands either of the government or of white settlers. The poorer, the more insignificant, the more helpless the band, the more certain the cruelty and outrage to which they have been subjected. This is especially true of the bands on the Pacific slope. These Indians found themselves of a sudden surrounded by and caught up in the great influx of gold-seeking settlers, as helpless creatures on a shore are caught up in a tidal wave. There was not time for the government to make treaties; not even time for communities to make laws. The tale of the wrongs, the oppressions, the murders of the Pacific-slope Indians in the last thirty years would be a volume by itself and is too monstrous to be believed.

It makes little difference, however, where one opens the record of the history of the Indians; every page and every year has its dark stain. The story of one tribe is the story of all, varied only by differences of time and place; but neither time nor place makes any difference in the main facts. Colorado is as greedy and unjust in 1880 as was Georgia in 1830 and Ohio in 1795; and the United States government breaks promises now as deftly as then, and with an added ingenuity from long practice. [...]

President after President has appointed commission after commission to inquire into and report upon Indian affairs and to make suggestions as to the best methods of managing them. The reports are filled with eloquent statements of wrongs done to the Indians, of perfidies on the part of the government. They counsel, as earnestly as words can, a trial of the simple and unperplexing expedients of telling truth, keeping promises, making fair bargains, dealing justly in all ways and all things. These reports are bound up with the Government's Annual Reports, and that is the end of them. It would probably be no exaggeration to say that not 1 American citizen out of 10,000 ever sees them or knows that they exist, and yet any one of them, circulated throughout the country, read by the right-thinking, right-feeling men and women of this land, would be of itself a "campaign document" that would initiate a revolution which would not subside until the Indians' wrongs were, so far as is now left possible, righted. [...]

However great perplexity and difficulty there may be in the details of any and every plan possible for doing at this late day anything like justice to the Indian, however hard it may be for good statesmen and good men to agree upon the things that ought to be done, there certainly is, or ought to be, no perplexity whatever, no difficulty whatever, in agreeing upon certain things that ought not to be done and which must cease to be done before the first steps can be taken toward righting the wrongs, curing the ills, and wiping out the disgrace to us of the present condition of our Indians.

Cheating, robbing, breaking promises — these three are clearly things which must cease to be done. One more thing, also, and that is the refusal of the protection of the law to the Indian's rights of property, "of life, liberty, and the pursuit of happiness."

When these four things have ceased to be done, time, statesmanship, philanthropy, and Christianity can slowly and surely do the rest. Till these four things have ceased to be done, statesmanship and philanthropy alike must work in vain, and even Christianity can reap but small harvest.

hectares) of land was held through free title and was therefore inalienable except through condemnation; the Meskwaki Settlement, as it became known, had grown to more than 7,000 acres (2,800 hectares) by 2000. In a number of other areas, native individuals simply refused to sign for or otherwise accept their parcels, leaving the property in a sort of bureaucratic limbo.

Despite its broad reach, not every reservation had been subjected to partition by the end of the allotment movement. The reservations that avoided the process were most often found in very remote or very arid areas, as with land held by several Ute nations in the Southwest. For similar reasons, many Arctic nations avoided not only allotment but even its precursor, partition into reserves.

Allotment failed as a mechanism to force cultural change: the individual ownership of land did not in itself effect assimilation, although it did enrich many Euro-American land speculators. Native social networks and cultural cohesion were in some places shattered by the dispersal of individuals, families, and corporate kin groups across the landscape. Many native institutions and cultural practices were weakened, and little to nothing was offered in substitution.

BOARDING SCHOOLS

The worst offenses of the assimilationist movement occurred at government-sponsored boarding, or residential, schools. From the mid-19th century until as late as the 1960s, native families in Canada and the United States were compelled by law to send their children to these institutions, which were usually quite distant from the family home. At least through World War II, the schools' educational programming was notionally designed to help students achieve basic literacy and arithmetic skills and to provide vocational training in a variety of menial jobs—the same goals, to a large extent, of public education throughout Northern America during that period.

However, the so-called Indian schools were often led by men of assimilationist convictions so deep as to be racist. One example is Carlisle Indian Industrial School (in Carlisle, Pa.) founder Richard Pratt, who in 1892 described his mission as "Kill the Indian in him, and save the man." Such sentiments persisted for decades; in 1920 Duncan Campbell Scott, the superintendent of the Canadian residential school system, noted his desire to have the schools "continue until there is not a single Indian in Canada that has not been absorbed into the body politic and there is no Indian question, and no Indian Department." Stronger statements promoting assimilation at the expense of indigenous sovereignty can hardly be imagined.

In pursuing their goals, the administrators of residential schools used a variety of material and psychological techniques to divest native children of their cultures. Upon arrival, students were forced to trade their clothes for uniforms, to have their hair cut in Euro-American styles, and to separate from their relatives and friends. Physical conditions at the schools were often very poor and caused many children to suffer from malnutrition and exposure, exacerbating tuberculosis

and other diseases that were common at the time. The schools were generally run by clergy and commingled religious education with secular subjects; staff usually demanded that students convert immediately to Christianity. Displays of native culture, whether of indigenous language, song, dance, stories, religion, sports, or food, were cruelly punished through such means as beatings, electrical shocks, the withholding of food or water, and extended periods of forced labour or kneeling. Sexual abuse was rampant. In particularly bad years, abuse and neglect were acknowledged to have caused the deaths of more than half of the students at particular schools.

Native families were aware that many children who were sent to boarding schools never returned, and they responded in a number of ways. Many taught their children to hide at the approach of the government agents who were responsible for assembling children and transporting them to the schools. Many students who were transported ran away, either during the trip or from the schools themselves. Those who escaped often had to walk hundreds of miles to return home. Some communities made group decisions to keep their children hidden; perhaps the best-known of such events occurred in 1894–95, when 19 Hopi men from Oraibi pueblo were incarcerated for refusing to reveal their children's whereabouts to the authorities.

Through these and other efforts, native communities eventually gained control over the education of their children. It was, however, a slow process. The first school in the United States to come under continuous tribal administration was the Rough Rock Demonstration School in Arizona in 1966, while in Canada the Blue Quills First Nations College in Alberta was the first to achieve that status, in 1971.

Many researchers and activists trace the most difficult issues faced by 20th- and 21st-century Indian communities to the abuses that occurred at the boarding schools. They note that the problems common to many reservations—including high rates of suicide, substance abuse, domestic violence, child abuse, and sexual assault—are clear sequelae of childhood abuse. In 1991 the assaults perpetrated upon Canadian children who had attended residential schools in the mid-20th century began to be redressed through the work of the Royal Commission on Aboriginal Peoples. The commission's 1996 report substantiated indigenous claims of abuse, and in 2006 Canada allocated more than $2 billion (Canadian) in class-action reparations and mental health funding for the former students.

REORGANIZATION

By the late 19th century the removal of the eastern tribes, the decimation of California peoples, a series of epidemics in the Plains, and the high mortality rates at boarding schools seemed to confirm that Indians were "vanishing." The belief that Native Americans would not survive

long as a "race" provided a fundamental justification for all assimilationist policies. It also supported rationalizations that indigenous views on legislation and public policy were immaterial. When it became obvious after about 1920 that Northern American's aboriginal populations were actually increasing, the United States and Canada found themselves unprepared to acknowledge or advance the interests of these people.

In the United States a 1926 survey brought into clear focus the failings of the previous 40 years. The investigators found most Indians "extremely poor," in bad health, without education, and isolated from the dominant Euro-American culture around them. Under the impetus of these findings and other pressures for reform, the U.S. Congress adopted the Indian Reorganization Act of 1934, which was designed to effect an orderly transition from federal control to native self-government. The essentials of the new law were as follows: (1) allotment of tribal lands was prohibited, but tribes might assign use rights to individuals; (2) so-called surplus lands that had not been sold or granted to non-Indians could be returned to the tribes; (3) tribes could adopt written constitutions and charters of incorporation through which to manage their internal affairs; and (4) funds were authorized for the establishment of a revolving credit program which was to be used for land purchases, for educational assistance, and for helping the tribes to form governments. The terms of the act were universally

FALSE SENTIMENTALITY ABOUT INDIANS

Theodore Roosevelt favoured a rational and equitable policy toward Native Americans, but he firmly believed that the Indian nations had no claim to the land they inhabited and were in fact nomadic people who by temperament had no desire to hold property. Roosevelt was disdainful of such zealous reformers as Helen Hunt Jackson because he thought they distorted the character of Native American-white relations.

The following excerpt is from Roosevelt's The Winning of the West, *Homeward Bound Edition, Vol. I, New York, 1910, Appendix A to Chapter 4.*

Theodore Roosevelt photographed while hunting in the West. Library of Congress, Washington, D.C.

It is greatly to be wished that some competent person would write a full and true history of our national dealings with the Indians. Undoubtedly the latter have often suffered terrible injustice at our hands. A number of instances, such as the conduct of the Georgians to the Cherokees in the early part of the present century, or the whole treatment of Chief Joseph and his Nez Percés, might be mentioned, which are indelible blots on our fair fame; and yet, in describing our dealings with the red men as a whole, historians do us much less than justice.

It was wholly impossible to avoid conflicts with the weaker race, unless we were willing to see the American continent fall into the hands of some other strong power; and even had we adopted such a ludicrous policy, the Indians themselves would have made war upon us. [...]

The purely sentimental historians take no account of the difficulties under which we labored, nor of the countless wrongs and provocations we endured, while grossly magnifying the already lamentably large number of injuries for which we really deserve to be held responsible. To get a fair idea of the Indians of the present day and of our dealings with them, we have fortunately one or two excellent books, notably Hunting Grounds of the Great West *and* Our Wild Indians, *by Col. Richard I. Dodge (Hartford, 1882), and* Massacres of the Mountains, *by J. P. Dunn (New York, 1886). As types of the opposite class, which are worse than valueless and which nevertheless might cause some hasty future historian, unacquainted with the facts, to fall into grievous error, I may mention,* A Century of Dishonor, *by H. H. (Mrs. Helen Hunt Jackson), and* Our Indian Wards *(George W. Manypenny).*

[...] Mrs. Jackson's book is capable of doing more harm because it is written in good English, and because the author, who had lived a pure and noble life, was intensely in earnest in what she wrote, and had the most praiseworthy purpose — to prevent our committing any more injustice to the Indians. [...]

The purpose of the book is excellent, but the spirit in which it is written cannot be called even technically honest. As a polemic, it is possible that it did not do harm (though the effect of even a polemic is marred by hysterical indifference to facts). As a history it would be beneath criticism were it not that the high character of the author and her excellent literary work in other directions have given it a fictitious value and made it much quoted by the large class of amiable but maudlin fanatics concerning whom it may be said that the excellence of their intentions but indifferently atones for the invariable folly and ill effect of their actions. It is not too much to say that the book is thoroughly untrustworthy from cover to cover, and that not a single statement it contains should be accepted without independent proof; for even those that are not absolutely false are often as bad on account of so much of the truth having been suppressed.

One effect of this is of course that the author's recitals of the many real wrongs of Indian tribes utterly fail to impress us because she lays quite as much stress on those that are nonexistent and on the equally numerous cases where the wrongdoing was wholly the other way. To get an idea of the value of the work, it is only necessary to compare her statements about almost any tribe with the real facts, choosing at random; for instance, compare her accounts of the Sioux and the Plains tribes generally with those given by Colonel Dodge in his two books; or her recital of the Sandy Creek massacre with the facts as stated by Mr. Dunn, who is apt, if anything, to lean to the Indian's side.

These foolish sentimentalists not only write foul slanders about their own countrymen but are themselves the worst possible advisers on any point touching Indian management. They would do well to heed General Sheridan's bitter words, written when many Easterners were clamoring against the Army authorities because they took partial vengeance for a series of brutal outrages: "I do not know how far these humanitarians should be excused on account of their ignorance; but surely it is the only excuse that can give a shadow of justification for aiding and abetting such horrid crimes."

applicable, but any particular nation could reject them through a referendum process.

The response to the Reorganization Act was indicative of the indigenous peoples' ability to rise above adversity. About 160 communities adopted written constitutions, some of which combined traditional practices with modern parliamentary methods. The revolving credit fund helped to improve tribal economies in many ways: native ranchers built up their herds, artisans were better able to market their work, and so forth. Educational and health services were also improved.

After 1871, when internal tribal matters had become the subject of U.S. legislation, the number and variety of regulatory measures regarding native individuals multiplied rapidly. In the same year that the Indian Reorganization Act was passed, Congress took the significant step of repealing 12 statutes that had made it possible to hold indigenous people virtual prisoners on their reservations. The recognition of tribal governments following the Reorganization Act seemed to awaken an interest in civic affairs beyond tribal boundaries. The earlier Snyder Act (1924) had extended citizenship to all Indians born in the United States, opening the door to full participation in American civic life. But few took advantage of the law, and a number of states subsequently excluded them from the franchise. During the reorganization period, many native peoples successfully petitioned to regain the right to vote in state and federal elections. The major exception to this trend occurred in Arizona and New Mexico, which withheld enfranchisement until 1948 and granted it only after a lengthy lawsuit.

A number of nations had for many years sponsored tribal councils. These councils had functioned without federal sanction, although their members had represented tribal interests in various ways, such as leading delegations to Washington, D.C., to protest allotment. Reorganization gave tribes the opportunity to formalize these and other indigenous institutions. Tribal governments soon initiated a number of lawsuits designed to regain land that had been taken in contravention of treaty agreements. Other lawsuits focused on the renewal of use rights, such as the right to hunt or fish, that had been guaranteed in some treaties.

These legal strategies for extending sovereignty were often very successful. The federal courts consistently upheld treaty rights and also found that ancestral lands could not be taken from an aboriginal nation, whether or not a treaty existed, "except in fair trade." The fair trade argument was cited by the Hualapai against the Santa Fe Railway, which in 1944 was required to relinquish about 500,000 acres (200,000 hectares) it thought it had been granted by the United States. A special Indian Claims Commission, created by an act of Congress on Aug. 13, 1946, received petitions for land claims against the United States. Many land claims resulted in significant compensation, including nearly $14,800,000 to the Cherokee nation, $10,250,000 to the Crow tribe, $12,300,000 to the Seminoles, and $31,750,000 to the Ute.

Even as many tribes in the United States were regaining land or compensation, the U.S. Bureau of Indian Affairs instituted the Urban Indian Relocation Program. Initiated within the bureau in 1948 and supported by Congress from the 1950s on, the relocation program was designed to transform the predominantly rural native population into an assimilated urban workforce. The bureau established offices in a variety of destination cities, including Chicago, Dallas, Denver, Los Angeles, San Francisco, San Jose, and St. Louis. Through program auspices, it promised to provide a variety of services to effect the transition to city life, including transportation from the reservation, financial assistance, help in finding housing and employment, and the like, although the distribution and quality of these services were often uneven. From 1948 to 1980, when the program ended, some 750,000 Indians are estimated to have relocated to cities, although not all did so under the official program and not all remained in urban areas permanently. Evaluations of its success vary, but it is clear that urban relocation helped to foster the sense of pan-Indian identity and activism that arose in the latter half of the 20th century.

Termination

The ultimate goals of assimilationist programming were to completely divest native peoples of their cultural practices and to terminate their special relationship to the national government. Canada's attempts at promoting these goals tended to focus on the individual, while those of the United States tended to focus on the community.

In Canada a variety of 19th-century policies had been emplaced to encourage individuals to give up their aboriginal status in favour of regular citizenship. Native people were prohibited from voting, serving in public office, owning land, attending public school, holding a business license, and a variety of other activities. These disincentives did not prove to be very strong motivating forces toward the voluntary termination of native status. More successful were regulations that initiated the termination of status without an individual's permission. For instance, until 1985, indigenous women who married nonnative men automatically lost their aboriginal status; undertaking military service or earning a university degree could also initiate involuntary changes in status.

Major adjustments to Canada's pro-termination policies did not occur until after World War II, when returning veterans and others began to agitate for change. In 1951 activists succeeded in eliminating many of the disincentives associated with indigenous status. After

THE DISILLUSIONED INDIAN

The discovery of gold on the reservation of the Nez Percé Indians in the Oregon country led to an overrunning of their land by miners in 1860. By coercion and bribery the government traduced some of the chiefs into signing away their land in a treaty three years later. Many of the Nez Percé remained, and when, in 1877, the government attempted to force them to leave, the tribe reacted, and under the leadership of Chief Joseph fought the U.S. Army for four months before being subdued in northern Montana. The Nez Percé were sent to the barren lands of the Oklahoma Indian Territory, where many of them fell victim to malaria and other diseases. Chief Joseph continued to plead the cause of his people, and eventually the remainder of the nation was allowed to return to the Northwest. In 1879 an account by Chief Joseph described the events leading up to the conflict of 1877 and its aftermath. The melancholy closing portion of his narrative, as published in North American Review *(April 1879: "An Indian's Views of Indian Affairs"), is excerpted here.*

[...] At last I was granted permission to come to Washington and bring my friend Yellow Bull and our interpreter with me. I am glad we came. I have shaken hands with a great many friends, but there are some things I want to know which no one seems to be able to explain. I can not understand how the government sends a man out to fight us, as it did General Miles, and then breaks his word. Such a government has something wrong about it. I can not understand why so many chiefs are allowed to talk so many different ways, and promise so many different things. I have seen the great father chief (the President), the next great chief (secretary of the interior), the commissioner chief (Hayt), the law chief (General Butler), and many other law chiefs (congressmen), and they all say they are my friends, and that I shall have justice, but while their mouths all talk right I do not understand why nothing is done for my people. I have heard talk and talk, but nothing is done. Good words do not last long unless they amount to something. Words do not pay for my dead people. They do not pay for my country, now overrun by white men. They do not protect my father's grave. They do not pay for all my horses and cattle. Good words will not give me back my children. Good words will not make good the promise of your war chief General Miles. Good words will not give my people good health and stop them from dying. Good words will not get my people a home where they can live in peace and take care of themselves. I am tired of talk that comes to nothing. It makes my heart sick when I remember all the good words and all the broken promises. There has been too much talking by men who had no right to talk. Too many misrepresentations have been made, too many misunderstandings have come up between the white men about the Indians. If the white man wants to live in peace with the Indian he can live in peace. There need be no trouble. Treat all men alike. Give them all the same law. Given them all an even chance to live and grow. All men were made by the same Great Spirit Chief. They are all brothers. The earth is the mother of all people, and all people should have equal rights upon it. You might as well expect the rivers to run backward as that any man who was born a free man should be contented when penned up and denied liberty to go where he pleases. If you tie a horse to a stake, do you expect he will grow fat? If you pen an Indian up on *a small spot of earth, and compel him to stay there, he will not be contented, nor will he grow and prosper. I have asked some of the great white chiefs where they get their authority to say to the Indian that he shall stay in one place, while he sees white men going where they please. They can not tell me.*

I only ask of the government to be treated as all other men are treated. If I can not go to my own home, let me have a home in some country where my people will not die so fast. I would like to go to Bitter Root Valley. There my people would be healthy; where they are now they are dying. Three have died since I left my camp to come to Washington.

When I think of our condition my heart is heavy. I see men of my race treated as outlaws and driven from country to country, or shot down like animals.

I know that my race must change. We can not hold our own with the white men as we are. We only ask an even chance to live as other men live. We ask to be recognized as men. We ask that the same law shall work alike on all men. If the Indian breaks the law, punish him by the law. If the white man breaks the law, punish him also.

Let me be a free man—free to travel, free to stop, free to work, free to trade where I choose, free to choose my own teachers, free to follow the religion of my fathers, free to think and talk and act for myself—and I will obey every law, or submit to the penalty.

Whenever the white man treats the Indian as they treat each other, then we will have no more wars. We shall all be alike—brothers of one father and one mother, with one sky above us and one country around us, and one government for all. Then the Great Spirit Chief who rules above will smile upon this land, and send rain to wash out the bloody spots made by brothers' hands from the face of the earth. For this time the Indian race are waiting and praying. I hope that no more groans of wounded men and women will ever go to the ear of the Great Spirit Chief above, and that all people may be one people.

years of prohibitions, for instance, native peoples regained the right to hold pow-wows and potlatches and to engage in various (if limited) forms of self-governance. The new policy also defined procedures for the reinstatement of aboriginal status, for which some 42,000 individuals applied within the first year of passage.

In the United States termination efforts were handled somewhat differently. In 1954 the U.S. Department of the Interior began terminating federal control and support of tribes that had been deemed able to look after their own affairs. From 1954 to 1960, support to 61 indigenous nations was ended by the withdrawal of federal services or trust supervision.

The results were problematic. Some extremely impoverished communities lost crucial services such as schools and clinics due to a lack of funds; in a number of cases, attempts to raise the capital with which to replace these services attracted unscrupulous business partners and further impoverished the community. The protests of tribal members and other activists became so insistent that the termination program began to be dismantled in 1960.

American Indians became increasingly visible in the late 20th century as they sought to achieve a better life as defined on their own terms. During the civil rights movement of the 1960s many drew attention to their causes through mass demonstrations and protests. Perhaps the most publicized of these actions were the 19-month seizure (1970–71) of Alcatraz Island in San Francisco Bay (California) by members of the militant American Indian Movement (AIM) and the February 1973 occupation of Wounded Knee, on the Oglala Sioux Pine Ridge (South Dakota) reservation.

During the 1960s and '70s, native polities continued to capitalize on their legal successes and to expand their sphere of influence through the courts; forestry, mineral, casino gambling, and other rights involving tribal lands became the subjects of frequent litigation. Of the many cases filed, *United States* v. *Washington* (1974) had perhaps the most famous and far-reaching decision. More commonly referred to as the Boldt case, after the federal judge, George Boldt, who wrote the decision, this case established that treaty agreements entitled certain Northwest Coast and Plateau tribes to one-half of the fish taken in the state of Washington—and by implication in other states where tribes had similarly reserved the right to fish. In addition, some groups continued their efforts to regain sovereignty over or compensation for tribal lands. The most important results of the latter form of activism were the passage of the Alaska Native Claims Settlement Act (1971), in which Native Alaskans received approximately 44 million acres (17.8 million hectares) of land and nearly $1 billion (U.S.) in exchange for land cessions, and the creation of Nunavut (1999), a new Canadian province predominantly administered by and for the Inuit.

DEVELOPMENTS IN THE LATE 20TH AND EARLY 21ST CENTURIES

Native American life in the late 20th and early 21st centuries has been characterized by continuities with and differences from the trajectories of the previous several centuries. One of the more striking continuities is the persistent complexity of native ethnic and political identities. In 2000 more than 600 indigenous bands or tribes were officially recognized by Canada's dominion government, and some 560 additional bands or tribes were officially recognized by the government of the United States. These numbers were slowly increasing as additional groups engaged in the difficult process of gaining official recognition.

The Native American population has continued to recover from the astonishing losses of the colonial period, a phenomenon first noted at the turn of the 20th century. Census data from 2006 indicated that people claiming aboriginal American ancestry numbered some 1.17 million in Canada, or approximately 4 percent of the population; of these, some 975,000 individuals were officially recognized by the dominion as of First Nation, Métis, or Inuit heritage. U.S. census figures from 2000 indicated that some 4.3 million people claimed Native American descent, or 1 to 2 percent of the population. Fewer than 1 million of these self-identified individuals were officially recognized as of native heritage, however.

The numerical difference between those claiming ancestry and those who are officially recognized is a reflection of many factors. Historically, bureaucratic error has frequently caused individuals to be incorrectly removed from official rolls. Marrying outside the Native American community has also been a factor. In some places and times, those who out-married were required by law to be removed from tribal rolls. Children of these unions have sometimes been closer to one side of the family than the other, thus retaining only one parent's ethnic identity; in some cases, the children of ethnically mixed marriages have been unable to document the degree of genetic relation necessary for official enrollment in a particular tribe. This degree of relation is often referred to as a blood quantum requirement; one-fourth ancestry, the equivalent of one grandparent, is a common minimum blood quantum, though not the only one. Other nations define membership through features such as

residence on a reservation, knowledge of traditional culture, or fluency in a native language. Whether genetic or cultural, such definitions are generally designed to prevent the improper enrollment of people who have wishful or disreputable claims to native ancestry. Known colloquially as wannabes, these individuals also contribute to the lack of correspondence between the number of people who claim Indian descent and the number of officially enrolled individuals.

A striking difference from the past can be seen in Native Americans' ability to openly engage with both traditional and nontraditional cultural practices. While in past eras many native individuals had very limited economic and educational opportunities, by the turn of the 21st century they were members of essentially every profession available in North America. Many native people have also moved from reservations to more urban areas, including about 65 percent of U.S. tribal members and 55 percent of aboriginal Canadians.

Although life has changed drastically for many tribal members, a number of indicators, such as the proportion of students who complete secondary school, the level of unemployment, and the median household income, show that native people in the United States and Canada have had more difficulty in achieving economic success than non-Indians. Historical inequities have clearly contributed to this situation. In the United States, for instance, banks cannot repossess buildings on government trust lands, so most Indians have been unable to obtain mortgages unless they leave the reservation. This regulation in turn leads to depopulation and substandard housing on the reserve, problems that are not easily resolved without fundamental changes in regulatory policy.

The effects of poorly considered government policies are also evident in less-obvious ways. For example, many former residential-school students did not parent well, and an unusually high number of them suffered from post-traumatic stress disorder. Fortunately, social service agencies found that mental health care, parenting classes, and other actions could resolve many of the problems that flowed from the boarding school experience.

While most researchers and Indians agree that historical inequities are the source of many problems, they also tend to agree that the resolution of such issues ultimately lies within native communities themselves. Thus, most nations continue to pursue sovereignty, the right to self-determination, as an important focus of activism, especially in terms of its role in tribal well-being, cultural traditions, and economic development. Questions of who or what has the ultimate authority over native nations and individuals, and under what circumstances, remain among the most important, albeit contentious and misunderstood, aspects of contemporary Native American life.

Although community self-governance was the core right that indigenous Americans sought to maintain from the advent of colonialism onward, the strategies they used to achieve it evolved over time. The period from the Columbian landfall to the late 19th century might be characterized as a time when Native Americans fought to preserve sovereignty by using economics, diplomacy, and force to resist military conquest. From the late 19th century to the middle of the 20th, political sovereignty, and especially the enforcement of treaty agreements, was a primary focus of indigenous activism; local, regional, and pan-Indian resistance to the allotment of communally owned land, to the mandatory attendance of children at boarding schools, and to the termination of tribal rights and perquisites all grew from the basic tenets of the sovereignty movement. By the mid-1960s the civil rights movement had educated many peoples about the philosophy of equal treatment under the law—essentially the application of the sovereign entity's authority over the individual—and civil rights joined sovereignty as a focus of Indian activism.

One, and perhaps the principal, issue in defining the sovereign and civil rights of American Indians has been the determination of jurisdiction in matters of Indian affairs. Historical events in Northern America, that part of the continent north of the Rio Grande, created an unusually complex system of competing national, regional (state, provincial, or territorial), and local claims to jurisdiction. Where other countries typically have central governments that delegate little authority to regions, Canada and the United States typically assign a wide variety of responsibilities to provincial, state, and territorial governments, including the administration of such unrelated matters as unemployment insurance, highway maintenance, public education, and criminal law. With nearly 1,200 officially recognized tribal governments and more than 60 regional governments extant in the United States and Canada at the turn of the 21st century, and with issues such as taxation and regulatory authority at stake, it is unsurprising that these various entities have been involved in myriad jurisdictional battles.

Two examples of criminal jurisdiction help to clarify the interaction of tribal, regional, and federal or dominion authorities. One area of concern has been whether a non-Indian who commits a criminal act while on reservation land can be prosecuted in the tribal court. In *Oliphant* v. *Suquamish Indian Tribe* (1978), the U.S. Supreme Court determined that tribes do not have the authority to prosecute non-Indians, even when such individuals commit crimes on tribal land. This decision was clearly a blow to tribal sovereignty, and some reservations literally closed their borders to non-Indians in order to ensure that their law enforcement officers could keep the peace within the reservation.

The *Oliphant* decision might lead one to presume that, as non-Indians may not be tried in tribal courts, Indians in the United States would not be subject to

prosecution in state or federal courts. This issue was decided to the contrary in *United States* v. *Wheeler* (1978). Wheeler, a Navajo who had been convicted in a tribal court, maintained that the prosecution of the same crime in another (federal or state) court amounted to double jeopardy. In this case the Supreme Court favoured tribal sovereignty, finding that the judicial proceedings of an independent entity (in this case, the indigenous nation) stood separately from those of the states or the United States; a tribe was entitled to prosecute its members. In so ruling, the court seems to have placed an extra burden on Native Americans: whereas the plaintiff in *Oliphant* gained immunity from tribal law, indigenous plaintiffs could indeed be tried for a single criminal act in both a tribal and a state or federal court.

A plethora of other examples are available to illustrate the complexities of modern native life. In particular, there are four issues that are of pan-Indian importance: the placement of native children into non-Indian foster and adoptive homes, the free practice of traditional religions, the disposition of the dead, and the economic development of native communities.

The Outplacement and Adoption of Indigenous Children

From the beginning of the colonial period, Native American children were particularly vulnerable to removal by colonizers. Captured children might be sold into slavery, forced to become religious novitiates, made to perform labour, or adopted as family members by Euro-Americans. Although some undoubtedly did well under their new circumstances, many suffered. In some senses, the 19th-century practice of forcing children to attend boarding school was a continuation of these earlier practices.

Before the 20th century, social welfare programs were, for the most part, the domain of charities, particularly of religious charities. By the mid-20th century, however, governmental institutions had surpassed charities as the dominant instruments of public well-being. As with other forms of Northern American civic authority, most responsibilities related to social welfare were assigned to state and provincial governments, which in turn developed formidable child welfare bureaucracies. These were responsible for intervening in cases of child neglect or abuse. Although caseworkers often tried to maintain the integrity of the family, children living in dangerous circumstances were generally removed.

The prevailing models of well-being used by children's services personnel reflected the culture of the Euro-American middle classes. They viewed caregiving and financial well-being as the responsibilities of the nuclear family; according to this view, a competent family comprised a married couple and their biological or legally adopted children, with a father who worked outside the home, a mother who was a homemaker, and a residence with material conveniences such as electricity. These expectations stood in contrast to the values of reservation life, where extended-family households and communitarian approaches to wealth were the norm. For instance, while Euro-American culture has emphasized the ability of each individual to climb the economic ladder by eliminating the economic "ceiling," many indigenous groups have preferred to ensure that nobody falls below a particular economic "floor."

In addition, material comforts linked to infrastructure were simply not available on reservations as early as in other rural areas. For instance, while U.S. rural electrification programs had ensured that 90 percent of farms had electricity by 1950—a tremendous rise compared with the 10 percent that had electricity in 1935—census data indicated that the number of homes with access to electricity did not approach 90 percent on reservations until 2000. These kinds of cultural and material divergences from Euro-American expectations instantly made native families appear to be backward and neglectful of their children.

As a direct result of these and other ethnocentric criteria, disproportionate numbers of indigenous children were removed from their homes by social workers. However, until the mid-20th century there were few places for such children to go; most reservations were in thinly populated rural states with few foster families, and interstate and interethnic foster care and adoption were discouraged. As a result, native children were often institutionalized at residential schools and other facilities. This changed in the late 1950s, when the U.S. Bureau of Indian Affairs joined with the Child Welfare League of America in launching the Indian Adoption Project (IAP), the country's first large-scale transracial adoption program. The IAP eventually moved between 25 and 35 percent of the native children in the United States into interstate adoptions and interstate foster care placements. Essentially all of these children were placed with Euro-American families.

Appalled at the loss of yet another generation of children—many tribes had only effected a shift from government-run boarding schools to local schools after World War II—indigenous activists focused on the creation and implementation of culturally appropriate criteria with which to evaluate caregiving. They argued that the definition of a functioning family was a matter of both sovereignty and civil rights—that a community has an inherent right and obligation to act in the best interests of its children and that individual bonds between caregiver and child are privileged by similarly inherent, but singular, rights and obligations.

The U.S. Indian Child Welfare Act (1978) attempted to address these issues by mandating that states consult with tribes in child welfare cases. It also helped to establish the legitimacy of the wide variety of indigenous caregiving arrangements, such as a reliance on clan relatives and life with fewer material comforts than might be found off the reservation. The act was not a panacea, however; a 2003 report by the Child Welfare League of America, "Children of Color in the Child Welfare System," indicated that, although the actual incidence of child maltreatment in the United States was similar among all ethnic groups, child welfare professionals continued to substantiate abuse in native homes at twice the rate of substantiation for Euro-American homes. The same report indicated that more than three times as many native children were in foster care, per capita, as Euro-American children.

Canadian advocates had similar cause for concern. In 2006 the leading advocacy group for the indigenous peoples of Canada, the Assembly of First Nations (AFN), reported that as many as 1 in 10 native children were in outplacement situations; the ratio for nonnative children was approximately 1 in 200. The AFN also noted that indigenous child welfare agencies were funded at per capita levels more than 20 percent under provincial agencies. Partnering with a child advocacy group, the First Nations Child and Family Caring Society of Canada, the AFN cited these and other issues in a human rights complaint filed with the Canadian Human Rights Commission, a signal of the egregious nature of the problems in the country's child welfare system.

Religious Freedom

The colonization of the Americas involved religious as well as political, economic, and cultural conquest. Religious oppression began immediately and continued unabated well into the 20th—and some would claim the 21st—century. Although the separation of church and state is given primacy in the U.S. Bill of Rights (1791) and freedom of religion is implied in Canada's founding legislation, the British North America Act (1867), these governments have historically prohibited many indigenous religious activities. For instance, the Northwest Coast potlatch, a major ceremonial involving feasting and gift giving, was banned in Canada through an 1884 amendment to the Indian Act, and it remained illegal until the 1951 revision of the act. In 1883 the U.S. secretary of the interior, acting on the advice of Bureau of Indian Affairs personnel, criminalized the Plains Sun Dance and many other rituals; under federal law, the secretary was entitled to make such decisions more or less unilaterally. In 1904 the prohibition was renewed. The government did not reverse its stance on the Sun Dance until the 1930s, when a new Bureau of Indian Affairs director, John Collier, instituted a major policy shift. Even so, arrests of Sun Dancers and other religious practitioners continued in some places into the 1970s.

Restrictions imposed on religion were usually rationalized as limiting dangerous actions rather than as legislating belief systems; federal authorities claimed that they had not only the right but the obligation to prevent the damage that certain types of behaviour might otherwise visit upon the public welfare. It was argued, for instance, that potlatches, by impoverishing their sponsors, created an underclass that the public was forced to support; the Sun Dance, in turn, was a form of torture and thus inherently harmed the public good. These and other public good claims were contestable on several grounds, notably the violation of the free practice of activities essential to a religion and the violation of individual self-determination. Analogues to the prohibited behaviours illustrate the problems with such restrictions. Potlatch sponsors are substantively comparable to Christian church members who tithe or to religious novitiates who transfer their personal property to a religious institution. Likewise, those who choose to endure the physical trials of the Sun Dance are certainly as competent to make that decision as those who donate bone marrow for transplant; in both cases, the participants are prepared to experience physical suffering as part of a selfless endeavour intended to benefit others.

By the late 1960s it had become increasingly clear that arguments prohibiting indigenous religious practices in the name of the public good were ethnocentric and were applied with little discretion. In an attempt to ameliorate this issue, the U.S. Congress eventually passed the American Indian Religious

Freedom Act (AIRFA; 1978). AIRFA was intended to ensure the protection of Native American religions and their practitioners, and it successfully stripped away many of the bureaucratic obstacles with which they had been confronted. Before 1978, for instance, the terms of the Endangered Species Act prohibited the possession of eagle feathers, which are an integral part of many indigenous rituals; after AIRFA's passage, a permitting process was created so that these materials could legally be owned and used by Native American religious practitioners. In a similar manner, permits to conduct indigenous religious services on publicly owned land, once approved or denied haphazardly, became more freely available.

If allowing certain practices was one important effect of AIRFA's passage, so was the reduction of certain activities at specific sites deemed sacred under native religious traditions. For instance, Devils Tower National Monument (Wyoming), an isolated rock formation that rises some 865 feet (264 metres) over the surrounding landscape, is for many Plains peoples a sacred site known as Grizzly Bear Lodge. Since 1995 the U.S. National Park Service, which administers the property, has asked visitors to refrain from climbing the formation during the month of June. In the Plains religious calendar this month is a time of reflection and repentance, akin in importance and purpose to Lent for Christians, the period from Rosh Hashana to Yom Kippur for

Devils Tower National Monument, also called Grizzly Bear Lodge, Wyoming. Courtesy of the Wyoming Travel Commission

Jews, or the month of Ramadan for Muslims. Many native individuals visit the monument during June and wish to meditate and otherwise observe their religious traditions without the distraction of climbers, whose presence they feel abrogates the sanctity of the site. To illustrate their point, religious traditionalists in the native community have noted that free climbing is not allowed on other sacred structures such as cathedrals. Although the climbing limits are voluntary and not all climbers refrain from such activities, a considerable reduction was effected. June climbs were reduced by approximately 80 percent after the first desist request was made.

REPATRIATION AND THE DISPOSITION OF THE DEAD

At the close of the 20th century, public-good rationales became particularly heated in relation to the disposition of the indigenous dead. Most Native Americans felt that graves of any type should be left intact and found the practice of collecting human remains for study fundamentally repulsive. Yet from the late 15th century onward, anthropologists, medical personnel, and curiosity seekers, among others, routinely collected the bodies of American Indians. Battlefields, cemeteries, and burial mounds were common sources of such human remains into the early 21st century, and collectors were quite open—at least among themselves—in their disregard for native claims to the dead.

Among others who freely admitted to stealing from recent graves was Franz Boas, one of the founders of Americanist anthropology, who was in turn sued by the tribe whose freshly dead he had looted. The rationale for such behaviour was that indigenous skeletal material was by no means sacrosanct in the face of science; to the contrary, it was a vital link in the study of the origins of American Indians specifically and of humans in general. Indigenous peoples disagreed with this perspective and used many tools to frustrate those intent on disturbing burial grounds, including protesting and interrupting such activities (occasionally while armed), creating new cemeteries in confidential locations,

officially requesting the return of human remains, and filing cease-and-desist lawsuits.

Despite their objections, the complete or partial remains of an estimated 300,000 Native Americans were held by repositories in the United States as of 1990. Most of these remains were either originally collected by, or eventually donated to, museums and universities. Inventories filed in the late 20th century showed that three of the largest collections of remains were at museums, two of which were university institutions: the Smithsonian Institution held the remains of some 18,000 Native American individuals, the Hearst Museum at the University of California at Berkeley held approximately 9,900, and the Peabody Museum at Harvard University held some 6,900. A plethora of smaller museums, colleges, and government agencies also held human remains.

The larger repositories had in-house legal counsel as well as a plentitude of experts with advanced degrees, most of whom were ready to argue as to the value of the remains for all of humanity. Lacking such resources, indigenous attempts to regain native remains proved generally unsuccessful for most of the 20th century. By the 1970s, however, a grassroots pan-Indian (and later pan-indigenous) movement in support of repatriation began to develop.

In crafting arguments for the return of human remains, repatriation activists focused on three issues. The first was moral; it was morally wrong, as well as distasteful and disrespectful, to disturb graves. The second centred on religious freedom, essentially holding that removing the dead from their resting places violated indigenous religious tenets and that allowing institutions to retain such materials amounted to unequal treatment under the law. The third issue was one of cultural property and revolved around the question, "At what point does a set of remains cease being a person and become instead an artifact?"

In part because many of the remains held by repositories had been taken from archaeological contexts rather than recent cemeteries, this last question became the linchpin in the legal battle between repatriation activists and those who advocated for the retention of aboriginal human remains. Native peoples generally held that personhood was irreducible. From this perspective, the disturbance of graves was an act of personal disrespect and cultural imperialism—individuals' bodies were put to rest in ways that were personally and culturally meaningful to them, and these preferences should have precedence over the desires of subsequent generations. In contrast, archaeologists, biological anthropologists, and other researchers generally held (but rarely felt the need to articulate) that personhood was a temporary state that declined precipitously upon death. Once dead, a person became an object, and while one's direct biological descendants had a claim to one's body, such claims diminished quickly over the course of a few generations.

Objects, like other forms of property, certainly had no inherent right to expect to be left intact, and, indeed, as mindless materials, they could not logically possess expectations. Thus, human remains were a legitimate focus of study, collection, and display.

These arguments were resolved to some extent by the U.S. Native American Graves Protection and Repatriation Act (NAGPRA; 1990), which laid the groundwork for the repatriation of remains that could be attributed to a specific Native American nation. Important attributes in identifying the decedent's cultural affiliation included the century in which death occurred, the original placement of the body (e.g., fetal or prone position), physical changes based on lifestyle (such as the tooth wear associated with labrets, or lip plugs), and culturally distinct grave goods. Remains that could be attributed to a relatively recent prehistoric culture (such as the most recent Woodland cultures) with known modern descendants (such as the various tribes of Northeast Indians) were eligible for repatriation, as were those from more post-Columbian contexts. However, some legal scholars claimed that NAGPRA left unclear the fate of those remains that were so old as to be of relatively vague cultural origin; tribes generally maintained that these should be deemed distant ancestors and duly repatriated, while repositories and scientists typically maintained that the remains should be treated as objects of study.

This issue reached a crisis point with the 1996 discovery of skeletal remains near the town of Kennewick, Wash. Subsequently known as Kennewick Man (among scientists) or the Ancient One (among repatriation activists), this person most probably lived sometime between about 9,000 and 9,500 years ago, certainly before 5,600–6,000 years ago. A number of tribes and a number of scientists laid competing claims to the remains. Their arguments came to turn upon the meaning of "cultural affiliation": did the term apply to all pre-Columbian peoples of the territory that had become the United States, or did it apply only to those with specific antecedent-descendant relationships?

The U.S. National Park Service, a division of the Department of the Interior, was responsible for determining the answer to this question. When it issued a finding that the remains were Native American, essentially following the principal that all pre-Columbian peoples (within U.S. territory) were inherently indigenous, a group of scientists brought suit. The lawsuit, *Bonnichsen* v. *United States*, was resolved in 2004. The court's finding is summarized in its concluding statement:

> *Because Kennewick Man's remains are so old and the information about his era is so limited, the record does not permit the Secretary [of the Interior] to conclude reasonably that Kennewick Man shares special and significant genetic or cultural features*

with presently existing indigenous tribes, people, or cultures. We thus hold that Kennewick Man's remains are not Native American human remains within the meaning of NAGPRA and that NAGPRA does not apply to them.

This finding frustrated and outraged the Native American community. Activists immediately asked legislators to amend NAGPRA so that it would specifically define pre-Columbian individuals as Native Americans. Many scientists countered that such a change would not reverse the need to specifically affiliate remains with an extant nation, and others lobbied for an amendment that would specifically allow the investigation of remains that lacked close affiliation to known peoples.

ECONOMIC DEVELOPMENT: TOURISM, TRIBAL INDUSTRIES, AND GAMING

Economic development is the process through which a given economy, whether national, regional, or local, becomes more complex and grows in terms of the income or wealth generated per person. This process is typically accomplished by finding new forms of labour and often results in the creation of new kinds of products. One example of economic development has been the transition from hunting and gathering to a full reliance on agriculture; in this example, the new form of labour comprised the system of sowing and harvesting useful plants, while the new products comprised domesticates such as corn and cotton. During the 19th century, much of the economic growth of Northern America arose from a shift in which extractive economies, such as farming and mining, were replaced by those that transformed raw materials into consumer goods, as with food processing and manufacturing. In the 20th century a broadly analogous shift from a manufacturing economy to one focused on service industries (e.g., clerical work, entertainment, health care, and information technology) took place.

Economic underdevelopment has been an ongoing problem for many tribes since the beginning of the reservation eras in the United States and Canada. Reservations are typically located in economically marginal rural areas—that is, areas considered to be too dry, too wet, too steep, too remote, or possessing some other hindrance to productivity, even at the time of their creation. Subsequent cessions and the allotment process decreased the reservation land base and increased the economic hurdles faced by indigenous peoples. Studies of reservation income help to place the situation in perspective: in the early 21st century, if rural Native America had constituted a country, it would have been classified on the basis of median annual per capita income as a "developing nation" by the World Bank.

Although underdevelopment is common in rural Northern America, comparisons of the economic status of rural Indians with that of other rural groups indicate that factors in addition to location are involved. For instance, in 2002 a national study by the South Carolina Rural Health Research Center found that about 35 percent of the rural Native American population in the United States lived below the poverty line; although this was about the same proportion as seen among rural African Americans, less than 15 percent of rural Euro-Americans had such low income levels. Perhaps more telling, rural counties with predominantly Native American populations had less than one-fourth of the bank deposits (i.e., savings) of the average rural county—a much greater disparity in wealth than existed for any other rural group. (Predominantly Hispanic counties, the next lowest in the rankings, had more than twice the deposits of predominantly Native American counties.)

Explanations for the causes of such disparity abound, and it is clear that many factors—geography, historical inequities, nation-within-a-nation status, the blurring of boundaries between collectivism and nepotism, poor educational facilities, the prevalence of post-traumatic stress and of substance abuse, and others—may be involved in any given case. With so many factors to consider, it is unlikely that the sources of Indian poverty will ever be modeled to the satisfaction of all.

Powwow dancers wearing jingle dance regalia. Blackfeet Indian Reservation, Montana. Travel Montana

Nonetheless, there is general agreement on the broad changes that mark the end of destitution. These typically involve general improvements to community well-being, especially the reduction of unemployment, the creation of an educated workforce, and the provision of adequate infrastructure, health care, child care, elder care, and other services.

During the late 20th and early 21st centuries, native nations used a suite of approaches to foster economic growth. Some of these had been in use for decades, such as working to gain official recognition as a nation and the filing of lawsuits to reclaim parts of a group's original territory. Extractive operations, whether owned by individuals, families, or tribal collectives, also continued to play important and ongoing roles in economic development; mining, timber, fishing, farming, and ranching operations were long-standing examples of these kinds of enterprises.

Highway improvements in the 1950s and '60s opened opportunities for tourism in what had been remote areas, and a number of indigenous nations resident in scenic locales began to sponsor cultural festivals and other events to attract tourists. Tribal enterprises such as hotels, restaurants, and service stations—and, more recently, golf courses, water parks, outlet malls, and casinos (the last of these is also discussed below)—proved profitable. At the same time, indigenous families and individuals were able to use traditional knowledge in new commercial ventures such as the production and sale of art. The powwow, a festival of native culture that features dancers, singers, artists, and others, is often the locus at which cultural tourism occurs. The provision of guide services to hunters and fishers represents another transformation of traditional knowledge that has proved valuable in the commercial marketplace, and ecotourism ventures were becoming increasingly popular among tribes in the early 21st century. Although the tourism industry is inherently volatile, with visitation rising and falling in response to factors such as the rate of inflation and the cost of travel, tourist enterprises have contributed significantly to some tribal economies.

The same transportation improvements that allowed tourists to reach the reservation also enabled tribes to connect better with urban markets. Some tribes chose to develop new industries, typically in light manufacturing. More recent tribal enterprises have often emphasized services that, with the aid of the Internet, can be provided from any location: information technology (such as server farms), accounting, payroll, order processing, and printing services are examples. More-localized operations, such as tribal telecommunications operations and

energy companies, have also benefitted from better transportation.

In a reversal of the extractive industries common to rural Northern America, some indigenous nations have contracted to store materials that are difficult to dispose of, such as medical and nuclear waste. For the most part, these projects were not initiated until late in the 20th or early in the 21st century, and they have generally been controversial. Factions within actual or potential host tribes often disagree about whether the storage or disposal of dangerous materials constitutes a form of self-imposed environmental racism or, alternatively, a form of capitalism that simply takes advantage of the liminal geographic and regulatory space occupied by native nations.

While these kinds of economic development are certainly not exhaustive, they do represent the wide variety of projects that indigenous nations and their members had undertaken by the beginning of the 21st century. At that time, mainstream businesses like these represented the numeric majority of indigenous development projects in Northern America, although they were neither the most profitable nor among nonnatives the best-known forms of indigenous economic development. Instead, the most important development tool for many communities is the casino.

In 1979 the Seminoles of Florida opened the first Native American gaming operation, a bingo parlour with

INDIAN GAMING

The term Indian gaming *refers, in the United States, to gambling enterprises that are owned by federally recognized Native American tribal governments and that operate on reservation or other tribal lands. Indian gaming includes a range of business operations, from full casino facilities with slot machines and Las Vegas–style high-stakes gambling to smaller facilities offering games such as bingo, lotteries, and video poker. Because U.S. laws recognize certain forms of tribal sovereignty and self-government, native-owned casinos enjoy some immunity from direct regulation by individual states.*

The first Indian casino was built in Florida by the Seminole tribe, which opened a successful high-stakes bingo parlour in 1979. Other indigenous nations quickly followed suit, and by 2000 more than 150 tribes in 24 states had opened casino or bingo operations on their reservations. The first years of the 21st century saw precipitous growth. By 2005 annual revenues had reached more than $22 billion, and Indian gaming accounted for about 25 percent of all legal gambling receipts in the United States. This was about the same amount generated by the country's aggregate state lotteries.

INDIAN GAMING STATES

States with casino gambling operations

© 2008 Encyclopædia Britannica, Inc.

U.S. states that allow Indian gaming, as of 2008.

Indian gaming has been at the centre of political controversy since the late 1970s. In many cases the debate has revolved around the morality or immorality of gambling; this issue, of course, is not unique to Indian gaming in particular. Controversies involving Indian gaming operations per se have generally focused instead on whether the unique legal status of tribes, which allows them the privilege of owning and operating such businesses, should be retained or discontinued; whether Indians have sufficient acumen or training to run such businesses; whether engaging in entrepreneurial capitalism inherently undercuts indigenous ethnic identities; and whether gaming is a desirable addition to a specific local economy.

jackpots as high as $10,000 (U.S.) and some 1,700 seats. The Seminole and other tribes surmounted a number of legal challenges over the next decade, principally suits in which plaintiffs argued that state regulations regarding gaming should obtain on tribal land. The issue was decided in *California v. Cabazon Band of Mission Indians* (1987), in which the U.S. Supreme Court found that California's interest in the regulation of reservation-based gambling was not compelling enough to abrogate tribal sovereignty. Gaming could thus take place on reservations in states that did not expressly forbid gambling or lotteries. The U.S. Congress passed the Indian Gaming Regulatory Act in 1988; the act differentiated between various forms of gambling (i.e., bingo, slot machines, and card games) and the regulations that would obtain for each. It also mandated that tribes enter into compacts with state governments; these agreements guaranteed that a proportion of gaming profits—sometimes as much as 50 percent—would be given to states to support the extra burdens on infrastructure, law

enforcement, and social services that are associated with casino traffic.

Although some Native American gaming operations have proved extremely profitable, others have been only minimally successful. To a large extent, success in these ventures depends upon their location; casinos built near urban areas are generally able to attract a much higher volume of visitors than those in rural areas and, as a result, are much more profitable. In order to expand their businesses, some tribes have reinvested their earnings by purchasing and developing property that is proximal to cities; others have filed suits claiming land in such areas. Some groups have petitioned the U.S. government for official recognition as tribes, an action that some antigambling activists have complained is motivated by a desire to gain the right to open casinos. In many such cases the group in question has a variety of reasons to press a claim, as well as ample historical documentation to support the request for recognition; in these cases recognition is eventually granted. In other cases, however, claims to indigenous heritage have proved bogus, and recognition has been denied.

INTERNATIONAL DEVELOPMENTS

In the early 21st century, while many of the efforts of Native American communities focused by necessity on local, regional, or national issues, others increasingly emphasized their interaction with the global community of aboriginal peoples. The quest for indigenous self-determination received international recognition in 1982, when the United Nations Economic and Social Council created the Working Group on Indigenous Populations. In 1985 this group began to draft an indigenous rights document, a process that became quite lengthy in order to ensure adequate consultation with indigenous nations and nongovernmental organizations. In 1993 the UN General Assembly declared 1995–2004 to be the International Decade of the World's Indigenous Peoples; the same body later designated 2005–2015 as the Second International Decade of the World's Indigenous Peoples.

In 1995 the UN Commission on Human Rights received the draft Declaration of the Rights of Indigenous Peoples. The commission assigned a working group to review the declaration, and in 2006 the group submitted a final document to the Human Rights Council. Despite efforts by many members of the UN General Assembly to block a vote on the declaration, it was passed in 2007 by an overwhelming margin: 144 votes in favour, 11 abstentions, and 4 negative votes (Australia, Canada, New Zealand, and the United States). Indigenous communities in the Americas and elsewhere applauded this event, which they hoped would prove beneficial to their quests for legal, political, and land rights.

CONCLUSION

At the dawn of the 16th century AD, as the European conquest of the Americas began, indigenous peoples resided throughout the Western Hemisphere. They were soon decimated by the effects of epidemic disease, military conquest, and enslavement, and, as with other colonized peoples, they were subject to discriminatory political and legal policies well into the 20th, and even the 21st, century.

Among the more insidious forms of discrimination that indigenous Americans face today is their often anachronistic representation. Depictions of their cultures are often "frozen" in the 18th or 19th century, causing many non-Indians to incorrectly believe that the aboriginal nations of the United States and Canada are culturally or biologically extinct—a misbelief that would parallel the idea that people of European descent are extinct because one rarely sees them living in the manner depicted in history museums such as Colonial Williamsburg (Virginia).

To the contrary, 21st-century American Indians participate in the same aspects of modern life as the general population. They wear ordinary apparel, shop at grocery stores and malls, watch television, and so forth. Ethnic festivals and celebrations do provide individuals who are so inclined with opportunities to honour and display their cultural traditions, but in everyday situations a powwow dancer would be as unlikely to wear her regalia as a bride would be to wear her wedding dress; in both cases, the wearing of special attire marks a specific religious and social occasion and should not be misunderstood as routine.

Despite challenges such as these, indigenous Americans have been among the most active and successful native peoples in effecting political change and regaining their autonomy in areas such as education, land ownership, religious freedom, the law, and the revitalization of traditional culture.

GLOSSARY

animism The belief that all things—animate or otherwise—have a living essence and are capable or either harming or helping human beings.

assimilation The process by which individuals or groups of a particular ethnic heritage are "mainstreamed" into a society's prevalent culture.

band A small, egalitarian, family-based group of people.

breechcloth A soft leather strip drawn between the legs and held in place by securing at the waist with a belt.

cartage Removing or transporting materials for an agreed-upon fee.

chiefdom The practice of having one individual or a small group of individuals in charge of the welfare of a community.

dugout A boat made from a single hollowed-out log.

ethnonym A name that a group of people attributes to themselves.

exogamous Used to describe a marriage outside of one's own group or culture.

hegemony A condition wherein a dominant group of individuals holds sway over all matters concerning the social, economic, political, and cultural welfare of another group.

hogan A traditional dwelling and ceremonial structure built by the Navajo.

indigenous Having originated in, or being the first to occupy, a particular area or region.

kachina Divine, ancestral spirit beings who interact with humans; often represented by doll figures.

kiva A subterranean ceremonial chamber that also functioned as a private gathering space for Pueblo men.

longhouse A long, rectangular domicile favored by indigenous peoples of the American Northeast.

matrilineal Based on the mother's heritage and familial lines.

megafauna The largest mammals of a given era.

mescaline A hallucinogenic substance used in traditional religious practices of some native North American tribes.

moiety A subdivision in a society that has a complementary counterpart.

pass law A law that restricts the movement of a particular ethnicity or culture.

patrilineal Based on the father's heritage and familial lines.

phratry A tribal subsection based on the division of clans.

potlatch A gathering used to mark a special occasion where individuals' social status was established or announced.

pueblo The communal, multistoried dwelling used by native peoples of the American Southwest.

shaman A man or woman who has shown an exceptionally strong affinity with the spirit world. Shamans also are considered healers and are thought to be adept at divination.

sovereign lands A geographic area over which a group holds authority.

subsistence A way of behaving that ensures survival.

syllabary A system of writing in which each symbol represents a syllable.

syncretism When multiple traditions, beliefs, and practices are fused into one.

travois A mode of transport consisting of two joined poles and a platform attached to both and draped between them that is dragged, most often by a horse or dog.

tribe A group of people who are politically integrated and shared a language, religious beliefs, and other aspects of culture; consists of several bands.

umiak Large boats used by indigenous peoples of the Arctic and subarctic to hunt whales.

vision quest A supernatural experience in which an individual seeks to interact with a guardian spirit, usually an anthropomorphized animal, to obtain advice or protection.

wattle A building cover consisting of poles through which reeds or branches have been woven.

wickiup A dome-shaped form of lodging favoured by Northeastern Native American peoples, constructed by draping bent samplings with rushes or bark; also called a wigwam.

BIBLIOGRAPHY

There are many syntheses of the traditional cultures of Native America. An excellent collection of photos and essays was commissioned to celebrate the opening of the Smithsonian Institution's National Museum of the American Indian, Gerald McMaster and Clifford E. Trafzer (eds.), *Native Universe: Voices of Indian America* (2004).

An encyclopaedic summary of knowledge, literature, and research on the principal cultural regions north of Mexico is provided by the multivolume William C. Sturtevant (ed.), *Handbook of North American Indians* (1978–).

Reference works include Carl Waldman and Molly Braun, *Atlas of the North American Indian* (1985), and *Encyclopedia of Native American Tribes* (1988); Barbara A. Leitch and Kendall T. LePoer (eds.), *A Concise Dictionary of Indian Tribes of North America* (1979); Barry T. Klein (ed.), *Reference Encyclopedia of the American Indian*, 6th ed. (1993); and Duane Champagne (ed.), *The Native North American Almanac* (1994), a combination of handbook, encyclopaedia, and directory.

Classic surveys of the native peoples of North America include Edward S. Curtis, *The North American Indian*, 20 vol. (1907–30, reissued 1978); Clark Wissler, *The American Indian: An Introduction to the Anthropology of the New World* (1917, reprinted 2005); A.L. Kroeber, *Cultural and Natural Areas of Native North America* (1939, reprinted 1976); John R. Swanton, *The Indian Tribes of North America* (1952, reprinted 1984); and Fred Eggan (ed.), *Social Anthropology of North American Tribes*, 2nd enlarged ed. (1955, reissued 1970).

Indigenous religions of the Americas as a whole are explored in Denise Lardner Carmody and John Tully Carmody, *Native American Religions: An Introduction* (1993). Religious beliefs and ceremonies specific to North America are described in Arlene Hirschfelder and Paulette Molin, *The Encyclopedia of Native American Religions* (1992); Sam D. Gill and Irene F. Sullivan, *Dictionary of Native American Mythology* (1992); Connie Burland, *North American Indian Mythology*, new rev. ed., revised by Marion Wood (1985); Omer C. Stewart, *Peyote Religion: A History* (1987); Weston La Barre, *The Peyote Cult*, 5th ed., enlarged (1989); and Gregory E. Smoak, *Ghost Dances and Identity: Prophetic Religion and American Indian Ethnogenesis in the Nineteenth Century* (2006).

Broadly comparative works include *Western Indians: Comparative Environments, Languages, and Cultures of 172 Western American Indian Tribes* (1980), on Northwest Coast, Californian, North American Plateau, Great Basin, and Southwest peoples; Christopher Vecsey and Robert W. Venables (eds.), *American Indian Environments: Ecological Issues in Native American History* (1980); Thomas E. Ross and Tyrel

G. Moore (eds.), *A Cultural Geography of North American Indians* (1987); Paul Stuart, *Nations Within a Nation: Historical Statistics of American Indians* (1987), with extensive tables and bibliography; *North American Indians* (1991), well illustrated; John Gattuso (ed.), *Native America* (1991), a description of people, places, history, and culture written and illustrated by Native Americans; Alice Beck Kehoe, *North American Indians: A Comprehensive Account*, 2nd ed. (1992); William T. Hagan, *American Indians*, 3rd ed. (1993); Shepard Krech III, *The Ecological Indian: Myth and History* (1999); and Julian Granberry, *The Americas That Might Have Been: Native American Social Systems Through Time* (2005).

Information on the United States alone includes Francis Paul Prucha, *Atlas of American Indian Affairs* (1990); and Arlene Hirschfelder and Martha Kreipe de Montaño, *The Native American Almanac: A Portrait of Native America Today* (1993).

Synthetic studies of Canadian peoples are Harold Cardinal, *The Rebirth of Canada's Indians* (1977), a study of government relations; Diamond Jenness, *The Indians of Canada*, 7th ed. (1977), a classic work; Jacqueline Peterson and Jennifer S.H. Brown (eds.), *The New Peoples: Being and Becoming Métis in North America* (1985); Bruce Alden Cox (ed.), *Native People, Native Lands: Canadian Indians, Inuit, and Métis* (1987), a study of economics with a bibliographic essay on Canadian native studies; J.R. Miller, *Skyscrapers Hide the Heavens: A History of Indian-White Relations in Canada*, rev. ed. (1991); Olive Patricia Dickason, *Canada's First Nations: A History of Founding Peoples from Earliest Times* (1992); and James S. Frideres and Lilianne Ernestine Krosenbrink-Gelissen, *Native Peoples in Canada: Contemporary Conflicts*, 4th ed. (1993).

INDEX

Loups (Wolves), 51
Lower Brulé, 80
Lower Creeks, 64

M

Macro-Algonquian languages, 66, 136
Maidu, 135, 140–141
Mandan, 70, 71–73, 74, 77, 81, 87, 90, 160
Mangas Coloradas, 105
Manitoba Act, 199–202
Maricopa, 101
marriage, colonization and, 21, 167, 168, 215, 219
Marshall, Chief Justice John, 194
Maskegon, 38
Massasoit, 50–51
Matthews, Washington, 71
Maximilian of Wied-Neuwied, 71
Mayan culture, 68
McDougall, William, 201–202
McJunkin, George, 144
Mdewkanton, 80
Medicine Dance Society, 53
Medicine Lodge, Treaty of, 88, 90
medicine societies (Midewiwin), 39, 47, 53, 55, 57
Mescalero Apache, 105, 106
Meshkwakihug, 56
Meskwaki, 56
Meskwaki Settlement, 209
Mesquakie, 56
Metacom/Metacomet, 51
Métis nation, 200–203
Miami, 57
Michif language, 70
Michigamea, 57
Micmac, 37
microblades, 28, 29
Midewiwin (medicine societies), 39, 47, 53, 55, 57
migration, 17–18
Miles, Gen. Nelson A., 121
Mimbreño Apache, 106

Miniconjou, 80
Minitari, 73
missionaries, 38, 68, 69, 121
Mississippian culture, 20, 76, 158–159
Modoc, 117, 123–125
Modoc language, 117
Modoc War, 125
Mogollon, 20, 152–157
Mogollon Apache, 106
Mohawk, 47, 51
Mohegan, 46, 51, 53
Mohican, 46, 51
moieties, 49, 97, 127, 128
Mojave, 101
Moki, 99
Monachi, 111
Mono, 111, 113
Montagnais, 28, 32, 37
Mooney, James, 161–162
Moqui, 99
Mountain Crow, 78
Muh-he-con-neok, 51
Munsee band, 51
Muskogean languages, 58, 62, 63, 65, 68
Muskogee, 64

N

Nadouessioux, 80
NAGPRA (Native American Graves Protection and Repatriation Act), 227
Nakota, 25
Nakota language, 80
Narragansett, 51
Narváez, Pánfilo de, 68
Naskapi, 28, 37
Natchez, 17, 58, 63, 66–67
Natchez language, 65
National Park Service, 225, 228
Native Alaskans, 27
Native American Graves Protection and Repatriation Act, 227